Love was central to Freud's project. And
contemporary field once more in touch wi'
psychic manifestations. Since Freud, many ...
disparate directions, while overlooking the power and centrality of this
psychobiological intersubjective force that binds us one to another and
sustains the generations. Celenza, with creativity and exquisite attunement to
individuality and the tensions of self-states, draws together many of her
exciting theoretical and clinical ideas into a beautifully written text, alive with
arresting case examples from life – in vivo and in cyberspace – dynamic
problems with innovative and classical therapeutic interactions. Her book
should be a part of every core curriculum in psychoanalytic training
institutes, and it will also be of great practical use and interest to teaching
trainees across all the mental health disciplines.

Rosemary H. Balsam, FRCPsych (Lond), MRCP (Edinburgh);
Yale Medical School; Training and Supervising Analyst,
Western New England Inst. for Spa; author of
Women's Bodies in Psychoanalysis (Routledge, 2012), Winner of
Sigourney Award for Excellence in Psychoanalysis, 2018

In these essays Andrea Celenza concentrates on those deep affective components that can at the same time constitute the source, the engine, the vital
energy of the analytic interchange, as well as the problematic area of human
beings in general, and of analytic patients in particular. The reader will find in
this book a broader, more exploratory and at the same time less frightening
way of observing and thinking about this area. I believe that this volume really
contributes to a useful advancement of the psychoanalytic instrumentarium in
a traditionally hostile and dangerous field. Andrea Celenza has been able to
[adopt] an authentic scientific attitude and with a natural, happy integration of
competence and humanity, without defensive academicism or hasty, scholastic
axiomatic formulations; this is perhaps one of the reasons why her work reads
so well and with pleasure, it is clear, touching and substantially convincing.

Stefano Bolognini, psychiatrist/psychoanalyst, Bologna, Italy;
Past President, International Psychoanalytic Association
and Italian Psychoanalytic Society; author of *Secret
Passages: The Theory and Technique of Interpsychic
Relations* (2010), *Psychoanalytic Empathy* (2004) and
Vital Flows Between Self and Not-Self (2022, Routledge)

With *Transference, Love, Being: Essential Essays from the Field*, Andrea
Celenza gives us a new chapter in her extraordinary journey in psychoanalysis. That it is rare and remarkable can be immediately guessed from the
richness and variety of topics addressed with depth but without lengthy
academicism. Interwoven with gripping clinical vignettes, Celenza translates
sophisticated theorizing into a vitalized and relevant real-world grounding.

Among the most intriguing essays: "The historically fetishized couch," "The inadvertent pluralist," "Diffuse attentional set"... and then, again, "The phenomenal experience of touch," "To be in it with" and, somehow affirmative and liberatory "'Yes and ...' dreams." Faithful to her Italian origins, she offers the menu of an exceptional chef, extremely careful to combine the best of tradition with experimentation with new flavors and aromas. That there really is a bit of Mediterranean cuisine is immediately apparent from the word "field" that significantly appears in the subtitle. *Transference, Love, Being* testifies to the vitality and creativity of the author and of psychoanalysis. I highly recommend this remarkable book to all professionals in the field of the treatment of mental suffering, but also to those who work in the humanities or who are curious to know more about contemporary psychoanalysis.

Giuseppe Civitarese, Psychoanalyst, Pavia, Italy and author of *Sublime Subjects: Aesthetic Experience and Intersubjectivity in Psychoanalysis* (Routledge, 2017)

Lieben, Erleben, Denken, To love, to experience within and between, and to think. Andrea Celenza is a master of all of these aspects of analysis and of being a human being. In this fine work, she shows us all how she does this and in so doing teaches us all more about what analysis is capable of being and doing. As in her previous work, we are treated to the way an incredibly talented clinician works. Every analyst and all therapists will grow by reading this book. Every analysand and every client and every patient will benefit as well.

Jim Herzog, Boston Psychoanalytic Society and Institute and author of *Father Hunger* (Routledge, 2001)

Reading this book is the literary equivalent of having dinner at the best tapas restaurant in town: You leave happy and full, having had a lovely time sampling a wide selection of appetizers, each one a little treat of its own. Celenza offers us 37 very brief essays on the subject of love in all the guises it takes in life and psychoanalysis – transference love, erotic desire, romantic love and so on. But the length of these little pieces doesn't limit their substance. The remarkable thing is that each one is satisfying. Celenza explodes the conventions that usually govern the length of essays without sacrificing a deep engagement with the issues she tackles. She uses the brevity of form she has adopted to skip over the usual preparatory paragraphs and plunge us directly into what she wants to tell us. The result is a highly stimulating collection that will delight clinicians, patients, teachers and scholars alike.

Donnel Stern, William Alanson White Institute and author of *The Infinity of the Unsaid: Unformulated Experience, Language and the Nonverbal* (Routledge, 2018)

Transference, Love, Being

Through a series of expansive essays, *Transference, Love, Being* explores the centrality of love in psychoanalytic practice. Starting with the immersion of the analyst, this book reimagines several aspects of the psychoanalytic process, including transference, countertransference, boundaries, embodiment, subjectivity and eroticism.

To love is to cultivate *to be*. Psychoanalysis, as essentially vitalizing, is a playspace for taboo subjects within clear and safe parameters. Interweaving loving, being and perceiving, this book provides challenging new perspectives on the analyst's subjectivity, receptivity and its immersive influence on the analytic process.

These essays refine theoretical understandings of the irreducible and omnipresent nature of love in psychoanalysis, thereby offering clarity to psychoanalysts, psychodynamic therapists and scholars through the often-prohibited love and eroticism, here viewed as indispensable to psychoanalytic theory and practice.

Andrea Celenza is a training and supervising analyst at the Boston Psychoanalytic Society and Institute and an assistant clinical professor at Harvard Medical School. She is also adjunct faculty at the NYU Post-Doctoral Program in Psychoanalysis. She has written numerous papers on love, sexuality and psychoanalysis. She offers two online courses and is the recipient of several awards. Her writings have been translated into Italian, Spanish, Korean, Russian and Farsi. She is in private practice in Lexington, Massachusetts, USA.

Transference, Love, Being

Essential Essays from the Field

Andrea Celenza

Routledge
Taylor & Francis Group

LONDON AND NEW YORK

Cover credit: MF3D, Getty Images

First published 2022
by Routledge
4 Park Square, Milton Park, Abingdon, Oxon OX14 4RN

and by Routledge
605 Third Avenue, New York, NY 10158

Routledge is an imprint of the Taylor & Francis Group, an informa business

© 2022 Andrea Celenza

The right of Andrea Celenza to be identified as author of this work has
been asserted in accordance with sections 77 and 78 of the Copyright,
Designs and Patents Act 1988.

All rights reserved. No part of this book may be reprinted or reproduced
or utilised in any form or by any electronic, mechanical, or other means,
now known or hereafter invented, including photocopying and recording,
or in any information storage or retrieval system, without permission in
writing from the publishers.

Trademark notice: Product or corporate names may be trademarks or
registered trademarks, and are used only for identification and explanation
without intent to infringe.

British Library Cataloguing-in-Publication Data
A catalogue record for this book is available from the British Library

Library of Congress Cataloguing-in-Publication Data
Names: Celenza, Andrea, 1954- author.
Title: Transference, love, being : essential essays from the field / Andrea
Celenza.
Description: Milton Park, Abingdon, Oxon ; New York, NY : Routledge,
2022. | Includes bibliographical references and index.
Identifiers: LCCN 2022002472 (print) | LCCN 2022002473 (ebook) |
ISBN 9781032205410 (hardback) | ISBN 9781032205434 (paperback) |
ISBN 9781003264095 (ebook)
Subjects: LCSH: Love. | Psychotherapist and patient. | Transference
(Psychology)
Classification: LCC BF175.5.L68 C45 2022 (print) | LCC BF175.5.L68
(ebook) | DDC 152.4/1--dc23/eng/20220120
LC record available at https://lccn.loc.gov/2022002472
LC ebook record available at https://lccn.loc.gov/2022002473

ISBN: 978-1-032-20541-0 (hbk)
ISBN: 978-1-032-20543-4 (pbk)
ISBN: 978-1-003-26409-5 (ebk)

DOI: 10.4324/9781003264095

Typeset in Times New Roman
by MPS Limited, Dehradun

To my husband, Bruce, for his unfailing affirmation and love, providing the foundation for this book. Along with our sons, Derek and Ethan, it is through all of you that I have learned the power of love reflected back in these pages.

Contents

Preface

Love, its roots in the past (transference) and how it is lived and experienced (in being) are the subjects of this book. These themes and concepts are of fundamental interest to psychoanalysts and are the constant preoccupation of poets, writers of literature, musicians, philosophers and scientists alike. This book contains a collection of essays on how these themes have interpenetrated my clinical practice for over 3 decades. How to live a full life, love with a full heart, feel one's life intentionally and with intensity. Theoretical refinements, always related to and explicated by clinical process, are included and interweave the narrations herein. Most of the essays are culled from prior publications that represent my most relied upon theorizing and, in some ways, favorites from within my own writing. These essays represent the way I work and reflect my theorizing, its influence on clinical process as well as its influences upon me.

This book has a strong clinical focus (and is thereby relevant for practitioners of all orientations and persuasions) yet also addresses much-needed theoretical refinements and correctives. There is a fair amount of confusion in the psychoanalytic literature and zeitgeist in the way we think about transference, love and how we live through our craft. This book addresses, clarifies and attempts to correct the many confusions in our literature making the practice of psychoanalysis and psychoanalytic psychotherapy accessible, seamless with the practitioner's being and consonant with the emotional care we provide.

Love, transference and the lived experience of each have had a vexed and confusing history in psychoanalysis. First erased, then devalued and disembodied, love in psychoanalysis has been (and continues to be) forbidden territory. Contemporary times have called for a clearer explication of this human phenomenon and basic need, indeed to place love squarely in the body/mind/being of the analyst without apology or qualification. This book writes and dreams psychoanalysis in its most human essence and form, allowing practitioners to call upon their most healing and infinite resource, their love for their patients and analysands.

Acknowledgments

A book is always an outgrowth from a moment in time, reflecting a history of cultivation and nurturance. This book has evolved from years of thinking, feeling, practicing and living under the influence of others. I have been graced with generously nurturant mentors who have demonstrated an unflinching belief in the power and salutary effects of love. In each, I found encouragement (some from a distance or only through their example, others through a profound and eternal relationship) to acknowledge love's power, without apology or doubt. I am indebted to the work of Harold Searles and Hans Loewald for their unqualified statements on the centrality of love in the work we do. Though I never met either of them personally, their influence on me can be seen from the way I work and through my writing.

More personally and directly, with boundless gratitude, I thank my mentors, colleagues and friends. I happily acknowledge their influence, especially: Gerry Adler, Salman Akhtar, Lew Aron, Rosemary Balsam, Stefano Bolognini, Mary Brady, Giuseppe Civitarese, Stan Coen, George Fishman, Glen Gabbard, Les Havens, Jim Herzog, Irwin Hirsch, Axel Hoffer, Howard Levine, Terry Maltsberger, Stephen Mitchell, Randy Paulsen, Alan Pollack, Martha Stark, Gerry Stechler, Lora Tessman, Don Stern and Richard Weinman.

I am particularly indebted to Stefano Bolognini, for his warm collegiality, for the influence of his work upon mine and I am honored by the words he has written in the Forward to this book.

I remain indebted to my peer group in whose trust I regularly place my clinical questions and conundrums: Jack Foehl, Ellen Golding, Chris Lovett and Joan Wheelis. Thanks especially to Ellen who provided invaluable feedback and critique. I also thank Lew Kirshner and Dawn Skorczewski for their enthusiastic interest in my ideas and writing.

As always, I owe a profound debt of gratitude to my patients who will remain necessarily anonymous. Thank you for entrusting your selves and souls with me and so generously sharing your innermost feelings and thoughts.

Thanks, as ever, to my faithful editor, Kate Hawes and her exceptional assistant Georgina Clutterbuck, both of whom are always responsive with unending respect for my voice.

Finally, to my husband, Bruce, my greatest fan and careful co-thinker, whose loving support provides the foundation for this book.

Many of these essays are part of previously published papers. I am grateful to the publishing companies for permission to excerpt and/or reprint from the following papers:

Contemporary Psychoanalysis: Celenza, A. (2010). Mutual influence in contemporary film. 46(2):215–223. Reprinted by permission of William Alanson White Institute of Psychiatry, Psychoanalysis and Psychology and the William Alanson White Psychoanalytic Society, www.wawhite.org. (Essay 35)

Journal of the American Psychoanalytic Association: Celenza, A. (2022a). Maternal erotic transferences and the work of the abject. 70(1):9–38. (Essays 19, 20 and 22)

Journal of the American Psychoanalytic Association: Celenza, A. (2022b). Stance, set, transference: The differentiation of two modes of clinical technique. 70(2):283–305. (Essays 14, 15, 16 and 17)

International Journal of Psychoanalysis: Celenza, A. (2005). Vis à vis the couch: Where is psychoanalysis? 86:1–14. Copyright © Institute of Psychoanalysis, reprinted by permission of Taylor and Francis, Ltd., http://www.tandfonline.com on behalf of Institute of Psychoanalysis. (Essays 3, 5–9)

International Forum for Psychoanalysis: Celenza, A. (2019). From relation to the field: Unconscious fantasy elaborations. 28(4):203–211. Copyright © 2019 The International Federation of Psychoanalytic Societies, reprinted by permission of Informa UK Limited, trading as Taylor and Francis, Ltd., http://www.tandfonline.com on behalf of The International Federation of Psychoanalytic Societies. (Essays 12 and 34)

Psychoanalytic Dialogues: Celenza, A. (2010). The analyst's needs and desires. 20:60–69. Reprinted by permission of the publisher (Taylor and Francis, Ltd., http://www.tandfonline.com). (Essay 2)

Psychoanalytic Dialogues: Celenza, A. (2016). Different strokes in boundary artistry. Commentary on Cooper's Blurring boundaries or Why do we refer to sexual misconduct with patients as "Boundary Violation." 26:215–222. Reprinted by permission of the publisher (Taylor and Francis, Ltd., http://www.tandfonline.com). (Essay 13)

Psychoanalytic Psychology: Celenza, A. (2017). Lessons learned on or about the couch. 34(2):157–162. Copyright © 2017 by the American Psychological Association. Reproduced with permission. (Essays 1, 10, 24 and 28)

Psychoanalytic Quarterly: Celenza, A. (2020). Embodiment and the perversion of desire. 89(3):369–398. Reprinted by permission of the publisher (Taylor and Francis, Ltd., http://www.tandfonline.com). (Essays 30–33)

Routledge and CRC Press: Celenza, A. (2021). Shadows that corrupt. In *Boundary Trouble: Relational Perspectives on Sexual Intimacy in Psychoanalysis.* Reproduced by permission of the Editor, Charles Levin and Taylor and Francis, a division of Informa plc. (Essay 11)

Karnac Books: Celenza, A. (2011). Touching the patient. In *Unusual Interventions: Alterations of the Frame, Method, and Relationship in Psychotherapy and Psychoanalysis* [pp. 165–176]. Reproduced by permission of the Editor, Salman Akhtar and Taylor and Francis, a division of Informa plc. (Essay 25)

Finally, I thank ***Penguin Random House*** for allowing me to print an excerpt from *Gift from the Sea* by Anne Morrow Lindbergh, copyright 1955, 1975, copyright renewed 1983 by Anne Morrow Lindbergh. Used by permission of Pantheon Books, an imprint of the Knopf Doubleday Publishing Group, a division of Penguin Random House, LLC. All rights reserved. (Essay 22)

Foreword

The vibrant scientific community of psychoanalysts has progressively internationalized in recent decades, thanks to a more widespread knowledge of foreign languages, more intense participation in congresses in distant locations and the integrative opportunity of internet connections.

We are no longer isolated researchers or professionals accustomed only to the restricted frequentation of our local "analytical family"; nor are we remote readers of other people's texts, without direct personal contact with our foreign colleagues.

This epochal development of openness and live acquaintance, abruptly interrupted by the misfortune of the pandemic that has traumatically prevented for a long, recent period to meet in person, has however allowed in many cases to give a face to our distant colleagues, to know their voice, expressions, ways of being and relational style, in addition to their ideas and their theoretical-clinical reports that we might have already known a little in the abstract and *in absentia*, through the mere reading of their writings.

I have had the opportunity to meet Andrea Celenza in several international meetings and congresses, participating with her and other excellent colleagues in panels and discussion groups on topics that I was then able to find and revisit in this beautiful book.

The first thing that came to my mind, coming into contact with these works of hers, is that there is in them an evident, appreciable continuity between the concepts presented, the clinical situations described, the way of transmitting observations and ideas, and the author's personal way of being: a coherence that is not always found in psychoanalytic authors, perhaps very brilliant but not always corresponding, on a personal level, to what they expound as a theoretical-clinical discourse.

In these essays Andrea Celenza concentrates with particular care on some essential components of analytic work and of the analyst-patient relationship: specifically, on those deep affective components that can at the same time constitute the source, the engine, the vital energy of the analytic interchange, as well as the problematic area of human beings in general, and of analytic patients in particular (sometimes due to lack, obstacle, disharmony or even excess).

This problematic area extends to the adult love life of most patients, and almost inevitably implies an experiential re-editing in the transference, with the corollary – as we know – of a corresponding countertransferential resonance.

The adjective "essential," present in the title of the book, is very appropriate in this case: Celenza's investigation aims to capture the emotional substance of the analytical experience, and to recognize the real deep conditions of the subject and the object in their encounter and their exchange in the session.

What is striking in many of these writings is precisely the positive tension toward the experiential knowledge of this "essence" of the analytic relationship and work, toward the fundamental nature of the inter-human bond that can orient the working couple toward a sharing of something humanly warm or cold, vital or deadly, creative or sterile; a bond that can rise or extinguish, flourish or wither, ignite or stabilize, depending on the events that primarily connected subject and object, and that may or may not further evolve toward a meaningful relationship between two people.

The seriousness of the author's commitment in this direction is confirmed, for example, by the depth and complexity of her reflections on the processes that generate and accompany the various forms of erotic or eroticized transference.

This attitude of research in such a specific field is not obvious: many previous works of even prestigious authors (especially European, I must say) have treated these themes emphasizing above all – and sometimes almost exclusively – only the resistive aspects of these transference-countertransference developments in the field of analytic treatment. A legitimate and in many cases plausible position, but also rather limited and limiting regarding the possibility of a deeper and more articulated understanding of them.

The reader will find in this book a broader, more exploratory and at the same time less frightening way of observing and thinking about this area; Celenza very consciously and appropriately uses specifically analytic tools, conceptualizations and perspective to approach the deeper meaning of the experiences, fantasies and phantasms that are involved in these transferential scenarios.

The mature result of this research is a perceptible progress in the understanding of many stories and intrapsychic scenarios that then unfold in intersubjective play, in analytic transference as well as in people's daily lives, and take on a new, different, broader and more humanized comprehensibility and tractability during treatment.

I believe that this volume really contributes to a useful advancement of the psychoanalytic instrumentarium in a traditionally hostile and dangerous field, and precisely for this reason approached with a certain contracted and understandably suspicious rigidity – or vice versa with superficial ease – by many psychoanalysts of the past.

I would like to underline how Andrea Celenza has been able to deal with it with an authentic scientific attitude and with a natural, happy integration of competence and humanity, without defensive academicism or hasty, scholastic axiomatic formulations; this is perhaps one of the reasons why her work reads so well and with pleasure, it is clear, touching, substantive and convincing.

It is therefore a pleasure for me to invite the reader to "enter" this book, sharing with the Author an essay that is both a source of knowledge and experience.

Stefano Bolognini
Bologna, Italy

Introduction

In some respects, I have always been writing about love. It's fair to say, I've always been trying to reckon with love and its relationship to psychoanalysis. Love in psychoanalysis has been my subject, the ways in which love can be expressed, nonverbally, in the veins of our being, in transference, in our natural being. And I've also been writing about the ways in which love in psychoanalysis has been erased. Perhaps I could not suppress this natural instinct of mine. Perhaps I was intellectualizing what would later be a full-scale surrender to the importance of love in psychoanalysis.

Still, I searched for complications – why was love erased from our theorizing? Freud was not immune from the strands of love that coursed through his care for his patients. Famously, he gave the Rat Man dinner (Lipton, 1977). In his early writings, he defined libido in its most general sense: "all manner of tender feeling ... lieben, to love" (1910, p. 91). A few years later, he elaborated:

> A strong egoism is a protection against falling ill ... in the last resort we must begin to love in order not to fall ill, and we are bound to fall ill if ... we are unable to love. (1914, p. 85)

And later, Freud acknowledged love's ubiquity:

> Even in its caprices the usage of language remains true to some kind of reality. Thus it gives the name of 'love' to a great many kinds of emotional relationship which we too group together theoretically as love; but then again it feels a doubt whether this love is real, true, actual love, and so hints at a whole scale of possibilities within the range of the phenomena of love. We shall have no difficulty in making the same discovery from our own observations. (1921, p. 43)

But then came the need to legitimize this budding new industry, to cast it in the scientism of Freud's day. The need to read the observer out of the

DOI: 10.4324/9781003264095-1

dyad – to observe *non-influentially*, to intervene *without participating*, to know our subjects *without our own subjectivity, bias or perspective*. The so-called God's eye-view (or view from nowhere, as we finally came to understand). This *pre*-postmodern view of our enterprise would ultimately be supplanted but not for many decades and much later than in other fields. (The rigidity of psychoanalysis, ironically, this process of liberation, cannot be understated.)

Soon there followed the ever-present tendency to construct a binary (between emotion and reason, the mind and body, to name the most prevalent), recruited now to erase love from our analytic setting. This tendency undergirded most of psychoanalysis during the 20th century. Following closely behind, and possibly driving the need to split in two, was the establishment of a hierarchy – the good and the bad. The elevation of reason over passion, the seeking of the rational over the irrational and the transcendence of the mind over the body.

Our patients have less trouble with it. Michael (Celenza, 2006, 2014) stated it simply, "You're a good analyst. You try to help me. *But it feels like love.*" Still, the analyst's love for her patients bristles with prohibition. When I began my training, I could not help but notice how I continued to have a very personal, emotional relationship with all my patients. A kind of *being with,* an affirmative receptivity that has a certain neutrality to it – openness to whatever my patients may bring – yet an emotional connection as well. Was I being unanalytic? Was the connection I felt an unfair seduction within the process or was it essential, the most important aspect, as I began to suspect it was? Neutrality and love – how to reckon with the two?

I like to think of the psychoanalytic process and the very personal relationship I craft between my patients and me as *unsaturated* – a blank, malleable canvas upon which we will paint their life. The medium, the process is an abstract painting upon which we will write their poetry of the mind. (It is not unusual for me to quote my patients back to themselves, selecting their prose as stanzas of a poem.)

Many of the precious conceptualizations learned during my training underwent an evolution in my mind. For example, we used to think about a *core self*, but these turned out to be fraught with essentialist, normative associations inevitably linked to power hierarchies. With the acceptance of the idea that a core self is an illusion, contemporary theorizing has embraced notions of multiplicity of selves "standing" in various relations to one another. Despite this, there is a persistent wish to reference self-experience in a continuous, holistic way. The need to sustain the pulls of multiple self-states creates a paradox inherent in the continual striving for wholeness; we are simultaneously split and divided while striving for unity and wholeness. Health, thereby, is access to a feeling of integration and this feeling needs recognition, a loving gaze upon it by the other.

This multi-faceted network of self-states, self-states that exist in some relation to one another with more or less integration, parallels neurophysiological research that continually reveal complex multiply-coded, embedded systems. It is the human condition to construct a multiply-organized, relatively coherent self, more or less continuous over time, despite divisions and splits.

This is the existential and ineluctable paradox of being, the universal givens of human experience. And these givens, these self-states are embodied. We do not exist except as embodied and sentient, another existential fact. Time was, being was parsed – to understand, to control, to reduce the sense of doom or threat. We are beings for whom *being* is an issue. Not so long ago, and most egregiously, we might have reduced phenomenal subjective experience to mechanistic explanatory systems, thereby erasing the particular for the universal, subject for object, I for me ... or worse, *it*. We might have studied the body in a way that considers a body without reference to *whose body that is*.

It is a short step to realize, then, that dualism is a form of objectification and in that sense, a defense against full, phenomenological immediate experiencing. Anything that takes us from the full experiencing of the here-and-now, the immediacy of love and life, is a distancing from the radical fullness of the present moment. Dialectical reasoning, the ways in which our emotional life implicates and affects our thought processes, came to me with this realization.

Love is central to healing these splits and to the work we do. Levin (2021) acknowledges love as central to the psychoanalytic project, stating, "Psychoanalysis deliberately sets out ... to play with loving feelings as organizers of human life ... place[s] every patient's love on the existential brink" (2021, p. 10).

In these ways, I continued to write about love and subjectivity. In my mind, there became an ever-present distinction between a positivist, descriptive account of a life and one that takes emotional reality into account, from the inside out, as it were. Computers cannot live a life, cannot experience in affective and sensate realms what it means *to be*. In short, "Computers are bad phenomenologists... The simulacrum is no substitute for the real Other" (Bakewell, 2016, p. 325). Striving for authenticity is the essence of phenomenological existentialism and one of the goals of psychoanalysis. This is not a new evolution within psychoanalysis, however the rebellion against abstinence and opaque anonymity has left us with a vexing challenge: how to be an authentic analyst, how to merge the role with one's person and emotional being.

Hans Loewald (1970) famously wrote about this transition in theorizing as well:

> Scientific detachment in its genuine form, far from excluding love is based on it. In our work it can be truly said that in our best moments of dispassionate and objective analyzing we love our object, the patient,

more than at any other time and are compassionate with his whole being. In our field, scientific spirit and care for the object certainly are not opposites; they flow from the same source. (p. 65)

Kristeva (2014a,b) writes of maternal eroticism not as sexual per se but as *vitalizing, life-giving* derived from libidinal forces and the fierce insistence of the primary caregiver's labor (pun intended) in giving the child its life.

Similarly, Jonathan Lear (1990) writes "The very activity of coming to understand love is itself a development, a unification, an act of love" (p. 13). Love's connection to being cannot be understated. *To love* is to promote *to be*. In welcoming her baby to the world, the mother says, "Hello! Yes, I see you! Hello!"[1] Love is infused in the work we do and characterizes transferences at all levels (see, for example, Bolognini, 1994).

Again, Lear states,

Psychoanalysis is the history of a series of battles that are fought and refought within the human soul .... However, insofar as [Freud] traced the route of love as it is manifested in human beings, Freud saw that it was *a force for individuation* ... Psychoanalysis, Freud once said, is a cure through love. (p. 27, italics added)

How love is imbricated in the experience and expression of one's being is also tied to the question of how reality is conceived. Loving, being and perceiving are all intertwined. Lear (1998) notes that Freud, in abandoning the seduction theory, opened the door to see the psyche as imaginative and active in structuring its experience. He then cites Loewald who worked through the significance that "reality is always reality *for a subject*, that its meaning is never simply given, nor can it ever be simply invoked" (p. 128, italics added). In our continual striving for wholeness, our striving to be, we construct the outside world through a loving reach, an erotic desire to find outside ourselves the "piece" of inside necessary for a sense of wholeness and integration.

Many other writers connect loving with the psychoanalytic process. "Between the couch and discourse ... yet another round of whispering on a bed" (Foucault, 1978, p. 5). The analyst's subjectivity is a seamless embodiment of the analyst's perspective, the vantage point from which everything flows and is experienced back. We take in and emerge from a place and moment, a space and temporal point. The *piece* of our subjectivity is actually a *moment* in time, situated and emerging from a concretized body that experiences the invisible through our emotional connectedness and tempo.

Ineluctable, irreducible and omnipresent, the limits are defined by the analyst's receptivity. What is to be included as fodder within the analysis, or better, what is to be made explicit, will depend on the analyst's attunement, attentive listening, affective experiencing of the other ... and *love* for his/her object.

Note

1 See Essay 23, *Le visage de la mère*, (this volume).

Part I

Transference

Chapter 1

Transference, real or unreal

No psychoanalytic concept exemplifies the need for greater clarity than our understanding of the phenomenon of transference, in particular, its real or unreal character. The ambiguity surrounding this concept, especially as it emerges in analysis, can result in a conscious rationale for segmenting the treatment, as if *real love* can be engaged *outside* the office while *unreal transference love* is engaged (and analyzed) *inside* it. Another way this segmentation is referenced is through the term *extra-transferential love*, referring to love outside the analytic setting. These misleading conceptualizations segment the experience of loving in a way that does not hold true on phenomenal and theoretical levels. Our patients constantly tell us, "But what I feel for you is *not transference*, it's *real!*" Further, the schisms in theorizing can be used in moments of perverse misuse, supporting conscious rationalizations and confusing all parties involved. These ambiguities need to be corrected for moments when such temptations arise but also for everyday theoretical discourse.

Though the concept of transference permeates almost all of Freud's writings, his paper on transference love (1915a) sets out the ambiguities with which we struggle in its most accessible form. As Humphrey Morris (2012) recently observed, this paper is structured around *the polarity of transference as real or unreal.* Since every practitioner needs a working definition of the phenomenon of transference from which to derive everyday technique, this is hardly an obscure point of interest solely for those who aspire to a high level of theoretical sophistication. Most importantly, conceptual clarity is necessary for any clinician facing the treacherous straits of erotic transferences and erotic countertransferences in order to derive sound technical strategies in moments of pressure and intense affective sway. It might surprise you to know that one of the rationalizations serving to justify sexual boundary transgressions is the analyst's conviction, "It was real love."

To put the question most simply, Is *transference love* as it arises in the analytic setting synonymous with *real love* or is the love that is experienced inside the analytic setting some kind of *unreal transference love*? In Freud's

DOI: 10.4324/9781003264095-3

paper on the subject (1915a), his resolution to this vexing question straddles both sides:

> It is, therefore, just as disastrous for the analysis if the patient's craving for love is gratified as if it is suppressed. The course the analyst must pursue is neither of these; it is one for which there is no model in real life .... *He must keep firm hold of the transference love, but treat it as something unreal....* (p. 166, italics added)

So is it real or not? In short, Freud seems to be saying, "Yes and no."

Underlying the derivation of the concept of transference, perhaps causing the schism between real and unreal dichotomous conceptions of it, is the axis of time and the phenomenal experience of temporality. Here, I believe it is most useful to consider transference as a structuring process, rather than a phenomenon with specific content. It is a process that wreaks havoc along the axis of time, but only if you think of time chronologically. Rather, transference engages our phenomenal experience of temporality in a cyclical manner, comprised of the condensed relationship between repetitions from the past and hopes for a new experience.

Transference, then, is a process comprised of affective memories and fantasies that are evoked by current reality. These structure the lens through which the past is retrospectively reconstructed and modifies the vantage point from the past to the present and future as well. In these ways, *transference is a process that telescopes time*[1] – it is a description of the process whereby *the past lives in the present*, in contrast to a sequential, linear, chronological view of time. The idea that what is past is past flies in the face of the work transference endeavors to perform. Neither do we live in the present in a way that discounts the reality of the past as past.

Transference is a shaping, a structuring that signifies, rather than a static phenomenon that might be deemed real or unreal. It is not that the past, as encapsulated by transference, is unreal but that transference structures meanings of the present. In this way, the past structures reality and signifies the present (and our dreams for the future as well). It is a paradoxical phenomenology that condenses and telescopes time – the past at once structures and signifies the present which simultaneously constructs an imagined future as well.

Questions are more aptly put, How does transference encapsulate the past such that it lives in the present? What is the effect of transference on the present such that the past is continually revived? The spiral trajectory of *nachtraglichkeit* is the process by which memories are constantly re-categorized and re-transcribed (Modell, 1990). This spiral trajectory (cyclical, forward and back) described in the Laplanchian notion of *après coup* (2017/2006) captures this cycle of temporality and memory re-transcription.

With these conceptual clarifications in mind, we understand this real/unreal polarity to be a false dichotomy. Transference (as in the history of our relationships and in particular, those that remain unresolved) is the lens through which we ascribe meaning to the present. In this way, *transference defines what is real.* It is the eye that sees (Schafer, 1983). We cannot step outside of it (in the analytic setting or elsewhere) nor experience reality without its structuring. Thus, there is no transference that is unreal and no mode of engaging where we do not call upon some historical antecedent for meaning and perspective. Each relationship emerges and develops as some amalgam of dreaded old patterning along with hopes for new resolutions. What we refer to as *the transference* is the particularly intense mode of relating induced by the analytic situation, i.e., those transferences that are structured around a power imbalance and that harken back to the earliest conditions of loving, desiring and fantasy production. It is the hope and dread of a new resolution to this particular old problem that psychoanalytic treatment aims to deconstruct. The treatment situation is designed to accentuate these patternings so that they may be analyzed.

The analytic task is to interpret the roots and meaning of these significations so that we may be freed of repetitive and neurotic (i.e., unhealthy) modes of engagement. It is not that transference is either real or unreal; indeed, *transference is what signifies realness* and what makes certain features of the present more important than others. We should more readily query whether these significations can be deconstructed or analyzed.

Psychoanalysis invites dreams of love.[2] The dreams that emerge in the analytic setting are responses to the seduction of the setting, a seduction parallel to the primal seduction of the mother (Laplanche, 1997) because the analyst *promises to maintain the boundary* between analysis and external life. As in all dreams (and all psychological phenomena), we understand transference on multiple levels, including the symbolic vs. presymbolic; ordinary, maternal/containing, or iconic (Modell, 1990); defensive or healthy and latent meanings beyond the manifest. Transferential modes of thinking and being in analysis are also seductions to more raw, unprocessed and *real* (in the sense of *undefended*) ways of being as more primitive modes of transference emerge. In the attempt to free associate, the analysand tries to disregard platitudes, social convention and especially forms of minimization in favor of more bald, undisguised assertions of desire. We could say that the analytic process is more truthful and, in that sense, edges closer to *real* feelings than the typical evasions that characterize polite social dialogue. The promise to hold social convention at bay (a promise made, responsibly guarded and maintained by the analyst) opens the space for the analysand to express archaic, fundamental and primal forms of desire. "The analyst holds open the presymbolic space so that the symbolic space, the usual conventional and defensive kinds of semantic closure, are avoided" (Morris, 2012, p. 9). Most importantly, *were this promise not made or trusted to be kept, these forms of desire would not emerge.*

So, I think we can definitively say that **transference love in analysis is more real than in ordinary life.** Thus, the question is not, Is transference love real or unreal? But more correctly put, Is the *analysis* of transference preserved? That is the promise and ethic. I would take this one step further and say that it is not that transference love within the analytic setting is unreal but that transference love within the analytic setting *is an **unhealthy**, incestuous form of loving*. It is a particularly intense and unprocessed form of love. The asymmetric structure of the analytic setting evokes forms of desiring that parallel incestuous loving with all the embedded significations. The resolution of the transference does not entail the recognition of it as unreal, but a living through this form of loving in order to transcend it, i.e., put it in perspective by recognizing and reconstructing meanings rooted in the past and mourning the losses inherent therein.

Notes

1 See many authors' (Freud, 1900, 1907; Laplanche, 1989, 1997, 2017/2006; Civitarese, 2008; Harris, 2009) discussions of *nachtraglickeit*.
2 For illustration and discussion of a variety of erotic transferences, see Celenza (2014).

Chapter 2

Paradox in the psychoanalytic stance

Rather than aspire to the conceptually problematic (and ultimately impossible) axes of the classical triumvirate (i.e., anonymity, neutrality and abstinence), I find it heuristic and more phenomenally accessible to structure my psychoanalytic stance around two dimensions of the psychoanalytic project: *mutuality* and *asymmetry* (Aron, 1996; Hoffer, 1996). Indeed, these two axes are definitional of the psychoanalytic contract and it is through these two dimensions that mental and behavioral roles are assigned and guided throughout the process. *These two axes function in dialectical relation; as one is engaged, the other is deepened. This dialectic greatly intensifies the experience and longing for intimate, sexual union in the psychoanalytic context.*

Psychoanalytic therapies take place within a highly seductive and potentially intimate context of this dialectic. However, the *asymmetry*, a potentially depleting and titillating axis, makes external supports and gratifications for the analyst - specifically sources of intimacy - crucial aspects of self-care, recalibration and equilibrium. The asymmetry, a complicated cross-current of deprivations for both analyst and analysand, is ambivalently held throughout the process. Both analyst and analysand are moved to disequilibrate, dismantle and simplify the engagement under the aspiration of *mutuality*.

On an intersecting axis to asymmetry is the background experience of *mutual, authentic engagement*. This dimension is bi-directional in the sense that there are two persons committed to working together and withstanding whatever emerges. This commitment holds out the hope for and promise of continued acceptance and understanding for the analysand or patient of even the most loathsome aspects of the self. Since the analysand is invited and encouraged to reveal areas of self-contempt and self-hatred, the promise of continued engagement in the face of these aspects of the self is simultaneously dangerous and seductive. The danger is inherent in the risk of rejection or withdrawal, despite the (sometimes overt) promise of sustained commitment. The seductive aspect coincides with the universal wish to be loved totally, without judgment or merit. Though rarely actualized, the wish

DOI: 10.4324/9781003264095-4

to be loved totally without having to give anything in return remains a lifelong wish.[1] These longings are never given up but can be set aside as life fails to fulfill them.

The seductiveness of unconditional acceptance and commitment is fueled and intensified by other fundamental and universal wishes as well. These include: a) the desire for *unity* (to be loved totally and without separateness), b) the desire for *purity* (to be loved without hate and unreservedly), c) the desire for *reciprocity* (to love and be loved in return) and finally, d) the desire for *omnipotence* (to be so powerful that one is loved by everyone everywhere at all times). All of these universals figure prominently in fantasies of romantic perfection and are stimulated in the treatment setting since the treatment contract partly institutes their gratification. It can be said that the treatment frame both stimulates and frustrates these universal wishes which will be freighted with the analysand's historical meanings and unresolved developmental trauma. As a background experience, *these aspects of mutuality are a given.*

A male patient with a history of subjugation to his single mother says,

> I want to flow with my emotions for you, but it's a trap. I can flow, but I don't want to because I'm always reminded that this is not life. I want to believe it is real between us and be able to say 'she really cares about me.' I ask myself, do I feel something personal between you and me? I would like to believe there's something flowing from you to me, but I don't trust it. Is it our purpose? Why is it relevant? Is it unprofessional? It's not our work, it's not your job. If I want to believe you care for me personally, then I'm in the analysis trap.

The analytic context is stimulating, seductive and frustrating for the analyst as well. The frustration for the analyst is inherent in the second dimension of the treatment context, *asymmetry*, defined by the asymmetric distribution of attention. This comprises the analyst's professional and disciplined commitment to the analysand. In the psychotherapeutic and psychoanalytic settings, the treatment context is defined by the asymmetric distribution of attention paid to the patient.

We are used to referring to the power imbalance in treatment to mean that the therapist has it and the patient does not, however the dynamics of power in the treatment setting is much more complicated. This axis of asymmetry is hierarchical in that it is constituted by several power relations, yet it is not straightforward or simple. It is an asymmetry that frames several power imbalances at once, each of which is ambivalently held by both patient and analyst. On the one hand, the analysand is positioned as special (and thereby of elevated status) and at the same time, in a desiring or needful state (thereby vulnerable and disempowered). The analyst, by contrast, is relatively contained in her or his need of the analysand (thereby empowered) yet also discounted in terms of the distribution of attention paid (and thereby dismissed, in terms of her or his personal needs). This asymmetry deepens and is concretized as the treatment progresses in the sense that the analyst continues to learn more about the patient while the reverse (relatively speaking) is not true. These forms of power are inherent in the structure of the setting, so neither participant necessarily feels subjectively empowered. Further, *the asymmetrical distribution of attention, definitional of the analytic setting, is not a given; it is a disciplined choice at every moment in the treatment.*[2]

As noted, these two axes, mutuality and asymmetry, function in dialectical relation. For example, the asymmetry deepens the analysand's need for mutual, affective engagement as a way to ameliorate the humiliating, disempowering aspects of being the continuous focus of attention. In this way, it is the facilitation and encouragement of the analysand's openness and vulnerability that makes the analyst's love and acceptance all the more important (Hoffman, 1998). Likewise, it is the extent to which the analysand reveals herself or himself, especially areas of self-hatred and self-loathing, that intensifies the analyst's power in relation to the analysand. In other words, it is the analysand's self-revelations that empower the analyst and intensifies the analysand's desire for a mutual, authentic engagement.

In these ways, the treatment setting is a complex structure that uniquely instantiates several contradictions. Especially interesting is the way in which the treatment setting combines these two contradictory axes: the axis of equality and mutuality (a *we're in this together* type of experience) along with the contradictory and imbalanced focus on the analysand (a *you are in this alone* type of experience). The treatment setting is the point at which these two axes converge, creating the paradox of a simultaneous feeling of mutuality and asymmetry, of intimacy and aloneness, and of equality and hierarchy. It is a mixture of existential givens and disciplined choices. These are tensions that the analysand is persistently moved to resolve, to disequilibrate or level the hierarchy, so to speak, and to make contact with the authentic person behind the professional role.

It can be said that psychoanalysis is a process by which the analysand attempts to both empower and disempower the analyst (and vice versa) in an ongoing, and increasingly more urgent way. By virtue of the special combination of mutuality and asymmetry, a tension is established that the analysand both desires and hates. This necessarily will reconstruct and recapitulate the analysand's relationship to authority and power in general. The psychoanalytic context and the analysand's experience with the analyst (given the power structures within it), is a particularly intense instantiation of this relation. Not surprisingly, in those for whom parental experiences are freighted with trauma and hypocritical or exploitative uses of power, the analytic process will be experienced with great mistrust and skepticism.[3]

Likewise, for the analyst, there is a powerful contradiction inherent in the intersection of these two axes. The constant dismissal of personal needs is frustrating and depleting yet the analyst is also partially gratified and titil-lated by the moments of attunement that the analysand offers. It might be said that *the frustration of asymmetry is counterbalanced by the seduction of mutuality and momentary attunements; we're in this together differently* mistakenly becoming *we're in this together the same.* These vicarious iden-tifications evoke and temporarily unsettle the analyst as she or he decenters and resonates with the analysand's experience. Recentering and thereby re-asserting separateness and difference are crucial aspects of this fluctuating dialectic that can become more muted, less sharp and only half-heartedly asserted over time.

For the analyst, the experience (and skill) is one in which her or his needs are constantly put aside. In this way, the analyst is disempowered and, it might be added, there is an attendant need to re-empower oneself that the analyst must continually resist. Idealization and seduction (by the patient) can be special temptations. The patient, on the other hand, is the central focus. The patient is thereby empowered but by a humiliation; there is the attendant need to become empowered in a different way, to be loved and to see perhaps, the analyst give up all other ties in an act of ultimate devotion, including those to her or his profession.

This is the nature and paradox of the psychoanalytic stance. There is the fluctuation of regressive and progressive emotional resonances, the inherent structured power imbalances, and the dynamic, resistive pressures to level the hierarchy from both within and without, i.e., from within ourselves and from the analysand/patient.

Notes

1 See, for example, S. Smith's (1977) discussion of *The Golden Fantasy.*
2 See Essay 10, *The nature of boundaries*, and Essay 13, *The art of the boundary* (this volume).
3 For a more elaborated discussion of the power dimensions of the analytic process, see Celenza (2007).

Chapter 3

The historically fetishized couch

In years past, the phrase "Are you on the couch?" has been shorthand for "Are you in analysis?" Today, no such shorthand exists. In contemporary practice, there is an expanded appreciation for the varieties of analytic experience. In line with Gill's (1984) helpful distinction between intrinsic and extrinsic features, psychoanalysis has come to be defined by process variables, such as the focus on transference and the exploration of unconscious meanings rather than external variables such as frequency of sessions or use of the couch. The widening scope of pathological conditions considered treatable with psychoanalysis has also brought with it a widening awareness of the various forms analyses may take, either with different analysands or for the same analysand at different points in time.

In 2020, the coronavirus pandemic forced analysts to become flexible in their ways of providing analysis. Virtual sessions became commonplace with some analysts encouraging or requiring analysands to use a couch in their home while placing their computer beside their head to mimic the visual experience of the analyst sitting behind the couch. Many analysts abandoned the couch during this time with a protracted phase of telephonic or virtual sessions sitting up during an otherwise couch-dominated experience. This modality has required exploration and legitimation. Indeed, all phases of sitting up in the analytic process were previously and have remained undertheorized. Some still view these phases as temporary departures from *real analysis*. Psychoanalytic models generally have not accounted for processes that occur within these so-called parameters (Eissler, 1953) resulting in sparse literature on these subjects, especially as sitting up (vis-à-vis) contrasts with lying down (on the couch). Telehealth (at home or on the patio) adds yet other extrinsic variables. Could it be that analysis can occur on a continuum: From virtual, to the patio, to the chair and ultimately to the couch?

Many relevant questions on both clinical and theoretical levels are raised. What is signified by the reluctance to use one modality over another? What are the analysand's fears? If sitting up is preferred, what is it that the analysand

DOI: 10.4324/9781003264095-5

needs to see in the analyst's face? What is the experience on the couch (both positive and negative)? And finally, What is the analyst's preference?

Originally, lying down on the couch was understood as an attempt to reduce the analytic action to the realm of ideas, associations or fantasies as these are expressed in words. This model of therapeutic action, Freud's hydraulic model (1895), was based on the idea that to the extent action is suppressed, free association and self-reflection are maximized. Since lying down on the couch inhibits motoric activity, free association was promoted by blocking discharge in one pathway thereby diverting the impulse to the ideational realm. Translated to the practice realm, if the analysand did not lie down, not much of significance would happen.

The assumptions underlying this hydraulic model have been called into question and it is now generally recognized that this model is not the appropriate analogue for therapeutic action. Any action or position can stimulate the evocation of memories. The dichotomy between words and actions breaks down further when it is considered that words themselves are actions, as in the performative action of speech (see, for example, Havens, 1997). Increasingly, analysts acknowledge that certain nonverbal experiences and phantasies may be initially available only through (motor-based) enactments. "Our emotions and thoughts are inextricably embedded in our bodies, so that our actions may connect with meanings and memories from all levels of mental functioning … conflicts being enacted in changes in posture" (Goldberger, 1995, pp. 38–9).

Recent neuroanatomical and neurophysiological studies support a different model of therapeutic action by demonstrating a dense interconnection of networks associated with motor control and affective states (Katz, 2004). These studies demonstrate intensive two-way communication from the cortex to the pons to the cerebellum and back through the thalamus to the cortex (Schmahmann and Pandya, 1997). On a theoretical level, a dialectical model of therapeutic action captures this two-way communication and illustrates the way in which a pathway from words to action is established. By encompassing enactments as one mode of communication, this model is applicable to the use of the couch and chair such that changes in body posture and/or visual access to the analyst's face and body will stimulate and enliven different experiences, memories, associations and modes of relating both in words and ways of being.

The increased acceptance of sitting up as part of or the whole of analysis has paralleled the increased acceptance of the intersubjective and interactional, participatory stance of the analyst (Weissman, 1977, for earlier reports; Goldberger, 1995; Moriatis, 1995). This shift in theory has deepened the appreciation of the function of the couch as well. In part due to bypassing shame and enhancing the freedom to associate, some analysands find it easier to access dissociated experience when facing away from the analyst. The couch is also implicated in the generation, experience, elaboration and utilization of the intersubjective analytic third (Ogden, 1996). Presumably owing to the lack of visual access to each other's face, the couch is a condition of the analytic setting that allows both analyst and analysand the privacy to render herself or himself optimally receptive to unconscious communications in order to jointly construct and experience the third subject of analysis. It affords both an area of privacy, in the sense of being alone in the presence of an "other" (Winnicott, 1958), and a playspace within which to generate and be receptive to overlapping states of reverie (Ogden, 1996).

The acceptance of these various functions of the couch has paralleled the shift in psychoanalytic theory from a focus on intrapsychic and, in particular, defensive transformations, to the intersubjective, enactive sphere. In addition, the pursuit of early preverbal or nonverbal material has directed the analyst's attention beyond *what is said* in the hour to *what is enacted* (Wrye and Welles, 1994; Aron and Anderson, 1998). In effect, the action of analysis has moved beyond words to bodies and likewise from one person to two. *Where* the body (of the analysand) is located has become significant, not as an inhibitor to action as in lying down but as a container and stimulant for affects symbolically communicated (Goldberger, 1995). In this way, the couch and chair can both play a part in setting the stage for a fuller exploration of intrapsychic and intersubjective meanings, always contextualized and embedded within the unconscious field.

Chapter 4

Changes in the frame[1]

There used to be a rule when starting an analysis: "Make no important decisions in your life until the analysis is over." But that was when analyses were shorter and marriages were longer. There have been many changes in the way we do our work since then, both within psychoanalysis and external to it. Psychoanalysis used to be so popular as to be a status symbol, a sign that you were among intelligentsia. There was a way in which analysts could rely on a certain level of commitment, even enslavement to the process both in length of treatments and frequency of meetings. Now it is primarily candidates who can be counted upon to submit to such an intense and lengthy venture.

It might be said that back then, cultural support for analysis allowed for a certain rigidity – everyone could be expected to use the couch, to be seen 4–5 times per week and to stay for years on end. With that cultural support, certain aspects of the process remained unquestioned and were assumed to be intrinsic to it. Now upon entering the office, a new patient might incredulously remark, "Oh, you have one of *those*?" As the economic climate has changed and the culture has shifted along with it, psychoanalysis has needed to defend itself and examine the essential features that define the process.[2] Gill's (1984) famous distinction between intrinsic and extrinsic features of analysis became the cornerstone in defining what we do at a process level. Aspects of the frame such as the length of treatments, frequency of meetings, fees and the use of the couch versus the chair took on the character of cosmetics, accoutrements of analysis but no longer intrinsic to it. Gill (1984) defined analysis by one inherent feature, *the analysis of transference.*

This was the 1980s and much has happened across a variety of cultures impacting psychoanalysis since, arguably much of it negative. For one thing, economic and cultural support for analysis has dwindled (although if training institute class size is any measure, a resurgence of interest might be discerned). In North America, the culture has become enamored of cognitive-behavioral techniques, neurophysiological explanations and biochemical intervention, all of which appear to promise quick changes and

DOI: 10.4324/9781003264095-6

nonthreatening processes (unlike the unknowable unconscious that captures us in our nightmares). There is a resurgence of interest with the publication of Shedler's (2004) and Luborsky's (2001) empirical reviews of studies supporting long-term, intensive work and multiple integrative efforts between the neurobiological and psychoanalytic perspectives (Schore (2018), Solms (2000, 2010) and Watt (1990) to name a few sources). These glimmers of empirical support may have helped the pendulum swing back, but the effects do not yet have a wide reach.

In the short run, the lack of cultural support for psychoanalysis has also required some selling of the craft. I often inform prospective analysands that psychoanalysis is the quickest and most effective way to address their symptomatology, even if it means sessions at a rate of 3–4 times per week for some period of time. I explain that the stereotype of analyses lasting years before termination is indeed accurate but not with regard to symptom relief. Analysands usually experience symptom relief within a few months and then choose to stay in analysis because *they become more ambitious,* desiring to address more areas of distress and to go deeper, i.e., beyond symptomatology to character change.

There are some positive developments, including those associated with the contemporary technological age that have helped support the survival of psychoanalysis. These changes in culture include an array of technological devises that make contact possible at great (almost without limit) distances.[3] With the coronavirus pandemic of 2020, remote sessions became a necessary alternative. These changes (expansions and restrictions) to the psychoanalytic frame are likely to persist. Even before the pandemic, it was not uncommon for analytic therapies to be conducted partially or even wholly on the telephone with a patient or analysand from a distant city. Most common is an interrupted treatment where a job or educational opportunity necessitates a temporary or even permanent move. These are practical impositions brought on by the reality that our patients (for good or ill) no longer feel the need to bind themselves in an unqualified way to the analytic process.

There are a multitude of useful tensions and dangers inherent in the unconscious potential space, all of which become part of the unconscious field. However, many of these tensions are not replicated virtually. These can have obvious or subtle implications on the 3-dimensionality of the analytic experience. Consider, for example, the fact that psychoanalytic therapies carry a mandate that we do not touch our patients, *despite that we could.* Only in-person sessions capture the tension of restraint this mandate instantiates. We could say the experience embodies a 3-dimensional way we *trust* our analysts. Another aspect is reflected in a comment made by a colleague where she noted the experience of *breathing the same air, a rhythmic interchange representing the dangers of intimacy* with in-person sessions. These examples highlight the embodied nature of being when with another person in both time and space. Our bodies exist as a concrete reminder of the intersubjective (and thereby threatening) nature of being with another person.

On the other hand, some persons would not enter treatment at all were it not for a variety of flexibilities of the (transitional) space. There can be a need for the safety of virtual meetings, *due to the reduction in dimensionality*, experienced as a necessary way station before some might venture the risks inherent with in-person contact. A poignant example is a man who asked if I would treat him without my knowing his name or location. He said he was too ashamed of what he had done to reveal these facts of his identity to me. I treated him via telephone for over a year in this way. I sent his invoices to a post office box in another state – not where he was – and then received payment by money order. He eventually did reveal who and where he was; we added sporadic in-person meetings to our work whenever we were in the same locale. I knew he would not have received help if I did not agree to these stipulations initially. In these ways, virtual meetings can be experienced as a helpful, if not essential preliminary step toward in-person meetings. Such flex extends the reach of our work.

I have written about the importance of postural changes and the visuospatial arrangements in the office as evocative of differing affective experiences.[4] The couch has historically been fetishized, yet today it is not necessarily true that a patient in analysis regularly or even *ever* uses the couch.[5] Preliminary data from a study of couch use by Lable and colleagues (2010) suggests that the effect of patient position (lying down or sitting up) is unique to each analyst/patient dyad. Beyond whether using the couch or chair pervades a treatment process, it is my view that *the capacity* to use both are signs of strength and health. The use of the chair (sitting up) is so conventional, it may be difficult to imagine fears centering on this posture, however there is evidence that some analysands will use the couch to hide from a more interpersonal, face-to-face exchange.[6]

Psychoanalytic approaches have continued to evolve. Some changes emerge from cultural trends that may not have a lasting life. In contrast, changes in *epistemology*, modifications in the frame and basic assumptions about our endeavor reflect critical, clear-sighted and indisputable truths that are bound to stand the test of time. Such changes are linked to the postmodern paradigm shift, i.e., perspectivism – the realization that the observer is never outside the field of study and thereby impacts the observed. This shift fundamentally undergirds and transcends cultural trends.

Evolutions reflective of this shift in epistemology impact the *intrinsic* features of the analytic process. These transformations have changed the way the frame and therapeutic action are conceived. It is now almost universally accepted that the analytic context is ineluctably relational, two-person, participatory and intersubjective, while embedded in an ever-expanding and deepening unconscious field. There is no standing outside of the process, nor a way to be uninvolved in it.[7] Given these transformations, it is not so much *analysis of* transference and countertransference that forms the essence of therapeutic action but *engagement with* these patterns. Describing the analyst's role or influence as *analysis of transference* can connote a stance that is outside of the process, nonreciprocal, nonaffective and unembedded. In contrast, *engagement with* captures the reciprocity, mutuality and embeddedness of the therapeutic relationship.

I also choose *engaging with* to describe the analyst's relationship to transference and countertransference because I believe *analysis of* (meaning *attention to, and/or interpretation of*) is an insufficient descriptor of the ways in which analysis facilitates change. The analyst engages the patient in a relationship that facilitates the emergence of multiply organized, shifting self-other identifications, characters in the field and various nonrelational props, all of which are *embedded in, emanate into and transform* an unconscious field. In this way, there is an emotional immersion with our analysands that represents our willingness to journey along with them, *feel with* and consciously and *unconsciously co-create something new.*

There are patterns that refer to the patient's unconscious convictions about the past, ways in which they have hermeneutically transformed memories and experience. Some of these convictions will be problematic (i.e., self-destructive), unresolved (i.e., conflict-laden, driven by unconscious processes or reflective of unmourned losses), dissociated or unrepresented. However, engaging transference and countertransference modes of relating, undergirded by ways the analysand interprets and transforms the unconscious field, stimulates and enlivens experience, memories, associations and states of being. These will only emerge when the analyst is authentically, lovingly[8] and vitally involved with the analysand, a *being with* rather than *knowing about* the analysand.[9] These are ways in which analysis nurtures growth and expands the analysand's capacities.

Other changes in the conception of therapeutic action have occurred as well. We no longer adhere to Freud's (1895) hydraulic model, the idea that immobilization would promote free association as thoughts are blocked from motoric expression. We now recognize the body as a container and conveyor of affective memories, some of which cannot be accessed except through action. This relates to the embodied nature of being[10] and the idea that actions or bodily position can stimulate the evocation of memory. The dichotomy between words and actions breaks down further when it is considered that words themselves are actions, as in the performative action of speech. Increasingly analysts acknowledge that certain *nonverbal* experiences and fantasies may be initially available only through motor enactments. Encompassing enactments as another mode of communication recognizes their stimulating and enlivening potential. All of this parallels the increased awareness and acceptance of the intersubjective, conscious and unconscious emotionally immersed and participatory stance of the analyst.

Finally, I would like to mention a rather old-fashioned belief, a way in which I believe psychoanalysis has *not* changed, that paradoxically may be one of the more radical statements I will make. I continue to believe that psychoanalysis is the treatment of choice and stands to cure most psychological disorders. I recently taught a class at my local institute and some students reacted strongly to my neglect of "inherent biological predispositions." They held the assumption that some people are born prone to depression and would need to take anti-depressants for life. I think this is a misreading of childhood temperament literature, perhaps inadvertently interpreted to line up with our pharmaceutically-oriented culture.

A blue-collar, Irish, young man had not been exposed to psychoanalysis in the circles he frequents but serendipitously was referred to me via his ex-girlfriend's therapist. John is the first and only member of his family to have gone to college. His father was a stonemason in Ireland who came to this country with his stonecraft and temper; John (one of five siblings) was diagnosed with ADHD at the age of 5, prescribed Ritalin by age 7 and then anti-depressants since age 16. (This is an all too familiar story.) John is remembered as inheriting his father's temper, though his other brothers seem to have gotten the gene too; one is now a heroin addict, another refuses to see the family at all.

John, now also a stonemason, has been attending sessions once weekly for over 2 years. A soft-spoken, intelligent man, he tells me he has struggled with a lifelong depression for which he believed he has a biological predisposition. Given that he is now 35 years old, he has been on anti-depressants for 19 years. Early on, after speaking with his psychopharmacologist, I told him that we might consider a goal of treatment to be "getting off his anti-depressants." He was intrigued, especially given that he had developed a homeopathic, Zen-like sensibility, practicing yoga several times a week and eating organic food. Anti-depressants did not fit with his culturally embedded self-ideal.

John is a hard worker. He toils 6 days per week and he is the manager of two crews who design and sculpt patios, ledges and pathways in a variety of yards in suburban Boston. He considers the coldest 3 months of winter to be his vacation time, when he tours around Ireland or sits at home cooking. In this, our second year of treatment, we took advantage of the 3-month hiatus and he attended sessions 5 days per week. We examined his self-criticism, his internalized parental identifications and his elusive anger in relation to his father. A nascently emergent, sensitive side to his character grew stronger. At the end of April, he took his last anti-depressant and has been reveling in the sharper, more intense experience of his feelings ever since. He says he now realizes drugs had dulled his emotions. This week, he mentioned that he has noticed the surfacing of anger in relation to people he does not like. He put another goal on the table yesterday when he reported, "I can be kind of a jerk. Our next project."

This is an example of how our patients become more ambitious when they see results. We should be ambitious too. We may have to sell it a bit, but nothing convinces like *feeling* affective changes, even when the wider culture does not support what we do.

Notes

1 A longer version of this paper was originally presented at the First Academic Lecture, *The Boston Psychoanalytic Society and Institute*, Newton, MA, September, 2011, with Steven Bernstein, Hans Agrawal and Chuck Henry.
2 See Essay 5, *Safety, danger, couch, chair* (this volume).
3 See Lemma and Caparrotta (2014) for a review of psychoanalysis through new technologies.
4 See Essay 5, *Safety, danger, couch, chair* (this volume).
5 See Essay 3, *The historically fetishized couch* (this volume).
6 See, for examples, Julie, Essay 8, *The analyst as subject* (this volume); Petra, Essay 19, *The maternal erotic transferences* (this volume) and Essay 20, *From a foreclosed void to usable space* (this volume).
7 See Essay 36, *To be in it with* (this volume).
8 Conveyed in our attentiveness, devotion and sometimes willingness to suffer with our analysands (see Celenza, 2014, 2022b and the multiple essays on love in this volume).
9 See Ogden's (2019, 2020) clarifying distinction between an epistemological vs. ontological conception of the mind and process in analysis. Bion (1965a) made a similar distinction in referencing 'knowing about' vs. 'being with.' See also Essay 17, *Stance, set, transference* (this volume).
10 See many essays on the nature of embodiment (this volume).

Chapter 5

Safety, danger, couch, chair

There seems to be a clearer sense of what analysis is when confronted with what it is not. We more frequently hear the phrase *This is not analysis!* than *This is analysis.* (Unlike pornography, we seem to know it when we *don't* see it.)

In contemporary psychoanalytic theory, we have generally abandoned the search for essences, as in the search for a core or unified self[1] (Mitchell, 1991; Grotstein, 1994; Davies, 1996; Harris, 1996; Bromberg, 1998;). Likewise, the search for the essence of psychoanalysis may be compared to the search for the real artichoke by stripping it of its leaves (Wittgenstein, 1953).

The aim of this essay is not to determine an unshifting, inherent essence of psychoanalytic action, but, through the use of a heuristic visuospatial metaphor, to find *where the action might be located* at any particular moment. The physical presence of both the analyst and the analysand is the foundation through which the psychic experience of the analytic process is mediated (Meissner, 1998), making the location of bodies a potentially anchoring metaphor for therapeutic action.

Perhaps the question, *What is analysis?* is more aptly posed, *Where is analysis?* Or, Where is the analysis for a particular individual? How is it best contained? From a postural perspective, how and where might it be embodied or enacted for a particular individual or dyad? How do shifts occur, both in time and space, over the course of treatment?

Here, and in several essays both theoretical and clinical,[2] I address the ways in which postural changes in relation to the analyst, as represented in the concrete icons of the couch and chair, intersect with and manage several relevant dialectics including danger/safety, engagement/privacy, interiority/exteriority and subject/object. The temptation to actualize internal conflicts by moving one's body is to experiment with unconscious wishes and fears in relation to the analyst's body and mind. As an analysand recently stated, "It's not that something changes; it just becomes easier to see."

There is no way to predict whether the couch or chair will evoke a particular state of mind or feeling state. For example, there is not a one-to-one correspondence between the use of the chair with engagement or the use of

DOI: 10.4324/9781003264095-7

the couch with privacy. One analysand may say, *I can't lie down because it's not safe!* while another may say, *I can't sit up because it's not safe!* The same analysand may experience danger (and safety) differently in different phases of the analysis as well.

When either the couch or the chair is viewed as dangerous (and thereby avoided), it is an indication of a defensive process, analogous to the creation of a phobic object. Identifying the danger as located *over there* establishes a boundary, so to speak, so that it may be imagined as controlled or sequestered. It is a defense against the dialectical nature of danger and safety in an effort to sanitize the therapeutic process and, for some, may eliminate danger too effectively. Once situated in the analysand's mind, the particular mode of experiencing may become phobically avoided or, conversely, fetishized.

The analyst may collude with this as well by not legitimizing the psychological processes that are being avoided or defensively managed. Some analyses are too safe and are thereby endless; others, too dangerous and never get going (Greenberg, 1986). In either case, there can be a lack of flexibility in the use of either the chair or the couch as these localize and psychically sequester unconscious dangers.

Finally, because lying down is also facing away, there are two variables to consider (from the analysand's perspective) in comparing the couch and the chair: one is the placement of the body, the other is having visual access to the analyst's face.

Analysands often say they sit up in order to see the analyst's face. Behind this may lie the fantasy that the analysand can know what the analyst is thinking and feeling. However, visual access to the analyst's face presents the analysand only with the surface of the analyst's experience from which the analysand must *infer* her or his internal experience. The analysand's perception of the analyst's facial expressions and body posture may foster the illusion that the analysand is controlling the potentially dangerous inner life of the analyst, creating an imagined safety and reducing the complexity of the analytic process. For some analysands, locating the other at this surface level can reduce the challenge of the analyst's presence from *what is fantasized* (i.e., in the analyst's subjectivity or internal world) to *what is seen* (i.e., on the exterior).

This is one of the ways that the preference for the couch or the chair presents the analysand with a visuospatial configuration wherein she or he may negotiate the dialectic of danger and safety as it is experienced within and collides with the dialectic of engagement and privacy. Yet, it is not possible to predict how lying down or sitting up will be experienced. For example, it is tempting to associate the couch, i.e., lying down and outside the visual sphere of the analyst, with the danger of abandonment (i.e., lack of engagement). Perhaps more typically, there can be an association of the couch with the danger of domination, as in the classical analytic icon of power, representing the asymmetry between analyst and analysand (analogous to a doctor's white lab coat). Potential dangers may also be associated with sitting up, such as confrontation with or fantasies of invasion.

Notes

1 See Essay 28, *The unbearable multiplicity of experience* (this volume).
2 See Essay 3, *The historically fetishized couch*, and Essays 6, 7, 8 and 9 (this volume) for theoretical and clinical applications of these conceptualizations.

Chapter 6

The analyst as objectified other

The particular ways an analysand experiences the analyst at any given point in time will determine an underlying structure that organizes various defensive postures and positions.[1] This brings to the foreground a dialectic: the extent to which the analysand experiences the analyst as an object, a subjective object or as a subject with an internal life and agency. This dialectic may be conceptualized along an axis of interiority/exteriority or the degree to which the analysand experiences the analyst as having an internal world. Here, I rely heavily on contemporary intersubjective theorists such as Ogden (1985, 1986, 1988, 1994, 1996), Benjamin (1988, 1995, 1998), Aron (1991, 1996, 1998, 2000), Slochower (1991, 1996a, 1996b), Modell (1993), Pizer (1996, 1998) and Bromberg (1998). These structures, the way defensive positions are unconsciously organized, can be formulated at different moments according to shifting intersubjective and intrapsychic pressures. In addition, these structures can be used to construct a developmental schematic of the progression of the analysis over time.

For some, especially in the early phases of analysis, the analyst is used as an object, a body, a bounded other from where the analysand sees or feels herself or himself from the outside in, as it were. One could say the other is experienced as having *exteriority*, a container but not an *other* with a separate and differentiated interiority. In this position, the analysand defends against being confronted with the analyst's separateness, difference and intentionality. The analysand is usually limited in the extent to which she or he can explore or become curious about the analyst's internal world as well. This parallels Ogden's (1986, 1994) notion of the autistic-contiguous position wherein the experience of the other is sensual, but not personal, or the various ways in which the analyst is used as a holding environment, protected from the disjunctive intrusions of the analyst's separateness (Slochower, 1991, 1996a, 1996b).

In these states of mind, the analysand requires concrete evidence of the analyst's presence, usually[2] more easily afforded in a sitting-up position, such that the analysand can see the outlines of the analyst's body and face, i.e., the *exterior* aspects of her or his person. In this context, concretization

DOI: 10.4324/9781003264095-8

as a defense establishes the illusion that one can relate in one mode and not another, i.e., that engagement is limited to what is physically seen. What is real is defined by what is tangible. In this way, a tension is collapsed and a boundary established, e.g., being seen and not being known or being known yet not being judged. The adaptive aspects of this defensive process may be understood as shoring up the boundedness of self and other, establishing the other as a reliable container, or challenging and maintaining separateness on a physical level.

Here, engagement is characterized by seeing the physical presence of the other as an object, but not as a subject. A female analysand, in the midst of tremendous marital discord, describes how she misses her husband's body when he travels. She says, "I miss the warmth, but just his physical presence, not his person." When he is home, they constantly fight, his domineering presence felt as a demeaning force against her. Through her analysis, she has realized that she needs and uses this type of contact as a concrete reminder of where he ends and where she begins. In effect, she knows her own presence by contrasting herself to him, as in *he is there and I am here*.

In her analysis, sitting up affords this analysand visual access to my face such that *seeing me* speak (more than hearing my words or their meaning) lends a tangible reality to my separateness and her difference from me. These are ways in which her experience of herself is embodied, located in space and is concretized. Likewise, my responses to her are experienced as tangible and thereby real. It is sensual but not personal. In turn, she knows herself by feeling her impact on me. In another hour, she explained,

> Face to face, I am aware I am talking to you, but I have low expectations of what I want from you. It's a question of how aware I am of your *you-ness*. With my husband, I might want physical contact, but that's not about *him*. I'm not present to his *his-ness*. It's not about wanting *him*.

In this way, she is aware of engaging with me (and her husband) in an impersonal manner, in an effort to manage and hold at bay the more particularized subjectivity of the other, the *he-ness* and *you-ness* of the other.

For this analysand, looking and seeing is a type of engagement that is essentially objectified, reflecting a mode of relating to me as an object but not as a subject. As she is becoming increasingly aware of her need to reduce my subjectivity, she has been able to explain,

> I am dependent on you to hold my thoughts, yet I don't have a sense of how you might hold me in mind. Since I can't know that, I don't think about it. But I notice you take notes—that means something to me. That you want to remember what I said. If I think about you thinking of me, I worry about your judgment of me. So I don't go there.

Here, she describes how concretization, reducing me to an object, serves as a defense, a way to limit our form of engagement since my internal life (my subjectivity) is dangerous to her. Consistent with this also is her ability to recognize my note-taking, my recognition of her in concrete form.

Notes

1 See Essay 5, *Safety, danger, couch, chair* (this volume).
2 The reader is reminded that preference for the chair or couch is always an individualized experience and cannot be predicted.

Chapter 7

The analyst as subjective object

In contrast to an objectified other,[1] *an aspect* of the analyst's subjectivity may be taken in by the analysand and psychically used. Here I rely on modes of relating described from a variety of theoretical perspectives, such as Ogden's (1994) subjective object, Aron's (2000) self-reflexive functioning, Bollas's (1987) transformational object, Kohut's (1977) self-object, the analyst as auxiliary ego (Greenson, 1967) and Fairbairn's (1952) part-object. Though there are subtle distinctions among these concepts, I emphasize here their major similarities and aim to describe ways in which the analyst is conceived by the analysand as not wholly separate. These concepts refer to the use of the analyst as an *other who performs certain functions* for the analysand but where the analyst is not experienced as *an other with separate subjectivity* or complex interiority. Over time, the analyst's subjectivity can take shape in the mind of the analysand, as needs and capacities are developed and become differentiated.

This experience of the analyst can affect the ability to lie on the couch, mainly in its requirement of turning away. The dangers experienced by the analysand in this case are illustrated in any number of *New Yorker* cartoons: the analyst's disengagement (as in clipping his toenails or sleeping); the analyst's intrusion or aggressive potential (e.g., poised with a dagger or about to strangle); or, the analyst's judging or shaming response (e.g., shaking his head or silently laughing). The point in elaborating these fantasies is to highlight the ways in which such fears can be differently elaborated, structured by transferences and may become anchored to one concrete aspect of the setting (i.e., behind one's back). Safety is often imagined by *never turning one's back* and many analysands choose to sit up for this reason.

For example, one analysand fears the couch because, if she were to lie down, she would no longer have access to signs in my gaze of my attentive listening. She imagines I might occupy myself with some quiet activity like reading or writing a paper (worse yet, not about her). But the question arises: Could she ever be sure I was listening? The analyst may appear to be listening, but is there a mode of interaction where the analysand can be

DOI: 10.4324/9781003264095-9

certain? *It is an existential condition that we never know the internal state of another being with certainty.*

Another analysand is reluctant to use the couch, not because of my feared inattentiveness or disengagement, but due to my imagined intrusion were he to lie down, organized by sadomasochistic fantasies of anal penetration as well as longed-for yet feared submission to enemas. Sitting up afforded him an illusory sense of control over the danger of domination, enacted in his way of rejecting my (penetrating) insights (Celenza, 2000a, 2000b, 2014). As in the previous example, danger was located on the couch but elaborated in an entirely different way, taking the form of domination and humiliation should he turn his back. Sitting up allowed the visual reassurance of where I was, physically at a safe distance from him.

Interestingly, the following case illustrates an analysand who used me as a subjective object for most of her analysis, conducted with her lying on the couch (and facing away). Julie, a 29-year-old female actor, came to treatment because of performance anxiety and, in particular, a reticence to "take the spotlight." She could recognize much positive feedback she consistently received for her talents, however, she had difficulty tolerating a feeling of self-esteem and confidence when she stood before a crowd. Julie also acknowledged problems sustaining a monogamous relationship but took care to state that her sexuality was not an issue. She saw her difficulty with intimacy as separate from her sexuality, preferring to view herself as sexually unconventional and uninhibited. She stated that she enjoyed sexual experiences with multiple partners and, at times, used recreational drugs (specifically marijuana and ecstasy) to enhance her sexual pleasure. She did not view either as problematic. I noted the apparent segmentation of her sexuality and intimacy needs. I noted the interesting contradiction of performance anxiety in front of a crowd and her ability to enjoy multiple partners (a crowd?) in her sexual life.

Julie easily approached the couch and spent the next several years revealing her inner thoughts and feelings to me in this mode. She uncovered an unconscious fantasy that amidst the stage lights and camera flashes, i.e., when she *could not see* people in the audience, she struggled with an irrational, split-second doubt about whether she was, in fact, alone. She associated this to the feeling of *aloneness in a crowd* that she had felt growing up among nine siblings, a depressed mother and a critical, yet often absent father.

Despite her insistence that her sexuality was not a problem, it became clear that Julie was trying to diminish fears of abandonment and rejection by using substances and having sexual relations with multiple partners, all persons she did not love. We also learned that keeping others at a distance, in an objectified way, protected her from the arousal of her hostility, linked to memories of her critical father. These angry feelings were inevitably evoked if she cared for a sole partner. Engaging with multiple partners diffused these feelings and tended instead to arouse wishful feelings of being touched and held, stimulated by nonverbal, bodily sensations. She stated that, in her quasi-hypnotic, drug-induced state, she was searching for *merger* (her word), the experience of being totally understood, known and cared for in a nonverbal, body-based way.

Julie's longing for merger coincided with her experience in the transference where she felt frustrated at the effort it took to verbalize her thoughts and feelings to me. She often expressed a desire for me to know her through some kind of body therapy, touch therapy or in some way to magically bypass having to speak. She expressed wishes that I could read her mind, get inside her skin and in many ways know her without her having to say anything. She made associations to analysis as too intellectual and left-brain. During this time, she frequently sought out extra therapies that were body-oriented, involving massage and "reading auras" around her body.

In general, I interpreted these wishes as her desire to have me understand her in a way her own mother had not, but in a way that also denied our separateness and difference. She often commented, "words divide us and do not describe what I want." She explained that she wanted to *feel* different and she wanted me to *make her feel* different by touching her concretely, through actual physical touch. I responded by suggesting that her desire for me *to be inside her* was a denial of our separateness and a bypassing of our external and internal differences.

In these various fantasies of her experience on the couch, the negotiation of sameness and difference can be discerned. Along similar lines, Julie's progression can be understood as the gradual establishment of self-boundaries as she learned to tolerate her frustrated desires for merger with me. Throughout, I believe the function I served was to help her play with my *internal* presence, the seductiveness of my potential understanding and, at the same time, the limits of my understanding. Though she was engaging my subjectivity, the process demonstrates the way in which my internal presence was used for this specific purpose, crafted by her needs, i.e., my presence for her as a subjective object.

Note

1 See Essay 6, *The analyst as objectified other* (this volume).

Chapter 8

The analyst as subject

It is reasonable to assume that, for most analysands, being outside the visual sphere of the analyst is a position that preserves and facilitates analytic complexity due to the ways in which this position requires the analysand to develop and rely upon their internal experience. In this position, it is more difficult to reduce complexity by attaching meanings with the exterior surface of the analyst. When facing away, the analyst's facial expressions are not visible, thereby forcing the analysand to imagine the feeling state of the analyst by relying upon internal experience. In this way, facing away provides fewer clues to the analyst's feeling state.

Because lying down is also facing away, *not seeing* can facilitate the expansion of the analytic play. In other words, facing the analyst may anchor the analysand's experience externally; facing away situates the analysand's experience internally. However, facing the analyst can also stimulate internal fantasies of the analysand if and when sufficient analytic work has developed the analysand's internal world. The stimulant of the analyst's presence (including the analyst's imagined internal life) can be a source of analytic material that facilitates this process.

The case of Julie (presented in the prior essay),[1] illustrates the development of internal capacities through the early phase of analysis in just this way. In a later phase of analysis, after Julie had terminated her analysis with me, she returned and requested to sit up. It became clear that facing me stimulated important, yet buried unconscious fantasies about my internal life and the ways in which Julie could experience me.

Julie had terminated her analysis after 5 years, having experienced increased feelings of inner strength, confidence in her performances and the ability to sustain romantic and sexual feelings in a monogamous relationship.[2] She was able to be more assertive in her goals and displayed greater enjoyment for the intensity of her passion. Her depression had lifted and she left the treatment feeling substantially strengthened.

Subsequently, after a year and a half, Julie returned. She acknowledged lasting changes from the analysis, yet a reticence to "take the spotlight" still lingered and she wanted to continue to explore this inhibition. She also

DOI: 10.4324/9781003264095-10

expressed discomfort at continuing with her previous reduced fee (though I thought she still needed one). We decided to reduce the number of sessions, thereby raising the fee per hour (though still at a reduced rate). She also chose to sit up. I had the fantasy that she wanted to *face me* more as an equal. We proceeded with a face-to-face treatment for the next year and a half, mostly exploring her feelings on the stage.

During one hour, Julie was describing the feeling of the curtain rising, the moment when she looks out at the audience and sometimes catches someone's eye. She described this moment as derailing her. She wondered about the earlier interpretation of her unconscious fantasy that "no one was there" and we speculated that perhaps this fantasy functioned in part as a wish, a protection from the potentially derailing connection to a particular other. (I was reminded of my own experience presenting papers at conferences where I feel less anxious peering out to a group of anonymous faces as opposed to the self-conscious feeling when someone I know is in the audience.)

This formulation was consistent with the ease with which Julie used the couch from the beginning, perhaps to protect her from the potentially de-railing awareness of *a particular other*. Now we wondered if being *alone in a crowd* represented both a fear and a protection: the fear of abandonment as we had initially understood as well as a protection against the awareness of a knowing, particular other. Her use of the couch and the chair elaborated both sides of this dialectical tension wherein safety, initially residing in a more diffuse type of engagement (like her sexual relations with multiple partners), was optimally experienced at a distance (i.e., on the couch). The couch protected her from the potentially disjunctive experience of my se-parateness and the complexity of my internal world (for her, as we would later discover, my potential as a competitor and object of envy).

In this later phase of analysis (sitting up), Julie's associations began to revolve around my external appearance. (We look and are about the same age.) She would comment on my body, weight and hair. She referred to my style of clothing, comparing her "funky, natural and unconventional" taste with my more professional, "less risky" appearance. In particular, she dis-liked my suit jackets, saying I dressed in an uncreative, consumer-driven fashion. She said she could not dress the way I do because show business required more flamboyance. I told her I thought she wanted to compare herself to me in order to find her own style. She spoke of memories of her mother repairing her older sisters' clothing and handing them down to her. She said she always wanted new clothing but there was not enough money. She admitted she still felt "not dressed up enough" and asked if I would view a video of a recent audition with an eye on her outfits. I told her it sounded like she wanted feedback on her appearance, especially for the stage. She mentioned acting coaches who help performers with their stage outfits. She added, "I've always disparaged that form of help as a waste of money, but I think I can tolerate someone examining me now." The analogy to this phase of treatment where I looked directly at her was obvious. Soon after, she hired such a coach. In her analysis, we focused instead on her competitive and envious feelings that were beginning to emerge.

Julie began to incorporate attention to her physical (external) appearance as part of her performance on the stage. She gradually came to tolerate the previously denied and unwanted reality that the way she *appeared in the spotlight* was part of her anxiety and fear of competition. She associated to her body as too big, too hungry, but also as an exterior container for her inner desires. I recognized her increasing capacity to tolerate competitive and envious feelings toward me based on her experience of both my inner and outer self.

The earlier wish to be inside my skin (or me in hers) now took on a different meaning in the *après coup* of the analytic process. Whereas in the early phases of the analysis Julie wanted a feeling of merger with me, by-passing my exteriority or separateness, she now gazed at me from a distance and imagined my inner life. She fantasized that I was internally powerful and strong yet worried that she was impoverishing me through the reduced fee. Omnipotent fantasies associated with her aggression emerged in competitive and envious forms. Would she tire me out or make me hate her? Would I envy her as she became strong? Was being strong the same as being too big or hungry? Was there enough in me to give to her along with my other patients? *Alone in a crowd* was transformed again, revealing another layer of meaning – she wanted to be my *one and only* among the crowd of my patients.

The illustration of the analytic process upon Julie's return serves to depict ways in which the analyst's presence, including her exterior appearance and the visual stimuli associated with it, can prompt the emergence of deep-seated feelings and associations within the analysand. Sufficient development of the analysand's interiority must precede this potential, so that the analytic process is not reduced to a surface, externally interactional rather than a bi-directional, intersubjective exploratory process embedded within a larger unconscious field.

Notes

1 See Essay 7, *The analyst as subjective object* (this volume).
2 It is important to note that developing a capacity for monogamy is not an imposition of the analyst's values. There is no assumption that the patient should live monogamously, only that the analysis can help to *develop the capacity for monogamy*, thereby expanding the analysand's choices for ways of experiencing intimacy.

Chapter 9

Where is psychoanalysis?

The process of psychoanalysis entails an exploration of intrapsychic and intersubjective engagement as it is expressed (verbally and through enactments) in the potential space created. The boundaries around this potential space as well as within the space (referring here to the demarcations around the analyst's and analysand's private spheres) fluctuate and shift according to the emergence of different transferences. Further, the potential space expands in all directions as analysis successfully proceeds and modes of relating (organized by transferences) are accessed and integrated.

The potential space can be symbolically demarcated and delimited by defensive retreats from intolerable aloneness (disconnection or annihilation) and overstimulating or engulfing engagement. The couch and the chair can each come to represent endpoints for the axis around which these aspects revolve and are anchored. It is not that the structural arrangement exclusively determines where this tension will be played out, but that, in locating the endpoints of this axis for a particular analysand, the couch and chair may come to concretely represent disavowed aspects of the danger/safety dialectic attributed to either placement.[1] These visuospatial configurations are elaborated in the experience and observation of the self in relation to the analyst as postural changes and views of each other's body, face and mind vary.

The analysand may sit up or lie down in an effort to control imagined psychic dangers that coincide with each body position. But these defensive postures are illusory psychic managements. Once situated in the analysand's mind, lying down or sitting up may become fetishized or, conversely, phobically avoided. While these defensive maneuvers effectively serve to temporarily manage anxiety or other dangerous affects, these affects may lurk unrecognized in the potential space whenever or however they may be demarcated. In other words, analysands who are reluctant to use the couch may sit up with greater ease; however, it is not unusual to find a fixity in their stare or a way in which their body posture belies a sense of danger nonetheless. Likewise, an analysand who cannot lie down for fear of being

DOI: 10.4324/9781003264095-11

dominated may imagine she or he is safe sitting up but may be unable to look away or *take in* the analyst's penetrating insights.

Here, it is useful to ask as well, Where is the analyst's subjectivity? Where is the analysand's desire and need for privacy in relation to it? For example, when Julie[2] came back to *face me as an equal,* I realized there was a way in which I had always felt she was *in my face.* Lying on the couch or sitting up, I recognized in retrospect that it had always been difficult to get into a dialogue with her without feeling as if I had to push her back, in effect, to fight to penetrate her. (This countertransference reaction became a relevant interpersonal factor in our increasing understanding of the strength of her hostility toward partners, a paternal transference that I was now experiencing with her as well.)

For me, the greatest obstacle in my countertransference with Julie was in *valuing* the processes that were becoming manifest in the sitting-up modality. I was aware of an internal battle within me as I felt simultaneously intrigued all the while minimizing the significance of the issues that were coming to the fore. I remember having difficulty giving Julie's comments, especially on my appearance, a level of importance and depth. I noted a tendency to dismiss her preoccupations with the exterior of my body as superficial and *not analysis.* For other analysands, an exchange in the waiting room, *on the way to analysis* so to speak, was sufficient to stimulate a variety of reactions and associations. Yet exploring these only when the analysand was on the couch seemed proper.

I also felt Julie's examination of me as intrusive and, at times, confrontational. I was aware of the imposition on my privacy as part of the modality of sitting up and, again, fought the tendency to dismiss its importance as *not analysis*, concrete or superficial. There was a way in which her reaction to facing me felt enactive, as if she was *doing something to me* rather than reflecting on her experience. The obvious polarization between action and words also fostered a minimization of these aspects of the process.

As I began to see an increasing flexibility in her examination of herself, including an increasing facility in moving from the exterior to the interior in her associations, I began to legitimize the process as analytic. When she spoke of changes in her ability to hold the audience's attention and to sustain her presence on the stage without undue anxiety, I began to take seriously, consistently and without conflict, the therapeutic action occurring in the treatment. It then became easier to link the ongoing processes with various unconscious fantasies that were arising.

I do not mean to suggest that the couch is dispensable. I am suggesting that the use of both the couch and chair are useful ways to explore the analysand's relation to the analyst, by varying body postures and through exposure to the analyst's body and face. In addition, avoidance of either the couch or the chair should be taken up. *Privileging lying down over sitting up is valuing one kind of psychic experience over another and may collude with a defensive avoidance that leaves important affective experience unexplored.*

I continue to believe that the couch is an invaluable stimulant of unconscious conflict and dissociated experience, primarily for the placement of the analyst outside the visual field of the analysand. The significance, however, does not rely on the impossible ideal of anonymity (Renik, 1995) but for the fact that placement of the analyst outside the analysand's visual sphere is a position that has more *plasticity*, i.e., contains a wider range of interpretability. Like a Rorschach blot with varying degrees of discrete or ambiguous features, the experience of the analyst outside one's visual sphere inherently contains less structure, thereby providing more possibilities for interpretation and construction of meaning. Any stance, visible or beyond the analysand's visual sphere, is consequential; the question is how and in what way it expands or constricts access to affective experience.

It is for these reasons that I continue to view lying down on the couch as the desirable mode to begin an analysis. As mentioned, it is reasonable to assume that, for most analysands, facing away is a posture and position that fosters self-reflection and fantasy about the analyst less tied to concrete factors. Also, lying down on the couch i is a position that inherently allows for greater plasticity due to the absence of concrete and potentially constraining visual cues. Finally, there is a greater sense of privacy (for both analysand and analyst) that can be at once freeing and constraining, requiring a focusing inward. However, for some analysands, this can foster a distancing and may obscure for some time important unconscious processes. The decisive factor revolves around the perception of resistance against one mode over the other, as indicated by some measure of anxiety in either facing the analyst or turning away. I have come to believe that every analysis *should, at some point, include both modalities* for some period of time, since it is often difficult to know what anxieties lurk where until they are enacted.

Notes

1 See Essay 5, *Safety, danger, couch, chair* (this volume).
2 See Essay 8, *The analyst as subject* (this volume).

Chapter 10

The nature of boundaries

There are certain frustrated, unmet desires that remain pre-symbolic, un-represented or unformulated. These can become accessible in concretized, body-based symptomatology or action. Sexual experience sometimes provides a conduit for such unformulated longings for which it can serve as a stand-in, a kind of hoped-for palliative. "If you can't see my being, then touch my body" one analysand may seem to be saying. Or, "If you can see me, I want you to touch *all* of me" says another. Each of these may fall into line with different types of misuses, perhaps the former with the classical analyst under the sway of a masochistic surrender and the latter with the relational analyst whose lovesickness refuses limit.[1]

When we touch another person, we do not solely touch a body, we touch a *being*. It is true that when we *see* another person, we see a body, but in a holistic way, we *experience a being*, the boundaries around which are invisible, and upon engagement, intermingled with our own. It is as if we are saying, "By you recognizing me, I become manifest, thereby your being has the power to evoke or pull me toward you." I emerge, come into being by virtue of your gaze and this power is reciprocal. I have a similar power for you. We then are manifest to each other and the mutual attention we pay to each other creates something between us, a feelingful connection that is something beyond you and me alone. Who am I in this moment? I know myself through your ability to evoke me, but you do not create me *de novo,* nor do you experience me wholly. Yet your ability to evoke me implies that the boundaries around our respective beings are not circumscribed, concrete or static (see Folkmarson Kall, 2009; Foehl, 2009).

There are no lines in nature. What, then, do we mean by boundaries? Boundaries, even in the physical world, are not lines, but *horizons,* those ever-elusive and ultimately illusory demarcations where one being ends and another begins in a moment of time and space. Each horizon shifts and is continually renegotiated with every change in perspective, every new facet of engagement.

Horizons note the temporal and spatial coordinates where difference meets. Often this moment is marked by speaking. As Winnicott (1971)

DOI: 10.4324/9781003264095-12

famously put it, the main reason the analyst makes an interpretation is so the patient knows the limits of his understanding (p. 116). To the extent that the therapeutic action revolves around the strengthening of subjectivity, i.e., becoming a subject, the process consists of moment to moment negotiations of self-other differentiation.

Consider the following vignette. A patient describes her excitement in having bought a new painting. She loves it and wants me to see it, imagining me loving it too, reflecting her experience, joining her in her enjoyment of the painting and having a similar experience as her own. Then she wonders, What if I don't like it? Would I tell her? That doesn't matter, she realizes. She would know. She decides she does not want me to see the painting after all, as she conjures the experience of me as other, disjunctive to her phenomenal experience and desires in the moment. She knows *she* loves the painting and suddenly that is enough.

Difference (separateness, the experience of the other *as other*) can engender discomfort and even hatred due to the ambiguity and uncertainty of the unknown. It is easy to mistake difference with disowned (or hated) aspects of oneself, making disjunction threatening. Yet, these boundaries, the *no* of the other, the experience of difference, leads to the sense of agency and selfhood. To know *not me* strengthens the experience of *me*.[2]

> Every frame – or margin, border … imposes an order on the story and defines a world within which characters move and plots are structured. The purpose of the performance is to help one of the two actors/protagonists to arrive at a better definition of himself and to construct his own identity – that is, to gain a broader consciousness of self. Identity, by definition, is made up of boundaries, of frontiers. (Civitarese, 2008, p. 68)

Similarly, to accept difference is to be open to the possibility of hierarchy, (e.g., *You are better or have something more than I*), wherein ensues the experience and tolerance of envy. This can become an opportunity for the birthing of desire, i.e., *I want*.

Thus, boundaries are defining of identity and being – this is their transformative power. The assertion of boundaries, the recognition of difference, provides that we have choices and is the result of an intersubjective negotiation. In the analytic setting, boundaries are a process, a commitment to a discipline that defines *the way* we engage with each other. The maintenance of boundaries is not static; it is a process and a capacity that is continually reasserted over time. As analysts, we make a commitment to face, deal, negotiate and *engage at the horizon of the unknown.* We promise to be present at the *edge of the emergent unknown other,* without knowing what we're going to feel, see or hear.

Notes

1 See Essay 11, *Sexual boundary violations and theoretical orientation* (this volume)
   for an elaboration of the unconscious dynamics of sexual boundary transgressions
   associated with theoretical orientation.
2 See Essay 33, *Internal psychic positions, healthy and perverse* (this volume) for an
   elaboration of the positions of subjectivity.

Chapter 11

Sexual boundary violations and theoretical orientation

I am often asked whether there is a difference in prevalence of sexual boundary violations according to theoretical orientation. There is, I often sense, a hidden, subtle, almost delicious anticipation .... *Please tell me the relational analysts are by far the bad actors and are single-handedly bringing down the profession!* kind of hope. I can almost touch their relish as they wait for my answer to which I calmly reply, "No, actually, there is no difference in theoretical orientation." However, that is not the end of the discussion.

Our theories fail us differently. Our theories, and derivations of technique from theoretical stance, all fail us, but in different ways so there actually may be some differentiations to be made in type of sexual boundary transgression and profile (correlated with theoretical orientation), but not in quantity or frequency of occurrence. These distinctions highlight different aspects of our beloved theories and their fallibilities, the different types of pressures on the analyst to maintain the appropriate stance, especially over time. How our theories are embodied and may I say, caricatured, can teach us much about the implications of certain theoretical stances and what is needed for us to live them out in humane and restorative ways.

We are all drawn to this infinitely interesting and compelling profession for very personal and characterological reasons. In an earlier paper on the analyst's needs and desires (Celenza, 2010b), I made the point that most of us have partly unconscious needs to find and heal ourselves. We identify in part with our patients to address these needs.[1] So, to varying extents, we are all here to find the good mother/father we have been searching out lifelong. *To be the good mother/father for our patients is in part to find salvation for ourselves.* These motivations will drive us to certain theories and repel us from others, finding us situated and perhaps entrenched in a way of performing our craft that is inextricably tied to what we ourselves need.

Our personal choice of theoretical orientation can also be informed by our relationship to countertransference, in that countertransference embodies the person of the analyst more than any other variable in technical stance. The degree to which one can let one's being or personhood enter the field reflects our preferences and comfort with this aspect of analysis. The history

DOI: 10.4324/9781003264095-13

of countertransference and its role in psychoanalytic theorizing bears this out and has affected how analysts were and are now trained. In the past, analytic training varied greatly depending on geographic locale. This was starkly reflected in how countertransference was taught.

In European and South American traditions, there was an *organic evolution* in the way countertransference became the focus of attention and was gradually integrated into the analyst's theoretical and technical stance. Through the works of Paula Heimann (1950) – from the British Psychoanalytic Institute – and Heinrich Racker (1957) – an Argentinian psychoanalyst – countertransference began to take center stage or at least enjoyed a legitimate place among the various "fields" where unconscious dynamics play out. This was reflected in gradual but significant changes in theorizing during the 1950s.

Not so in North America where the medical establishment held a stranglehold on the training of psychoanalysts. In North America (and especially the United States), theorizing maintained a conservative, "purely Freudian" or ego-psychological constriction. It took a *decisive revolution* in psychoanalytic theorizing, a revolution from a one-person psychology to a two-person perspectival epistemology, to allow the personal, unconscious affective experience of the analyst onto the stage.[2] Due to the medical establishment's resistance, this revolution could only take root much later and outside of the American Psychoanalytic Association's auspices, where certain "non-certified" institutes – the William Alonson White Institute and the New York University Post-Doctoral Training Program in Psychoanalysis – germinated and nurtured the radical thinking of the Interpersonal and Relational Traditions [see Stern and Hirsch (2017) for a detailed review of this history and Celenza (2017) for a book review].

Thus, theorizing became geographically localizable and assertively nonintegrative. In recent decades, however, psychoanalytic theorizing has become internationalized, such that these polarized differences have led to integrative efforts and a wider teaching of various technical stances. The full range of theorizing now plays a part in the conscious and unconscious choices one makes.

Some of us have a concordant relationship to our theoretical persuasion in that we identify with the (usually idealized) preferred stance of the analyst of a particular orientation because it fits with our personality tendencies, going *hand in hand*. It's easy to see how the attuned, naturally empathic and emotionally expressive analyst, perhaps a bit less loved than she might have needed, would be drawn to the relational tradition to make good use of her empathic skills and propensities. Others have a compensatory relationship to their preferred theoretical persuasion in that the correlate analytic stance gives them cover, something that they need but do not readily have in their armamentarium. We could say this group has a complementary relationship to their theory of choice, like a *hand in a glove*. The classical analytic stance as a blank screen can serve as a protection for the more schizoid and in-hibited among us. I am not saying this is true for all, but that it can function this way. You may think that the latter example is much worse for our patients than is the former, however *both fail us* in great measure.

For the relational analyst, the problem is in the idealization of love and its healing power. While of course, the emphasis on the mutuality and hu-manness of the analytic relationship is a much-needed corrective to the wooden, inaccessible classical caricature, the emphasis on mutuality to the exclusion of the disciplined restraint of asymmetry is problematic, especially as this imbalance evokes *omnipotent rescue fantasies*. This is the dynamic in a certain profile of sexual boundary transgressor where the subjectivity of the analyst can be stirred to a level of grandiosity that knows few limits.

On the other hand, the problem in the idealization of anonymity and the supposed freedom to fantasize such a striving affords, fails to guide the more schizoid, narcissistically impaired analyst when things heat up. Like a boat in a storm without a mooring, intense erotic transferences can overwhelm the more schizoid, inhibited analyst who has only classical theories with their one-person epistemology – a mandate to "act like you're not there" – to rely on in these times.

Or, the almost exclusive emphasis on the asymmetry in the analytic re-lationship (through the lens of neutrality, anonymity and abstinence[3]) can be interpreted as permission to hide behind the analyst's authority. A *ma-sochistic surrendering* to the patient's intensely driven demands is more likely to derail this kind of limited analyst whose subjectivity finds safety in the hidden, mysterious shroud of anonymity. We might be tempted to think this would only happen to the young and unseasoned. However, our fantasies of seniority feed our omnipotence as well, in ways that blind us to the most basic existential limitations in a time where fears of mortality loom.

Most sexual boundary transgressions are a composite of both; one com-pensating where the other falls short at one time, the other compensating when rationalizations are needed. This is a special fallibility in these plur-alistic times. The omnipotence derived from the idealization of love can easily address gaps in our clinical armamentarium when intense erotic passion seems to break down the screen behind which lurks our own guilty schizoid longings.

Notes

1 See also Essay 2, *Paradox in the psychoanalytic stance* (this volume).
2 Some theorists cite Kohut's (1977) self-psychological revolution in theorizing as a middle step from a one-person psychology toward a two-person psychology where the analyst embodies a needed psychic figure, a *self-object*, representing a one-and-a-half person psychology.
3 See Essay 2, *Paradox in the psychoanalytic stance* (this volume).

Chapter 12

The inadvertent pluralist

The psychoanalytic literature is a major source of exposure to different clinical approaches, modes of technique and theoretical orientations. Comparative studies of theoretical orientations are one way to learn about how to approach clinical dilemmas from different points of view, how different theoretical systems view the nature of therapeutic action and what methods of intervention are associated with each system (Celenza, 2019). Techniques and technical stances are often discussed in association with particular theoretical orientations and their concomitant foundational assumptions, modes of therapeutic action and theories of change. However, comparative studies among theoretical perspectives are often not well described by those outside of a particular tradition and are sometimes set up in stereotypic, if not exaggerated ways to elucidate a particular polemic. These discussions can devolve into caricatured arguments among various straw men as proponents of one viewpoint make their case in contrast to another. Alternative technical possibilities and the hope of expanding one's clinical lexicon and repertoire for the less theoretically pure can be lost.

As examples, American relational approaches are often reduced in complexity to theories that focus on the interaction between analyst and analysand. Through these oversimplified descriptions, there arises a criticism that relational analysts are environmentally distracted and pay little attention to unconscious factors. Italian field theories are similarly distorted by descriptions of imaginative play disregarding repetitive themes in the here-and-now relationship that may relate to the analysand's historical narrative.

Sometimes comparative discussions engender debates about how to define each theoretical orientation (especially regarding essential elements, clinical stances and modes of technique associated with each), which version is under scrutiny (classical, contemporary or neo) and finally, who belongs to which. These are not easy lines to draw and it is not unusual for a particular psychoanalyst to have difficulty placing herself or himself within a specific tradition as characterized. In the worst-case scenario, descriptions of each theoretical orientation and their corresponding clinical stances become

DOI: 10.4324/9781003264095-14

caricatured and ultimately describe an orientation to which no one would subscribe.

Donnel Stern, for example, is allied with the interpersonal/relational tradition yet his stance is characterized by continuous receptivity to emergent process, as reflected in his longstanding emphasis on unformulated experience and courting surprise. Indeed, my reading of the papers included in the two-part panel (Cooper, 2013; Carnochan, 2013; Ferro and Civitarese, 2013; Foehl, 2013a, 2013b; Levine, 2013a; Peltz and Goldberg, 2013; Stern, 2013a, 2013b; Troise, 2013) leads me to categorize Stern as a relational-field theorist.

It is my view that technical choices often do not require an allegiance to a particular model, but at the phenomenological and clinical levels, may, like various other technical approaches, straddle multiple theoretical models such that many having an unwitting reach to several orientations (Cooper, 2015). Some theoretical orientations may prioritize one technical stance over another, while other orientations make use of both in an oscillating or variable fashion. In the latter case, individual psychoanalysts are likely to have developed a "personal core theory" made up of multiple part theories (LaFarge, 2017) that characterize the way their practice is conducted such that they no longer fit neatly into pure theoretical systems.

There are also debates about jargon where similarities in technical stances arising from disparate geographical regions or longstanding theoretical traditions employ idiosyncratic terminology. This jargon is usually viewed as belonging solely within its own theoretical province. Sometimes subtle differences yield important distinctions (e.g., Bion's (1967) *negative capability* as a fundamental attitude or capacity versus Laplanche's *tub* [1999b] as a feature of the setting, inclusive of the analyst's attitude, but not only). In other cases, it is possible for reasonable analysts to wonder if certain technical language deriving from different theoretical systems is not aiming at a similar phenomenon, despite widely divergent linguistic referents, (e.g., unformulated experience and unrepresented states,[1] bastion and enactment,[2] mutual recognition and at-one-ment). A question is inevitably raised, Are these discussions nit-picking and if so, do they render the debates about them a rhetoric of minor differences?

At the same time, another, perhaps more widely accepted consensus is emerging involving the recognition that many psychoanalysts utilize a multiplicity of models and theoretical orientations (Cooper, 2015, 2017; LaFarge, 2017; Zimmer, 2010, 2017). Stimulated by particular types of interactions and experiences with analysands across time, different understandings and experiences of what is occurring in the analytic process can evoke divergent or even contradictory theoretical lenses at different times, requiring a shift in models. While it is generally accepted that different theories have their own limitations and excesses, it is suggested that in actual practice, most psychoanalysts are likely to be *inadvertent pluralists*, borrowing from many theoretical viewpoints while maintaining theoretical ideals and commitments in word or theoretical discourse. Some writers are recognizing the possibility of flexibility in theoretical commitments (LaFarge, 2017; Cooper, 2017) while others consider such theoretical shifts to be moments that foreclose exposure to deeper truths that a single, multi-faceted model may offer. The argument here is that some models are sufficiently comprehensive and multi-faceted that shifts in stance do not reflect a concomitant shift in model but fall within deeper layers of the same model (see Blass, 2017).

It may be, for example, that in varying clinical moments, a psychoanalyst will utilize differing clinical *stances* that are associated with several different models. An approach or stance resides at a relatively low level of abstraction and does not introduce a clash at the theoretical level, (a higher level of abstraction), because many models utilize the same or similar clinical stances. When a higher level of abstraction is explicated, (for example, in discussing the foundational assumptions associated with the nature of the unconscious), the clash in theoretical models emerges. In certain instances, the problem is not one of multiplicity or plurality in technique; it is the comprehensiveness of the model in mind (see Blass, 2017, for further discussion). In contemporary times, it may be fruitless to attempt to describe any theoretical orientation as representative of its tradition, which in current models is likely nonetheless to be a hybrid (see, for example, Harris' (2011) definition of relational theory and technique). The choice to debate in clinical discourse at the level of stance over model may lead to greater consensus (Bernardi, 2017), especially when the discourse revolves around clinical material.

Notes

1 The interested reader is referred to Levine (2013b).
2 See Stern's (2013a) comparison of these two concepts where he claims differences in emphasis in the understanding of the analyst's conduct.

Chapter 13

The art of the boundary

The concept of boundary is used in many ways in psychoanalytic theorizing, some of which belong to different registers and dimensions of psychic experience. We can easily commit a category error when we speak of boundaries from one and then another domain. Cooper (2016) draws two distinctions among these domains: boundaries in the psychic realm versus those that demarcate behavioral mandates.

Redrawing these distinctions, I prefer not to separate the psychic from the behavioral under the assumption that the two implicate each other (our behavior follows or reflects our psychic experience). For my palette, one way in which boundaries do their psychic work is by demarcating internalized self and object relations which then become actualized in interpersonal, lived experience. When forensic discourse is invoked, I believe we can (with sufficient analysis) trace back from the behavior (the violation) to the drama of the psychic realm and see how internal identifications/psychic experiences are or were implicated, including how or why the behavior went awry of ethical commitments.

The two registers that I find heuristic to the concept of boundary and how it is used in our discourse refer to the mutual and asymmetric modes of relating inherent in and definitional of an analytic process (respectively).[1] To my palette, these registers differ but are dialectically related and both involve the concept of boundaries on psychic and behavioral levels. Further, these dimensions are either *given* (in the mutual realm) or are *asserted* (in the asymmetric realm), the latter being definitional of the psychoanalytic project and a choice we make moment to moment based on our ethical commitments.

What, then, is a boundary in the most general sense? A paint stroke? A sentence? An experience? Since there are no lines in nature, I prefer to think of boundaries as *horizons,* those ever-elusive and ultimately illusory demarcations where one being ends and another begins in a moment of time and space.[2] Each horizon shifts and is continually renegotiated with every change in perspective, every new facet of engagement. Boundaries are invisible constructions, sometimes blurred, sometimes a given, sometimes

DOI: 10.4324/9781003264095-15

negotiated and sometimes choices we make, again depending upon the register. To me, this is the canvas upon which our boundary art is painted.

Boundaries, emergent in the mutuality register, demarcate the activity of self-other differentiation. It is here where the sorting out of projective identificatory mechanisms and various co-creations of the process come to the foreground. In this register, boundaries can be blurred, invisible and illusory yet, in the sorting out process, we rearrange and co-create them such that these illusory demarcations emerge with greater clarity as self-states and defenses become differentiated. I believe the *givenness* of these boundaries can be presumed, however, *only in retrospect* as they emerge through a clarifying process that rearranges self and other authorship. In this context, boundaries aid in defining which and what is whose. (Through this writing I am realizing an aspect of what is meant by authorship; we have been making use of another artistic metaphor in describing how we *write* as opposed to *paint* the contours of the self.) In whatever metaphor, these abstract demarcations refer to invisible but phenomenally experienced contours that then are linked to behavioral stances or expressions.

In the asymmetric register of the psychoanalytic process, however, the concept of boundaries is used in a different way. These are also abstract demarcations but they reflect and link to a concrete attitude that is not a given but that is *intended to be actualized in behavior*. In the asymmetric register, boundaries define our choices and guide our behavior more explicitly in the sense that they prescribe certain modes of thinking, listening and behaving while prohibiting others. They are integral to the social contract of the analytic set-up involving at least three dimensions: our asymmetric *focus* which demarcates and instructs where our attention is directed; behavioral *abstinence* (especially sexual, but other emotional desires and needs as well) referring specifically to a prohibition, i.e., all talk, no action; and, the *purpose* of the meeting, to help the patient evolve in psychic development (in contrast to, for example, talking for the purpose of erotic arousal).

These commitments guide us toward what and where our responses are geared. This is our discipline, *it is not a given but a choice we make* and it must be asserted and reasserted in an ongoing way throughout the process. Boundaries in this dimension are abstract demarcations that help keep us on course by reflecting our commitments, attitudes and, by extension, behaviors aimed toward maintaining an ethical position. They serve to differentiate our role in an overall way, made up of our focus and purpose, all reflected in our behavior.

A boundary is an abstract demarcation rooted in a fantasy. When self-boundaries are blurred through defensive rearranging (such as projective identification), it might be that the patient is engaging in a wish-driven, defensively constructed fantasy. When boundaries are selected in role definition, they are created through a reality-based choice and are meant to be actualized in behavior. Though they may be initially rooted in a fantasy, they are concretized in a social contract to maintain certain attentional and behavioral commitments. These may begin as an abstraction or fantasy but are purposefully concretized in order to actualize the analytic set-up. I believe this is why we can talk about the analyst's responsibility in this realm.

The act of a boundary violation refers, then, to a (conscious or unconscious) choice to use these abstract demarcations for purposes other than what was agreed upon, i.e., to pervert the purpose of the process by actualizing something else via a means/end reversal that upends the psychoanalytic project.[3] By pairing the concept of boundary with violation, we pinpoint a specific kind of ethical breach that connotes perverse usage. To substitute the term *ethical* violation, we only know that a mistake was made. To use the term *boundary* violation, we know some perversion of the process has occurred.

We could say the psychoanalytic process sometimes entails a vigorous enactment of *No, you! No, **you**!* kind of interchange. Perhaps this is why this kind of disclaiming occurs so often in the aftermath of a boundary violation where each member of the dyad wants to disown the failure of maintaining commitments. (For the patient, it is an inevitable confusion whereas for the analyst, it is a perverse disclaiming of responsibility.)

There is no doubt that there is a disturbing tendency to think about sexual boundary violations in a concretized black/white, either/or manner, abundantly displayed in the literature and formal and informal discourse on the subject. This has been identified and written about extensively (Schoener, 1989; Gabbard, 1994, 2016; Celenza, 2007). In addition, the furor over sexual boundary violations has sometimes caused anxiety, reductionism and constraint in our ability to be with our patients in flexible, playful and unpredictable ways. Yet, at the same time, it is by virtue of maintaining our commitments in focus, purpose and behavior that boundaries make play and flex possible; the safety that comes about through the consistent maintenance of our (asymmetric) commitments sets the stage for flexible play within the psychic (mutual) register.

Having continuously made this promise, the patient and her desires and needs emerge in a more undefended form than they otherwise might. Archaic patterns, desires, thoughts and memories are given freer expression *due to the promise that there will be no contingencies.* Herein lies the nature of the dialectic and the nature of the seduction – an invitation to one-wayness with special accommodations and safeguards tempts the analysand toward more openness, authenticity, baldness and vulnerability. Our patients travel deeper into forbidden terrain, deepen their affective engagement with us *because of* our continuous commitment to the social contract.[4] I suggest this is where Cooper's (2016) felicitous idea of boundary art has its place, especially as the process evokes this dialectic, i.e., how one realm makes the next possible (like the play of shadows in an M.C. Escher painting).

All of this invokes our relationship to uncertainty. Cooper (2016) tells us (and I agree) that boundaries allow us to get lost. When self-boundaries are blurred, what we really mean to convey is that we psychically and unconsciously shift what we own (who we think we are) in a particular moment. These allow the patient to take more risks. It is not that boundaries do not exist in this moment, but that they shift and are rearranged as defensive, adaptive and creative demands push them this way and that. Self-boundaries are different from the rules of the game which basically say, "You'll do this and I'll do that" or "You are allowed X whereas I am not." But this also amounts to a rearrangement of who one is (and how one will behave) in this particular dyad at this particular time. The multiplicity of self-other relations does not reduce this complexity when we focus on role boundaries; rather, the analyst's challenge is to keep these different registers in mind, simultaneously, despite their inherent contradictions.

It is the analytic contract that makes it possible to explore psychic boundaries and results in a depth that otherwise would not occur. But the compact (the commitment by the analyst) must be reasserted continuously throughout the treatment. At the same time, it is the real possibility of failing that makes these commitments more meaningful.

Notes

1 See Essay 2, *Paradox in the psychoanalytic stance* (this volume).
2 See also Essay 10, *The nature of boundaries* (this volume).
3 See Essay 31, *Perversion and its qualities of being* (this volume).
4 See Essay 24, *The promise that seduces desire* (this volume).

Chapter 14

Stance and attentional set in analytic listening

In examining different theoretical systems from a metapsychological perspective, it can be discerned that different models *imply a prioritization of certain modes of listening*, yet clear guidelines for how analysts put this into practice or intervene at the clinical level remain lacking. What exactly does the analyst *do* when functioning under a particular theory and not another? How does one theory differ from another and are there ways to integrate various techniques (despite different theoretical and epistemological assumptions underlying different systems)? Are there different priorities in modes of listening that can be identified and put into practice?

In this essay, I introduce two clinical listening stances that are associated with *different attentional sets*.[1] In the subsequent essays, a clinical application is described through a patient, Molly, in different phases of her treatment where I primarily utilized one listening stance over the other.[2] These attentional sets reside at a relatively low level of abstraction and are experience-near. The two attentional sets are: 1) *a directed attentional set* aimed at the identification of conscious and unconscious repetitive patterns, defensive tendencies or personality organization, and 2) *a diffuse attentional set* receptive to emergent phenomena for the purpose of elaborating unconscious fantasy as it arises in clinical process.[3] These attentional sets correspond to the analyst's mode of listening at any particular clinical moment and naturally occur in most analytic process in an oscillating fashion as clinical phenomena emerge and then are analyzed. It is worth emphasizing here that both sets utilize unconscious fantasy, however the first primarily *identifies* unconscious fantasy while the second set aims at *elaborating* unconscious fantasy. These aims shape the a priori readiness of the analyst in divergent ways.

Analysts do not listen in only one way. Nor do I want to suggest that either of these stances is solely associated with a particular theoretical orientation. Such an assertion would not be accurate and would imply a polarization between various theoretical approaches that does not exist in clinical practice. At the phenomenological, clinical level, both modes are found in all theoretical models, providing an "unwitting reach" across different models (Cooper,

DOI: 10.4324/9781003264095-16

2015). By differentiating these modes of listening for heuristic purposes, however, analysts can discern (often in retrospect), the oscillation and/or prioritization (in a foreground/background kind of way) of one mode of listening over another in any particular clinical moment.

Further, the differences between these listening stances become most obvious in certain theoretical orientations that tend to prioritize one mode of listening over another, especially as these relate to the interpretive choices subsequently taken. *In this way, these attentional sets are purposive and correspond to different attitudinal intents in relation to the analytic process.* For example, an analyst interested in historical reconstruction or repetitive defensive processes may foreground more frequently a directed attentional mode and listening stance. In contrast, analysts interested in elaborating unconscious fantasy or inscribing heretofore unrepresented states would, for the most part, listen more diffusely and nondirectively.[4]

This is not to suggest that either listening stance is applied solely from within each perspective. These technical stances do not require an allegiance to a particular model. I believe, however, that within a particular theoretical orientation, one may be emphasized and placed primarily in the foreground while the other is more in the background. As noted, I am articulating the clear differentiation of these attentional sets for heuristic purposes. My aim is to help analysts examine and discern differences among theoretical models at the level of listening stance, especially as these guide subsequent interpretive choices.

Analytic listening

The literature on analytic listening reveals it to be a multi-dimensional and varied process. Some authors view analytic listening as a structure of the mind (Parsons, 2007), providing a holding function for dissociated parts (D'Agostono, 2011), involving empathy through mirror neurons[5] (Aragno, 2008; Gallese, 2001), transient identification (e.g., numerous ego and self psychologists, summarized by Jacobs, 1992), a capacity that involves all five senses (Yamaguchi, 2012; Griffin, 2016; D'Agostino, 2011) and that integrates the analyst's authentic affective experience (e.g., Ella Freeman Sharpe and the numerous analysts associated with the British Independent/ Middle Group, summarized by Antonis, 2015).

From a descriptive standpoint, the nature of attention as part of analytic listening is also variously described. At this level, it is possible to discern a continuum ranging from free-floating attention to a more sharply focused listening mode (Helm, 2000; Miller, 2004). Ferro puts this in terms of grasping and casting, (2009), along with others who describe an oscillation between evenly hovering attention and judgment (Hamelmann-Fischer, 2016) or "hearing and marking" (Miller, 2004, p. 1486). LaFarge (2000) makes a distinction between *interpretation* and *containment*[6] as the analyst imagines the analysand's inner world.

Elaborating on Freud's (1912) "evenly suspended attention" (p. 112), one end of the continuum is variously described as listening without memory or desire (Bion, 1965b, 1970; Faimberg, 2019), immersion in reverie (Ogden, 1997) or waking dream thought (Ferro, 2009) or the analyst as "listening-accompanist open to something new" (Wilson, 2018). At the other end of the continuum is a mode of listening that seeks to uncover associative linkages (Meissner, 2000), clarifies affects, defenses and forms of resistance (Helm, 2000; Goodman et al., 1993) and is a mediated, disciplined response to emergent experience (Aragno, 2008), catching hold of significant clinical moments (Wilson, 2018) or a selected fact (Bion, 1970).

In this essay, my choice to focus on attentional sets or listening modes was informed by Ricardo Bernardi's (2017) Three-Level Model for Observing Patient Transformations (3-LM). Although intended for a different purpose, Bernardi's model was helpful to me in realizing the importance of examining clinical technique at a relatively low level of abstraction. Bernardi's model was designed to study the level of agreement among a group of analysts with different theoretical affiliations when presented with common clinical material. The study revealed greatest agreement when the discussion remained at the lowest level of abstraction, i.e., when experiencing clinical material in the *phenomenological* moment.[7] Agreement among diverse analysts could also be found when a higher level of discourse was invited, e.g., among different theoretical explanations, but only as long as the common clinical material was used as a foundation for the discussion.[8]

Bernardi's 3 L-M approach was initially conceived to address the plurality among differing theoretical frameworks and, in particular, to propose an observational procedure that might help clarify similarities and differences among them. "Shared resonances" among clinical understanding were found at the phenomenological level, making communication possible in efforts to conceptualize patient changes and when identifying "personal implicit theories." I hope to offer another clinical axis (the listening stance) around which communication can occur among analysts adopting divergent theoretical models. In addition, because most analytic practitioners today are *inadvertent pluralists*,[9] the prioritization of one attentional set over another may occur at different times or in different phases of an analysis along with subsequent interpretive choices as the analytic material evolves. For such pluralists, this shift in prioritization will not necessarily require a shift in theoretical allegiance.

In the next several essays,[10] I utilize Bernardi's 3-LM to clarify what the analyst *actually does* in clinical practice. Drawing on Bernardi's 3-LM, this discussion applies a "bottom up" approach in examining different modes of psychoanalytic listening, both of which reside at the lowest level of abstraction. For my purposes here, the two clinical listening stances are described with reference to experience-near defining characteristics. These include different attentional sets that I believe are a useful way to describe the analyst's mode of listening in any particular clinical moment. This does not mean the analyst makes a conscious choice in these moments, but in retrospect, attentional sets can be identified along with their impact on clinical process.

These two modes of listening are distinguishable for heuristic purposes, but in clinical practice, they are not so clearly separable. At any given moment, it may not be possible to differentiate the two modes of analytic listening as these modes tend to oscillate. However, I believe when one mode is actively prioritized in a more sustained way, differences evoked in the clinical material can be discerned and thereby coordinated with different analytic goals.

I also purposefully use the language of *attentional sets* in order to more clearly identify the purposive action and mode of readiness in the analyst's mental state. I believe this language points more clearly to what the analyst's stance is at any particular clinical moment.[11] Further, I have selected this terminology (and these two attentional sets) because neurophysiological studies identify these sets as divergent and governed by different neurophysiological substrates.

Notes

1 By *attentional set*, I refer to the analyst's cognitive readiness and focus. At the same time, *listening modes* and *stances* refer to similar aspects of the analyst's mental state. All of these terms reside at the lowest level of abstraction, are thereby experience-near, and refer to perspectives on the analyst's mental state. I use all three interchangeably.

2 Though not clearly demarcated and generally oscillating throughout, I primarily foregrounded a *directed attentional set* in the first years of Molly's analysis and then, a *diffuse attentional set* in later years.

3 There is neurophysiological research that supports the differentiation of these divergent attentional sets. Two networks, the dorsal and ventral attentional systems, govern one or the other mode of attentional processing (see Bressler and Menon (2010), Vossel et al., (2014), Chica et al., (2013), Balchin et al., (2019) and Watt, 1990, 2019).

4 The prioritization of *directed* and *diffuse* attentional sets may, in broad strokes, correspond to Levine's (2020) two-track perspective on psychoanalytic process, namely *archaeological* and *transformational* (respectively). Similarly Ogden (2019, 2020) and Bion (1965a) make a distinction between epistemological (knowing about) and ontological (being with) psychoanalytic processes. See also Essay 17, *Stance, set, transference* (this volume).

5 Defining the process as bypassing representational or cognitive/linguistic systems (Gallese, 2001).

6 These, then, are associated with whole-object transferences and part-object transferences, respectively.

7 The other two levels, residing at increasingly higher levels of abstraction, are *conceptualization* and *theoretical explanation* (Bernardi, 2017).

8 "Discussions show the existence of frequent agreement among analysts with varied theoretical backgrounds ... [when they are] not aimed at answering general, abstract questions linked to psychoanalytic theory but to solve specific clinical problems identified in the previous levels" (p. 1302).

9 See Essay 12, *The inadvertent pluralist* (this volume).

10 See Essay 15, *Directed attentional set,* Essay 16, *Diffuse attentional set* and Essay 17, *Stance, set, transference* (all this volume).

11 See Helm (2000) for differentiations based on a continuum of states of consciousness in the analyst.

Chapter 15

Directed attentional set

The first stance, a *directed attentional set*, involves the identification of relational patterns and/or defensive tendencies and personality organization that are the focus of clinical attention. These will usually emerge in the transference/countertransference experience and may reflect repetitions linked to the analysand's historical narrative. In this attentional set, the analyst *searches, recognizes* and *identifies* patterns of relating in the here-and-now. The analyst's mode of listening (and experiencing) is aimed at the *identification* of conscious or unconscious repetitious modes of relating that constrict the analysand's subjective experience and, consequently, the interactional field. These can also surface or develop through the experience of mutual enactments and are then scrutinized by the analyst in one of two ways: 1) through the recognition of constricting repetitions based on expectations from past experience (as in historical reconstruction); or, 2) as novel experience with the analyst, facilitating growth through the introduction of new understanding of old relational patterns and consequently, freeing the interpersonal field. Both of these analytic processes revolve around the *recognition* of unconscious relational patterns or defensive repetitions in the here-and-now that structure the unconscious transference/countertransference matrix.

For example, Katz (2015) refers to a *detailed inquiry* into the emerging personal myths of the analysand and, quoting Levenson (2005), describes how analysands recapitulate relationships with primary caregivers. Here, the mode of readiness in the analyst foregrounds a *directed* attentional set for the purposes of identifying such patterns. Most importantly, the recognition and identification of these patterns is a *search for a fit* between experience in the here-and-now and past repetitive patterns that correspond with the analysand's historical narrative.

Similarly, a neo-Kleinian approach would be geared toward recognizing and interpreting an enacted internal object relation, including an appreciation of the ways in which unconscious fantasy interweaves with such a pattern. Forging links to the analysand's historical narrative is part of the interpretive strategy that guides this attentional set along with the analyst's ability to recognize the enacted internal object relation. Likewise, defenses

DOI: 10.4324/9781003264095-17

are instantiated in unconscious fantasies that include wish/defense compromise formations (Erreich, 2003). The attention to defenses and the active parsing of the analysand's compromise formations, especially the ways in which these are entwined with veridical or constructed historical narratives, requires a more directed attentional set.

A significant way in which the analyst evolves a sense of the patient's early object relations is via understanding the here-and-now transference experience. Repetitious patterns in the here-and-now may correspond to internalized self- and object-configurations that structure the transference/countertransference relationship. Through this directed attentional mode of listening, the aim is to elaborate and re-transcribe the analysand's historical narrative or personal myths[1] about her or his history. These will play a part in the evolving process of historical re-transcription and the creation of new meanings.

While this stance also includes an ongoing receptivity to emergent, (and perhaps novel) ways of being, there is an emphasis on *recognition and identification* of maladaptive defensive repetitions or old relational patterns that emerge in the here-and-now. This latter area of therapeutic action represents an aspect of the stance that is oriented toward the development of a deeper understanding of the past, but not in a manner that implies past memories exist in some static, preformed, or internally localizable way, nor are they constructed without the shaping from unconscious fantasy. Historical references are not assumed to be in a one-to-one relationship with what actually occurred nor do enacted scenarios replicate the past in some faithful way. Old patterns emerge and develop, becoming re-transcribed and reconstructed in the après coup of analytic process. New experience is particularly oriented toward countering past maladaptive expectations and fixed scenarios. In this way, historical narratives change as the analytic process evolves.

In a directed attentional mode, the analyst preconsciously holds the analysand's evolving historical narrative. This readiness aids in the identification of modes of relating that may constitute repetitions of the past. Once such relational patterns are identified, various types of transference interpretations may be offered to further understand these patterns.[2] The *recognition* of relational patterns, reflective of unconscious, fantasied expectations, dreads and/or traumatic repetitions, is an interpretive strategy distinguishing this directed approach[3] from that of the sustained and diffuse openness to emergent process for the purpose of *elaborating* unconscious fantasy.[4]

This approach may also lead to interventions that correct, repair and/or integrate traumatically dissociated parts of the self where split-off or dissociated self-states can emerge. However, the turn to the analysand's historical narrative (a narrative that continues to evolve through the analytic process) often guides the associational links. At the level of abstract theorizing, a polemic has arisen where traditions utilizing this approach are sometimes viewed as *delimiting unconscious fantasy production, resulting in an impoverishment of unconscious fantasy in favor of identifying historical repetitions.*[5] (Though erroneous, since historical reconstruction is always inextricably shaped by unconscious fantasy [see Erreich, 2003], this is the argument put forth).

Clinical illustration, Molly

Molly is a highly self-critical woman, sullen and withdrawn, who carries a sense of grievance and disappointment in others that quickly is turned upon herself. Indeed, when I greeted her for our first session, I sensed a silent accusation and wondered if I was late. I asked if she had been waiting long and she immediately chastised herself for being early. This became a familiar pattern of expectation, disappointment and self-criticism.

Molly came to analysis for incapacitating depression and difficulty in interpersonal relationships that have stood in the way of maintaining steady, satisfying work and a love life. She grew up in a regimented upper-class home, where there was much attention to appearances and "doing things right." Her mother was highly sensitized to the imagined gaze of others upon her, the family, their home and especially their material wealth. Molly's father was a warmer presence but traveled extensively for work.

Molly initially contacted me in great distress. She described an inability to think without feeling internally reprimanded and put-down, eventuating in an incapacitating depression. She felt no pleasure, had never orgasmed (she is a woman in her late 50s) and the numbness of existence made her want to die. She requested to be seen 5 times per week because of her distress and used the couch immediately. She was in analysis with me for 6 years.

Below is a vignette (occurring about a year into the analysis) that illustrates a technical stance of identifying patterns of relating that correspond to self- and object-configurations in the transference. In these clinical moments, my attention was focused primarily on how these repetitious patterns were linked to expectations from her past. These repetitious patterns served to affectively constrict Molly and prompt her self-criticisms:

P: ……..…..… I am thinking of a picture of my mother from the beach house. It was never relaxing. Everything had to be done properly. Even relaxing had to be done properly. My cousin reminded me that her mother and mine were there together and my cousin thought she'd help so she laid out the table for dinner. My mother asked her, What are you doing? She said I'm laying out supper. My mother said, You know we don't do that before drinks! So my cousin had to take it all apart. She went outside and screamed. My mother was so bound by rules. By the book. ……..… …..…..

(I'm thinking about Molly's wish that I would tell her what to do, give her a book on how to do analysis, a maternal transference. It's familiar territory, so I don't interpret it here.)

P: I contacted my cousin by What's App – she didn't respond yet.
A: Sometimes we get responses, sometimes we don't.
P: Like me yesterday.

(Yesterday's session was frustrating for Molly. She criticized herself for wanting me to tell her what to do about a problem with a friend.) I didn't think I'd be okay yesterday. I thought it would worry me all day, but it didn't. I can start with a clean slate. Have a relationship with myself. I didn't understand. The problem is ..... no! It's embarrassing to think about good when it comes to oneself. Or sharing it at least. I know I shouldn't. It's clinical in here.

A: It's impossible to share something good about yourself with me?
P: Yes, I shouldn't brag. .... What happens if I die before ending this?
A: Maybe we'll give birth another way …
P: I meant it literally. I finally put my mother and sister in their own place. Maybe I'm fighting my own demons now. Sounds grandiose. Biblical proportions. Like Munch's scream.
A: It *is* dramatic – there's a scream inside.
P: Hm. It's a wonderful painting … .... I can't do this, what do you want from me? You never say and it's hard having you sit there, witnessing this …. You must think I'm awful, pathetic, and you'd never say it.

In this vignette, my thinking revolved around Molly's experience of me (and the stories of her mother that were on the surface) as conjuring a silent image of expectations and rules. This stimulates in her a desire to please, yet she does not know how and feels resentful for the impossibility of succeeding. At this point in the analysis, this was familiar terrain where I had previously drawn her attention to her past narratives and how dominated by them she was. I think her comment, "I've finally put my mother and sister in their place" refers to a new perspective (and distance) she had developed in relation to these erstwhile persecutory internal objects. Linking her present experience with me as a maternal figure who "does not give her a book to follow" has evoked anger and resentment yet over time has also given rise to a feeling of liberation from externally imposed rules.

At the same time, I sensed a scream, referenced through her cousin, for which I wanted to create a space. My comment that she has a scream inside, following her association to Munch's painting (as "wonderful," heard by me as a denial of her rage) and a more direct complaint about my not letting her know what I want from her left her wondering and uncertain. All of the above observations primarily engaged a directed attentional set.

P: I can't be sure. It's hard. …. I don't know what good this is doing. I have demons. Or you are! (She laughs.) Biblical. Trying to get it out of me.

What we're trying to do. You know that. You know everything. It's dramatic like Shakespeare. *The Scream*. The whole thing. Do you get it?

A: I do now.

P: Are you laughing at me?

A: Is that a kind of scream?

P: I'm being laughed at. Yes. I was skyping my brother and reminded him how he called me [a degrading nickname]. He apologized! He never has before. Parents never stopped the hurt. Did they see it? I don't know. It's important not to make mistakes.

In our last session of the week, just before my vacation, the following vignette took place:

P: I'm in a mood and it's getting worse. I'm blaming you for not helping me enough. Isn't there a book you can give me to read? You have all these books, isn't there one that would help me?

(I think Molly is wanting something concrete to hold onto while I'm away, not surprisingly a book, one that might hold a secret – perhaps how to keep me in place, perhaps instructions on how to be the little girl no mother would criticize or leave).

P: Yesterday, a co-worker pointed out a problem. I collapsed in on myself. Now I'll find out that everything will fall apart. How I have destroyed myself. All the good work I've done will go to waste. The firm has insurance. ... I didn't practice fraud. Still, a voice says, "You're a failure. Everything about you is a fraud." I just want out. I want everything to stop. I'm panicking. Why can't I be reasonable, analyze it through. I'm being ridiculous!

A: These are your fears .... That you're a fraud, a failure – what you fear will happen when I leave.

P: Oh, it's all about you. ... It's almost worse. Why haven't you helped me with them.

A: They are coming through with a stronger intensity. You're letting your fears surface – you're articulating them directly to me – trusting me to hear them.

P: The feelings are stronger but not nicer. How do I stop it? You'll say, talk about it. Or maybe it goes back to my mother.

A: You're afraid if you weren't nice, you'd cause her to withdraw, maybe that you've done something to cause me to leave, you're afraid your world will collapse.

P: It's my inability to do anything about it .... Just want to stop everything. Close the books. Walk away from everything. ... This is all so melodramatic. I think I'm making this into a huge thing. Making the problem huge.

A: It *is* huge when a child can't find her mother ... ...

P: I don't remember being confused. I don't remember much. The fear, the anxiety, but we didn't know it. It was normal life. .... I hate this! I don't know what this is that I'm hating .... I've shut down. I just told myself to stop exposing this.

Much of the above process utilizes the directed mode of listening where my attention was oriented toward recognizing familiar patterns emerging between us that structured our interaction. These served to prompt and replicate Molly's angry, fearful feelings that she had done something to disappoint me and push me away. There were many instances of longing for a "book" from me (some system of regulations) that would both guide her yet also frustrate and constrict her. While the process allows for emerging fantasy production in the intersubjective experience, the identification of these patterns requires a directed attentional set.

The formulations above involve the identification of defensive processes that weave together elements of Molly's narrative history. My responses tend to engage a directed attentional set in the way links are constructed from past to present, making use of the stories Molly has told me. This work with Molly revolves around attempting to provide new intersubjective experience in the dyadic interplay while recognizing historical repetitions and her sensitivity to the resultant affects in the here-and-now with me.

Notes

1 See also Laplanche's (1994) ideas on the child as hermeneut.
2 See Roth (2001) for an explication of four levels of transference interpretation aimed at linking the patient's history to current or external events, unconscious fantasies and enactments in relation to the analyst/analysand relationship.
3 The theorists associated with this particular attentional mode include (but are not limited to) Freudian and neo-Freudian theorists, Kleinian and neo-Kleinian theorists, interpersonal/relational theorists and ego psychological theorists.
4 See Essay 16, *Diffuse attentional set* (this volume) for a discussion of this contrasting mode of analytic listening.
5 For articulation of this polemic, see Foehl (2013a,b); Stern (2013a,b); Ferro and Civitarese (2013) among other discussants in a two-part panel.

Chapter 16

Diffuse attentional set

In contrast to the previous essay,[1] the second stance revolves around a *diffuse attentional set* in relation to emergent process. This mode of listening engages an *unfocused, nondirected receptivity* that is primarily aimed at expanding the play of unconscious process, encouraging its emergence in all its forms so as to facilitate the psychic growth of the mind. This attentional set is one of *patience, openness, waiting* and *tolerance of uncertainty* in relation to what may emerge. The allowance for unconscious processes can take any form and are assumed to be ubiquitous in the here-and-now experience. This mode of listening corresponds to Freud's evenly hovering attention, Bion's listening without memory and desire and Ogden's immersion in reverie.

In a diffuse mode of listening, unconscious experience and data are not necessarily configured relationally, however there is great emphasis on the here-and-now experience within the analytic dyad. An openness to non-relational symbols as potentially indicative of unconscious emanations is characteristic of this approach, with the emphasis on expanding the play and growth of the mind. The recognition of repetitive patterns in the analytic dyad is explicitly *not* part of this stance, nor is the turn toward the analysand's historical narrative. This process is held as "enriching and transforming in itself" (Ferro and Civitarese, 2013).[2] Here, the analyst maintains an uncritical attitude toward emerging experience with the analysand, especially in relation to those experiences that may *not* fit with past repetitious patterns or the analysand's historical narrative.

An example of this analytic stance is seen when Bion (1965b) writes of listening to a married patient and appreciating that this patient was "talking in a way which is quite appropriate to his not being married at all" (p. 15). Winnicott says to his analysand,

> I am listening to a girl. I know perfectly well that you are a man but I am listening to a girl, and I am talking to a girl. I am telling this girl: "You are talking about penis envy". (1971, p. 98)

Another way this stance is put into practice is by viewing the session as a

DOI: 10.4324/9781003264095-18

dream experience, comprising the lens through which every session is both understood and constructed. The session itself is held as a new experience created through unconscious mechanisms that use the entire setting as props or characters in the field (Ferro, 2009).

A diffuse attentional set engages a form of nonlinear thinking associated with analogic, synthetic modes of cognition, a "this is like that" type of cognitive process, globally receptive to affective shifts and emergent experience. Analogic thinking is metaphoric, poetic and momentarily disregards differences.[3] This is a receptive mode of attention, especially for visuospatial (pictorial) images and affect-laden forms of processing that may emerge in the analyst's reveries as well.[4]

This stance privileges the *elaboration* of the field so as to facilitate emergent growth processes. These may or may not involve their verbal expression. Projective identificatory processes may emerge and define functional roles for each member of the dyad, yet both are viewed as part of a single dynamic process that encompasses the entire context (Baranger and Baranger, 2008). Attention to these processes is viewed as emergent properties of the joint internal fantasy of the couple or dream-field. This is an *expansive view* and privileges efforts toward growth and creative elements.

Sustained receptivity to emergent process is engaged in a more or less continuous manner to generate and elaborate unconscious fantasy as a primary and desired outcome of the analytic exchange. When primarily engaging this listening stance, the analyst seeks to address the analysand's concerns by more fully elaborating them, thereby containing and symbolizing heretofore unrepresented, "undreamt" states. The pursuit of dream-like images is privileged, with the goal of transforming the analysand's anxieties and the meanings derived from them. Because the privileging of this attentional set favors the generation of unconscious imagery in a dream-like context, the argument is sometimes made that analysts primarily utilizing this approach *neglect or even dismiss the analysand's historical narrative* and its concomitant myth-making, i.e., personal hermeneutic.[5]

Clinical illustration, Molly (continued)[6]

I offer the following vignette, occurring several years into the analysis of Molly and also during a session right before my vacation. It demonstrates a more diffuse attentional set, an imaginal mode of listening that elaborated the clinical process with her.

Molly begins a session reporting a dream:

P: You had a daughter. She was fat and you hated her. You had a small son. You got fat. You lent me a belt. You wanted my paddle tennis racquet. I lent it to you. There was a lot of chaos, small spaces, people.

Your husband appeared. You lived in a basement. All my friends wanted to meet you. I said "No, she's not very nice."

Molly had some ideas about this dream:

P: Your daughter was obviously my daughter who is also fat. She had your hair but it was red. We were living underground where everything was low. Below street level. Everything is open. (I'm thinking this represents going deep into the unconscious.) Molly continues:

Maybe the daughter is my daughter or maybe it is me. Fat obviously. Makes sense. Living underground …. Oh here! Oh! (My office is half below the landscape line, almost a basement.)

A: And the unconscious is deep.
P: Yesterday, I bought an expensive paddle, yet not playing worries me.
A: Paddle, belt …
P: Punishment. My mother whipped me once. She denied it. I don't remember if she really did. Another time she whollopped me with a hairbrush and used the prickly side. She denied that too.

While Molly continued associating to her dream, the image of the paddle stuck with me. I imagined its wooden structure, the hardness of it and the punishment she associated to it. The red hair of my (her? me?) daughter in the dream came into focus as well, making me think of anger, hardness and a wooden, i.e., unfeeling thing. I imagined Molly suddenly standing straight and rigid, like a Flamenco dancer, with her arms straight above her head, making sudden, sharp movements, perhaps hitting? She appeared to have an angry expression on her face. Her Flamenco dress was decorated with beads all around, especially in the back of the dress, perhaps in line with her backbone. Then the beads began to fall off. I said:

A: Anger can stiffen a thing, harden against feelings.
P: Yes, and hatred too. It was the way you looked at this little girl. She indicated you didn't like her. It was just there. She didn't want to be near you. She sensed you hated her. … I don't think you hate me. I do sometimes think this is boring for you. You might say, "You're done. You've had enough. I have more important people." I think you tolerate me. I know you don't hate me.
A: How do you know this?
P: If I sensed you hated me, you'd see me packing. You seem to be engaged. But I do wonder if you're faking it. Maybe it's about my mother hating me? I don't think so. I was easy. I don't feel she hated me.

Molly struggled with weekends and separations from me. I have wondered if one meaning of the dream was that she hated her dependency on me, leading her to feel that she hated me. My own meanderings about the paddle, the red color, the beads and my image of her as a rigid, angry Flamenco dancer helped me see the strengthening function of her projected anger and hatred. I wondered if the hardness of all of this imagery led to a feeling of strength in her, unlike the dependency and vulnerability she was feeling, especially given our impending separation. Perhaps the beads falling off was symbolic of her loosening defenses, making her dress less stiff, perhaps less capable of "holding her up."

From a different angle, I wondered, too, if Molly was trying to express a fear of my hating her, despite her negations. I suspect there is truth in this. My imaginative meanderings described above helped me with this line of thinking as well. Rigidity, woodenness (lack of feeling) and anger were ways to feel strong and if I hated her, paradoxically I acquired credibility in her mind. Hate was strong, love was weak. In this context, perhaps the beads falling off were symbolic of her fears that she would break apart during our separation.

These reveries can also be viewed as representing Molly's erotic (and sadomasochistic) attachment to me. The Flamenco dancer is a stiff, phallic image and the beads falling off may represent an undressing, perhaps in an attempt to seduce me into staying with her. Though the various ways in which these emergent images might be interpreted are too many to enumerate, the diffuse attentional set illustrated above demonstrates the way in which the field was elaborated, expanding the imagery available to me as Molly's analyst. Then, the choice about what to express and fold into the process depends on the proclivities of the analyst and nature of the process at any point in time.

The diffuse attentional set demonstrated in the above vignette engaged predominantly analogic and associative processes in me, favoring metaphoric modes of processing. This is open-ended and receptive to unbidden, nonrational affective states and symbol formation. In employing a dream model of the field, this stance sustains the engagement of analogic modes of processing as I attended to images and affective experience that arose. These may relate to Molly's past history, but I did not use the imaginal material in a consciously directed attempt to find such patterns. Rather, the immersion in my own associative reveries helped me notice imagery in a nonlinear, dream-like scene where new meanings were elaborated and then used in the clinical process.

Notes

1 See Essay 15, *Directed attentional set* (this volume).
2 The theorists typically associated with prioritizing this clinical stance are those associated with the variety of field theories, Winnicottian-inflected orientations and child play therapies.

3 This form of cognition corresponds to the form of thinking governed by the nondominant (right) hemisphere (Watt, 1990, 2019). This form of cognition is referred to as visuospatial, nonlinear and imagistic. It is also strongly associated with dreaming.

4 Stern (1990) might refer to this mode as the analyst as conduit, an active receptivity to unconscious communication, in line with Bion's (1967) negative capability or Laplanche's (1999b) conception of the tub. Indeed, Stern's (1990) attentiveness to dissociated self-states and unformulated experience would categorize him as a bridge theorist, a relational-field theorist balancing attention to repetitions from the past and emergent elaborative content in the here-and-now.

5 In his emphasis on elaborating the unconscious in these ways, the Italian field theorist, Giuseppe Civitarese acknowledges that it is almost inevitable to pay attention also to historical and material reality – after all, what are our patients going to talk about? However, the elaboration of the field is needed to explain how the unconscious works (personal communication, 2020).

6 Molly is introduced in Essay 15, *Directed attentional set* (this volume).

Chapter 17

Stance, set, transference

Differences among technical stances such as the attentional stances and sets discussed in the previous three essays[1] can also be viewed by identifying *which type of transference is being realized*. Prioritizing a directed attentional set is well-suited to evoke and explore a repetitious transference identified by Freud (1916–17). Transferences of this sort are constituted by the projection of figures of the primary objects of love, hate and identification in line with the effort at historical reconstruction.

Alternatively, transferences constituted by projective identificatory mechanisms in the moment, creating a pathology of the field (Baranger, Baranger and Mom, 1983), initially engage a diffuse attentional set. This allows unconscious emanations to become manifest. These may warrant interpretive clarification, at which point the "second look" (Baranger, Baranger and Mom, 1983, p. 2) engages a more causal, directed attentional set as the analyst identifies a possible enactment through projective identificatory mechanisms (Baranger, Baranger and Mom, 1983). These then can be identified and interpreted in line with other forms of defense analysis.

As noted in this series of essays, these two attentional sets tend to oscillate in everyday clinical process. Yet sometimes a particular attentional set will be prioritized, depending on the nature of clinical process, the analyst's clinical goals and the treatment phase. The immersed analyst primarily engages a diffuse attentional set in order to be receptive to unconscious emanations as they occur in the dynamic field. Then, an observational, directed and causal attentional process can be engaged, depending on the way in which the analyst organizes the unconscious phenomena that have arisen. Historical re-transcription is one such use, but another would be a redistribution of projected splits, while another involves the re-integration of dissociated self-states. Still another may involve the naming (and thereby symbolizing) heretofore unrepresented states. Much of these differentiations occur in retrospect, as the oscillation occurs naturally within clinical process.

A diffuse attentional set is primarily engaged in the effort to integrate dissociative phenemona, eloquently described by Stern (1997) as

DOI: 10.4324/9781003264095-19

unformulated experience, the receptivity to which requires more diffuse attentional processes. Dissociated splits can be comprised of split-off affects, a sense of something as yet unstructured and nonsymbolized, or as unrepresented self-states. Unformulated experience is not limited to the verbal register and it is experience that does not yet exist except as potential. It is what experience *can become* (Stern, 1997, 2015). These previously unformulated self-states then emerge in the transference/countertransference experience.[2]

A similar distinction between the two sets, though not a one-to-one correspondence, can be made between Laplanche's filled-in transferences (*transfert en plein*) and the hollowed-out transference (*transfert en creux*) (1999b). The former involves the repetition of childhood imagos and scenarios whereas the hollowed-out transference represents the emergence of the analysand's originary relation to the enigmatic (m)other. The former (filled-in transferences) are interpreted through directed associative links with the analysand's historical images and memories in order to make room for the "hollowed out space" of the analytic setting (see also Scarfone, 2015). This form of transference requires the analyst *not to know, not to fill in the space* and instead to have a receptive, diffuse attentional set ready to receive unconscious emanations.

Ogden (2019, 2020) distinguishes epistemological and ontological processes, the former oriented toward "knowing and understanding" in contrast to "being and becoming." Bion (1965a) discussed this shift, moving from "knowing about" to "being with" the patient. Levine's (2020) *archeological* and *transformational* perspectives parallel this discrimination. In broad strokes, this distinction aligns with directive versus immersive processes (respectively), as discussed in this series of essays.

In this post-pluralistic era of psychoanalytic theorizing (Cooper, 2015), there is a growing consensus that many analysts make use of "partial theories" as they attempt to make sense of the complexity and multiplicity of clinical moments, discourse in theorizing and analytic process (LaFarge, 2017; Zimmer, 2017). Along these lines, this series of essays[3] aims to describe specific approaches and mindsets of the analyst that can be primarily associated with disparate moments in clinical process. I have attempted to describe sometimes oscillating, sometimes eliding approaches that involve both immersion and observation with their respective attentional sets.

I also suggest that in actual practice, many psychoanalysts are likely to be *inadvertent pluralists*,[4] borrowing from many theoretical viewpoints while perhaps maintaining specific theoretical ideals and commitments in word or theoretical discourse. Some writers are recognizing the possibility of flexibility in theoretical commitments (Akhtar, 2000; Aron, 2018; Cooper, 2015, 2017; LaFarge, 2017; Stern, 2015; Zimmer, 2017). I believe this is especially true at the level of clinical listening stance and attentional set.

Though formal theories are implied by the way an analyst tends to listen and intervene, I have based the discussion in the previous several essays at the level of clinical stance and attentional set in order to clarify a basic way an analyst works in the clinical moment. Taken together, these moments may imply an implicit theory or theories that can be discerned in retrospect. As Birksted-Breen (2008) has stated, "To be psychoanalysis, the two person situation must include a theory as its 'third object' ... the setting itself implies a theoretical structure which comes from outside and is essential to it" (p. 1). Adding to this claim, Tuckett (2008) continues, "This is why the theories underlying how the analyst listens, thinks about the patient and intervenes, which may vary with practitioners but must always be there in at least implicit form are an inherently necessary feature" (p. 243).

As noted in this series of essays, some analysts claim that "part-theories" engaged at the clinical level (i.e., at lower levels of abstraction) need not be consistent with one another at a metapsychological level (see, for examples, LaFarge, 2017; Cooper, 2017). LaFarge states,

> Part-theories ... develop in the course of any analysis and are based upon pieces of broader theories, experiences with analysands, identifications with teachers and other analysts, and commonsense beliefs about behavior. Residing in the analyst's preconscious ... [part-theories] are stimulated by the analysand's material and the analyst's subjective responses. (p. 830)

LaFarge goes on to state that these part-theories are subordinated to an implicit *personal core theory* that comprises a constant framework of *what analysis should be* in an overarching way. These are tied to an analyst's hierarchy of values as well, such that a particular implicit core theory is unique to each analyst. This line of thinking may also allow for a broader range of technical choices at the clinical level.

In drawing the distinctions between these two clinical stances, the methods of each approach stand out more clearly. Beyond this discursive purpose, it is important for psychoanalysts to understand the distinctions among differing technical stances. It is my hope that the distinctions drawn between associated attentional sets and types of transferences will help in the translation of theory into practice.

Notes

1 See Essays 14, *Stance and attentional set in analytic listening*, Essay 15, *Directed attentional set* and Essay 16, *Diffuse attentional set* (all this volume).
2 Stern's interest in history is not as explanation, but rather on the consequences of what we know for the field. It is a freeing of the field that reveals new aspects of history (D. Stern, personal communication, 2021).
3 See Essay 12, *The inadvertent pluralist*, Essay 14, *Stance and attentional set in analytic listening*, Essay 15, *Directed attentional set* and Essay 16, *Diffuse attentional set* (all this volume).
4 See Essay 12, *The inadvertent pluralist* (this volume).

Part II

Love

Chapter 18

The erotic field

There is an unmistakeable desexualization that pervades psychoanalytic theorizing, occurring from the beginning of the field itself. Even Freud, whose discovery of infantile sexuality should have paved the way for a frank recognition of the erotic throughout development, played a part in the first wave of desexualization as an unintended consequence of his immersion in the scientism of the Enlightenment era. His commitment to construct a vision of the psychoanalytic project as a one-person enterprise, in his mind, an attempt to remove bias from the field of study, caused the erasure of the analyst's presence, at least at a theoretical level. As the patient became the sole focus of attention – subjectivity in a vacuum and decontextualized – erotics became part of a defensive picture and not an intersubjective creation. This conception of the erotic as a defensive manifestation is a form of desexualization, an erasure of the natural erotic and sensual aspects of intersubjectivity.

The next wave of desexualizing came with the love affair we all have with the unconscious, where manifest content was always interpreted by searching for something behind, latent or deep. Everything always meant something else. Once, psychoanalysis was scandalously viewed as "*all about sex.*" Then, it was viewed as "*all about sex, except for sex … that's about aggression*" – another desexualization.

Even recently, the pervasive desexualization of our literature prompted André Green (1995) to write, "Has sexuality anything to do with psychoanalysis?" A few decades ago, there was a turn to preoedipal manifestations in psychoanalytic process, but it was a desexualized preoedipal, a *non-erotic maternal* engagement. This was the typical understanding of object-relations theorizing, causing Muriel Dimen (1999) to comment, "Where libido was, therefore *objects* will be" (p. 417). Similarly, Peter Fonagy (2008) measured the current decline in interest in sexuality by examining word usage in electronically searchable journals of psychoanalysis. He found that the decline in *sexual* word usage is inversely related to the rise in *relational* word usage.

DOI: 10.4324/9781003264095-21

How to capture the erotic, including our love for our object, without taking the spark, the arousing and vitalizing potential, from our engagement with the other? In this essay, an inclusive, totalistic view of erotic love is utilized as a way to capture and sustain the erotic in the psychoanalytic process and field. We desire to know the other, the object of our attention and in so doing, express our love. Here, I draw on Hans Loewald, who wrote,

> Scientific detachment in its genuine form, far from excluding love is based on it. In our work it can be truly said that in our best moments of dispassionate and objective analyzing we love our object, the patient, more than at any other time and are compassionate with his whole being. In our field, scientific spirit and care for the object certainly are not opposites; they flow from the same source. (1970, p. 65)

Freud (1910), as well, embraced a totalistic view of the erotic in his paper on "*Wild*" *Psycho-analysis,* written in 1910, (possibly written in response to Jung's sexual involvement with Sabina Spielrein [(Morris, 2012]).

> In psychoanalysis the term "sexuality" comprises far more… than the popular sense of the word…we reckon as belonging to "sexual life" *all expressions of tender feeling* which spring from … sexual feelings….we prefer to speak of *psychosexuality* … the mental factor [which] should not be overlooked or underestimated. We use the word sexuality in the … comprehensive sense: *lieben* (to love). (p. 91)

What is it about the nature of love, psychosexuality and our interest/desire to know the other that so irresistibly draws us to it and yet threatens us to the extent that we back away at the same time? Perhaps a turn to other fields will help. The poet Rilke (1923) famously paired beauty with terror and death in the first of his *Duino Elegies,* beauty being the object of desire:

> And even if one were to suddenly take me to its heart,
> I would vanish into its stronger existence.
> For beauty is nothing but the beginning of terror,
> that we are still able to bear,
> and we revere it so,
> because it calmly disdains to destroy us.

It is no coincidence that Eros is described[1] as the son of **Chaos**, the original **primeval emptiness** of the universe. Since ancient times, Eros has been associated with chaos, emptiness, sexual love, beauty and battle. *Eros is the god of passion*; passion defined as the sufferance or submission to *intense* *feeling* (i.e., love or hate). As son of the divine messenger, we might also surmise that these are the messages sexual desire may send.

We can feel the terror to which Rilke refers upon encountering, seeing and in some way knowing beauty and desire. Freud (1915b, 1917) noted the cannibalistic, devouring nature of object choice, denoting these characteristics of object choice as preliminary stages, when the ego incorporates the object into itself, thereby devouring it.[2] Erotic love is more recently described as at once irresistible, excessive (Stein, 1998; Celenza, 2014, 2022a; Saketopoulou, 2019), a mysterious message (Laplanche, 1997), and *a passionate imperative that threatens annihilation* (see, for example, Lichtenberg, 2008; Pajaczkowska and Ward, 2008; Celenza, 2022a). With erotic desire comes a threat because it is in its very nature to arouse primitive anxieties. What is it and what do we mean by beauty that threat inheres within it? Here I quote the existential philosopher Merleau-Ponty (1962):

> The body of the other is not perceived as an object, but rather as inhabited by a secret perception, by a sexual schema that is strictly individual ..... the body [of the other] is enigmatic ... it is connected with [a] personal life and is like the habitat in which the human being seeks closeness and union with others ... corporeality ... [it is] our surface of contact with being. (Merleau-Ponty, cited in Moya and Lorrain, 2016, p. 744–5)

The relationship between knowing and desiring is an eternal problem and has been addressed since ancient times. In the Judeo-Christian creation myth, the serpent tempts Adam and Eve into eating the forbidden fruit of the Tree of Knowledge, which allows them to "see" their nakedness, and therefore to experience shame (Tutter, 2018). From this, Adam and Eve acquire the capacity for self-knowledge, the knowledge of their own frailty, desires and potential for death. But what did Eve do? She offered Adam a bite of an apple, tempting him with the forbidden sexual – in a combined epistemophilic erotic scene. It is through the apple, she beckons him not solely to know her, but *to take her in*. To desire is to long for union, to be inside the other, and thereby, to risk death.

Eroticism calls inner life into play (Bataille, 1957/1986). The erotic is one's personal aesthetic, the way we *take in* life and the world. In this way, sexuality is one's manner of receptivity to the world in its sensuous aspects, transmitted to our unconscious as we translate our experience and are sometimes overcome by it. Then there is the *grasping* nature of our relation to the world – the way in which we capture our experience by directing our gaze outward and taking what we desire from it. In this manner, we select the particularities we desire (or do they select us?), we translate and thereby constitute and transform our conscious and unconscious experience. In this way, we penetrate the outside world with our gaze. "*To see* is *to have* at a distance" (Merleau-Ponty, 1961, p. 127).

Our gaze into the world is comprised of a *taking in/grasping dialectic*, a *receptivity to* and *penetrating into* dialectic. In an overall way, and from within the position of the experiencing self (what I refer to as the embodied subject[3]), individual experience can be described as some amalgam of *receptivity and potency* – in the language of sexuality, *holding and penetration* or, in the language of the body, *openness and backbone*. Put as now an outdated stereotype: the feminine and masculine. I realize articulating this binary can be misunderstood as promoting one pole over the other, in line with the ways in which Western culture traditionally organized sexual and gendered splits. I am not supporting the traditional delegation of a host of (gendered and nongendered) relations associated with each pole to either female or male (e.g., femininity with passivity, to name the most prevalent). Risking this misunderstanding, I am proposing the articulation of this binary to pose it as a false dichotomy and as a developmental challenge for us all, a kind of psychic bisexuality – after all, who would choose between having receptive capacities and potent abilities? *We all must have both*, we could say the feminine and masculine within us all, in a manner not associated with any particular gender binary. (Indeed, the prison of two ideas should be expanded to a psychic multi-sexuality.) Still, to recognize the extent to which some of our patients may be trapped in gender polarities and splits can be helpful, especially when the clinical aim is to transcend these.[4]

In 2014, I suggested the engagement of this polarity (receptivity and potency), stereotypically definitional of femininity and masculinity, in order to expose it as a false dichotomy, the poles of which are not actually opposite and thereby are not mutually exclusive. These reckonings and the particular individual's negotiation of each can define the ways in which gender is instantiated, experienced and expressed from within the embodied subject. They may also vary *intra*-individually as relational patterns shift and self-experience multiplies and expands. *Most importantly, I view these poles as liberated from any hierarchic power relation, in that neither pole is privileged*, though in any particular individual one may be.

This individualized amalgam of *receptivity and potency* reckons with the feminine and masculine, representing bi-gendered aspects of the self. This is what I mean to convey (Celenza, 2014) with the play on Faulkner's (1951) phrase, *The binary is not dead; it is not even binary*. I intend to invoke a *psychic multi-sexuality* (expanding on Elise, 2002; Perelberg, 2018a[5] and Chodorow, 2011) or, in this instance, *a psychic multi-gendered sexuality*.

Here, the threat of eros is implicated in the ancient tendency toward dualism that long predates Descartes, derived from a desire to transcend the body – to segregate and idealize pure reason and linear, abstract thought. In an outmoded view of scientism, reasoning became associated with masculinity; emotionality and body-based experience with femininity, re-flecting a certain distaste for and fear of our embodied, sexual selves.

This dualism arises inevitably from fearing sexuality, not only because we are afraid of incest (as in sexual boundary violations) but because of the threat associated with eros itself. We resist erotic transferences and erotic countertransferences because we resist the exposure of narcissistic, oedipal-level wounds, our patient's as well as our own. But perhaps most threatening is the mysterious other … sexuality is transgressive – we cross the boundaries of the unknown and penetrate a new frontier. Our vulnerability *is* our body, our nakedness, our desires in the face of the unknown other.

So, as Rilke suggested, beauty and passion ignite the terror of death. I believe it is this terror that leads to a persistent desexualization in our work, including our theorizing, as we attempt to manage the overwhelming threat that desire risks. Constructing binaries and dualisms can indicate the management of this threat, splitting the threat in half, as it were.

This bears on the treatment situation in a nongendered way (Celenza, 2014). It is an intimate relationship (albeit, asymmetric) that easily lends itself to sexual metaphor. To hold is to grasp; to probe is to transgress. Our work is penetrating and enveloping, incisive and containing, a firm re-ceptivity that retains, envelops and holds the other in mind. The word is the touch is the affect is the knowledge.

This is consistent with a totalistic view of the erotic, based on a dialectic, and one that implicates sexuality at every moment and from the beginning of life. A visual, aesthetic encounter where the analyst or other attempts to get inside, a probative receptivity awaiting an unfolding process, penetrating the depths of the unknown other, risking the loss of oneself in the depths of the wilderness, the unconscious. Thus, we see Eros ignites life and we also see that with every desire comes a dread, a threat to one's being and very existence, *because to encounter the other is to encounter a mystery*. The mystery of the unknown, the challenge of separateness and difference and the threat of the other's intentionality.

These are some of the elements that make the analytic situation threatening. The wish to know the other through a receptive and penetrating dialectic is the seduction and threat of the analytic context. And we must never forget how seductive and titillating this probing can be to our analysands.

Because of its ubiquity, indeed the field is an erotic field, the threat linked with the beauty of sexuality and desire moves us to desexualize, de-eroticize the field. The persistent problem of desexualization of our theories and practice leaves us unprepared for the intensity of sexual material and feeling that will inevitably arise in our work. We de-eroticize the maternal trans-ferences and also de-eroticize countertransferences, a stance in collusion with and hidden by the striving for neutrality and abstinence. Instead, I suggest we strive for transparency of process, i.e., how the analyst is thinking and experiencing the process, especially in relation to our own receptivity to reverie and feeling. I do not view the absence of erotic feeling toward my patient as a relief or an easy route to neutrality or abstinence; rather I believe the absence of erotic arousal in my countertransference is a *present absence* that should be problematized.

As analysts, we are the objects that will not be had, upholding the incest taboo and thereby cultivating a setting where early forms of desire can safely emerge. We must have the full range of affectivity at our disposal, but we must also help our patients reckon with, interpret and be unafraid to experience the excitements and mysteries of the unknown other, including from within themselves.

Notes

1 A primeval god of Greek mythology. Later tradition made Eros the son of Aphrodite, goddess of sexual love and beauty, with his father as either Zeus, (the king of gods), Ares (god of war and of battle), or Hermés (divine messenger of the gods). (In the Theogony of Hesiod [c. 730-700 BC/2018].)
2 See Essay 22, *Identificatory Love and object love* (this volume).
3 See Essay 33, *Psychic positions, healthy and perverse* (this volume).
4 See Dimen (1991) and Benjamin (1995, 1998) for further discussion of splitting and its interface with gender polarities.
5 See also Perelberg and others in a series of papers on *Psychic Bisexuality* (2018a).

Chapter 19

The maternal *erotic* transferences [1]

In 1931, Freud beckoned female analysts to gain access to pre-oedipal transferences in analyses with female patients. Over the past century, many female analysts have done just that. At the same time, *erotic* transferences (presumably, oedipal) seemed to remain the purview of male analysts. As I have written elsewhere (Celenza, 2006, 2014, 2022a), clinical lore included the mistaken idea that female analysts did not (perhaps could not) evoke erotic transferences and it was surmised that, at least with male patients, this was related to the intolerable helplessness associated with dependency longings in the maternal transference (Lester, 1985; Person, 1985; Kernberg, 1994). I have suggested that female analysts (and male analysts as well) can collude with this clinical phenomenon by taking refuge in a de-eroticized maternal transference and countertransference. There may be several reasons for this defensive move, including discomfort with erotic material in the transference/countertransference interplay and/or various kinds of discomfort in combining the maternal with the erotic.

Such de-eroticization and specifically *desexualization* have been identified in psychoanalytic theorizing of the maternal. Balsam (2012, 2019) addresses the neglect of the female body in the psychoanalytic literature; Litowitz (2014) wonders if the mother's body has been *denatured* in object relations theories; Fonagy (2008) identifies a desexualization in contemporary relational theorizing; and Green (1995) noted a more general absence of clinical interest in sexuality, as if its presence were "'beyond' sexuality, or … 'before' sexuality" (p. 872).

The recognition of the maternal transference *as erotic* is emerging in the literature (see, for example, Chassaguet-Smirgel 1970, 1976; McDougall 1986, 1995; Kulish, 1989; Wrye and Welles, 1994; Benjamin, 1995; Elise, 2002, 2015, 2017, 2019; Dimen, 2003; Harris, 2005; Fonagy and Target, 2007; Balsam, 2003; 2012, 2014, 2019; Salomonsson, 2012; Kristeva, 2000, 2011, 2014a,b; Celenza, 2014, 2022a; Litowitz, 2014; Widawsky, 2014; Wilson, 2014; Atlas 2016; Coen, 2021). These authors and discussions have marked an important shift in analytic theorizing.

Wrye and Welles (1994) are notable in their description of how the erotic is implicitly experienced in maternal body and maternal activity [the realm of

DOI: 10.4324/9781003264095-22

Khora (Kristeva, 2014a)]. Many of these reports revolve around descriptions of the mother and infant in the mother's nonverbal, body-based ministrations that involve looking or gazing at each other and various kinds of touching, stroking, sucking, licking, being inside the other and the overall enveloping nature of the maternal touch. These body-based ministrations defy physical boundaries as the mother and baby *take each other in* – all of which combine to another version of erotic desire. The baby's *taking in* of the mother's ministrations is counterposed with the baby's active demands on its mother, culminating in a mutual regulatory interaction. Much of this mutual regulatory interaction is nonverbal, dependent on what the baby sees, touches and feels through the mother's caregiving (CPSG, Bruschweiler-Stern et al., 2002; see also Bolognini, 2011c).

All of these ministrations can be viewed as having, perhaps at an unconscious level, erotic dimensions. At this level, there includes two sides of a dialectic that might be termed *receptivity/penetration* (Celenza, 2014, 2022a), a *taking in* and *penetrating into* interplay that can capture the ways in which the erotic is conveyed in a mutual regulatory fashion. Consistent with these explorations is Laplanche's (1997) general theory of seduction, in which he claims that the mother, the universal driving force of all scenes of seduction, presents the infant with her enigmatic, sexual unconscious. These affects and longings are then rekindled in later genital sexuality yet retain the maternal-infant dyad to serve as their template.

In our first telephone call, in which Petra requested analysis, she let me know that she did not want to look at me, *ever*. Indeed, she entered each session gaze averted and rushed to the couch, so as to quickly turn away. As she would lie there, she placed her hands over her eyes and face. She did not want to see me age, she explained. Consciously, her fear of my aging was related to the terrible deterioration of her mother, suffering with a blood disorder that eventually involved cognitive dementia. Her mother's blood was the site of her disease, coursing through her body, her platelets in short supply, failing to nurture her brain.

Petra chose to lie on the couch immediately, turning away as her hands remained covering her face. Her posture reminded me that some patients can use the couch as a psychic retreat (Steiner, 1993, 2015), to hide rather than reveal.[2] Petra had spent the last years of her mother's life in close proximity with her, ministering to her as she coped with a gradually encroaching dementia. By the time she started treatment with me, Petra had researched her maternal relatives and found a preponderance of brain-related diseases, many of whom died at a young age (Male transgenerational transmitters of such disease did not cross her mind.). Though she surrounded herself with these facts of her family tree, she consciously tried to keep them out of her awareness. I did not realize until much later in the analysis that seeing me age carried with it a fear not only that I would become demented (and unable to hold her in mind) but that *she would be the contaminant who gave the germ to me*.

Petra is a psychiatric nurse, married and at the time of beginning treatment, in her early 30s. She and her husband had begun talking about having children prompting Petra to enter treatment when she began to experience significant anxiety, almost to the point of panic. She assumed this had something to do with impending motherhood, but could not say how or in what way. She had always thought she wanted children.

Petra grew up in a middle-class home where her family lived well beyond their means, oriented toward presenting a wealthy appearance to the outside world. This required a frugal lifestyle in the home, so that money was spent primarily in ways that could be ostentatiously displayed to others. Unsurprisingly, Petra requested a reduced fee from me which I knew was the beginning of an enacted scenario related in some way to her childhood experience with money. I agreed to a modest reduction to meet her halfway. This is how we began our work, the beginning of what I hoped would be a 4 times per week analysis. This came to be.

Petra told me she had few female friends. She had experienced eroticized relationships with both male and female teachers – the erotic longings for a beloved female teacher puzzled her and raised questions in her mind about her sexual orientation. Erotic longings toward men countered this confusion. At the beginning of our treatment, Petra told me she was uncertain about being in analysis with me because she "wasn't sure she could trust me." She linked this to my being a woman and added, "There's something about women." Sensing an important area for exploration, my queries did not yield further fantasies or feelings at this initial stage. Though I suspected important links between this ambiguous statement, the absence of female friends and fantasies linked with her early experience with her mother, she was unable to offer much beyond an idealized picture of her mother (as wholly empathic) and puzzlement about her friendships. The specter of her erotic attachments to female teachers also remained in the background of my mind. Within this early phase of a maternal transference, I also did not know if Petra's mistrust was linked to me as biologically, anatomically female or to my femininity (whatever this might mean to her).

Throughout her analysis, Petra often raised the issue of her reduced fee, stating a wish to pay my full fee. Over the years, I adjusted and readjusted her fee – she would pay my full rate for a period of time, then she reversed this for another period of time. An example of this play occurred one day when she once again suggested paying my full rate for the next several months due to an anticipated surplus in her savings. We examined her fantasies around this and she revealed a fear that she was draining me of my resources, depleting my strength, and she feared I would become ill. She wished to see, touch and know me but feared the damage she might cause in doing so. Feelings of closeness through the treatment process seemed to trigger these obsessive worries. Would her germs penetrate me? Was my receptivity to Petra dangerous? *Looking, gazing upon and seeing* immediately conveyed powerful channels to project damage and thus were dangerous, contaminated and contaminating modes of connection, as the transmission of germs seemed to go both ways.

Many psychoanalytic theories speak to this clinical process. Maternal figures, through various maternal transferences, tend to arouse early and intense anxieties associated with desire along with a passivity and helplessness in relation to an all-powerful, enviable other. If all goes well, the infant develops the capacity for receptivity to the good-enough other. This refers to an active, receptive stance toward receiving maternal care just as the analysand gives herself or himself to the analyst's care (Green, 1986).[3] Depending on the child's experience, the child then develops a basic receptivity to, idealization of, or expelling tendency to the seduction of the other and to the outside world.

We can see the vitalizing energy a mother offers her infant (on both psychic and bodily levels) in the invitation *to be,* through being delivered, seen and touched. Instinctively, the good-enough mother (Winnicott, 1960) says to her infant some version of "Hello! Yes! I see you!" in a reflexive, lilting, high-pitched tone, all the while stroking, physically holding and rhythmically soothing her baby. This is the mother's invitation *to be* as well as *to have (her)* as an object of love.[4] She invites the baby's presence in both body and being, (however undifferentiated and nascent).

With its libidinal force (tenderness) as its basic (but certainly not only) affect, "[maternal eroticism] is a *fabulous investment in the state of emergency in life*" (Kristeva 2014a, p. 77). Similarly, Elise (2015, 2017, 2019) refers to the erotic as embodied affective energies including "libidinal vitality, tempestuous passions, unruly urges, vigor, ardor and a stimulating, vibrant frame of mind" (2019, p. 1).

This is the conscious and unconscious seduction by the mother, with all its excitations and inflections, the mother's enigmatic message conveyed in the Khora's sensory surround (especially from her body) through *touch, gaze and tonalities.* The baby "takes in" the mother even when the mother transmits mixed messages, perhaps does *not* invite the baby in, or obstructs and frustrates the baby's seeking, pleas, needs and demands. The mother is a complex *bodily* force to the baby, mysterious and erotic, serving as a launching pad for seeking closeness with or being repelled by others.[5]

Merleau-Ponty writes, "The body of the other is not perceived as an object, but rather as inhabited by *a secret perception*, by a sexual schema that is strictly individual" (Merleau-Ponty, 2012/1945, pp. 158–9).

And further:

> The body [of the other] is *enigmatic* … it is connected with [a] personal life and is like the habitat in which the human being seeks closeness and union with others … corporeality … [it is] our surface of contact with being. (see Merleau-Ponty, 1964/1945, p. 229; cited in Moya and Lorrain 2016, pp. 744–5, *italics added*)

The baby's complex experience with the mother's body will be internalized and bear its imprint, referenced as a template for experience with others throughout life.

The translation of these experiences, conveyed through psychic *messages* begins in infancy (Salomonsson, 2012), consistent with Laplanche's thesis:

> An adult faced with a child is particularly likely to be deviant and inclined to perform bungled or even symbolic actions because he is involved in a relationship with his other self, with the other he once was. The child in front of him brings out the child within him. (Laplanche, 1989, p. 103; quoted in Salomonsson, 2012, p. 637)

And further,

> [A]n adult profers to a child verbal, non-verbal and even behavioral signifiers which are pregnant with unconscious sexual significations. (Laplanche, 1989, p. 126; quoted in Salomonsson, 2012, p. 637)

These messages are translated by the child and become embedded within the structures of subjectivity in nonverbal, imagistic forms. In addition, these messages are internalized with varying degrees of ego-syntonicity, a distinction among processes of internalization that draws on the theorizing of Schafer (1968), Green (1986), Perelberg (2018a,b) and Zeavin (2019). Unresolved mourning, derived from a traumatic loss of the mother, can indicate faulty internalizations of the maternal introject, resultant from an attempt to cope with traumatic loss in real life. Introjection or incorporation are types of internal psychic presences that exert an influence on the body and mind in an undigested, raw manner in order to preserve the object as a living thing inside. This inner presence can attack from within, from the inside out, as it were. For Petra, the living presence of her mother took the form of an illusory genetic predisposition to her mother's blood disease. This led to fears of her own decline and potential destructiveness to me as these were projected into me, resulting in fantasies of my imminent demise, unconsciously caused by her.

Questions are raised, What did Petra have, in this concretized form, transmitted from her parents? How did she translate and internalize the confusing and mysterious messages of her mother's sexuality presented to her through her mother's ministrations (Laplanche, 1989, 1997, 1999a,b)? Though there is no scientific basis for this, Petra wondered if the gene for her mother's illness is a *sex-linked trait*, as if linked to *femaleness* and/or *femininity* and transmitted through touch. Irigaray[6] artfully states, "The girl has the mother ... in her skin, in the humidity of the mucous membranes, in the intimacy of her most intimate parts, in the mystery of her relation to gestation, birth and to her sexual identity." Not sex-specific, Bolognini (2011c) evocatively states, "*Through the bodily openings coated in mucous membrane, the 'inside' of an individual is placed in direct communication with that of another individual*" (p. 108, italics in original). How the child experiences and translates the ways in which her mother relates to mystery, the unknown and the unspeakable (where sexuality often resides, at least in Western societies[7]) determines the nature and qualities of these internalizations.[8]

In the early months of the treatment, Petra spoke of contamination – does she make her *patients* sick, will her patients make *her* sick and she worried about making *me* sick. Germs were a regular character in the field (Ferro, 2009) and she was alert to my voice sounding congested, if I sneezed or coughed, if I was late or, worst of all, if I forgot something. She talked about a *pit in her stomach* that she chronically sensed, along with an anxious dread of being overcome by it. She worried if she would give this sense of dread to me. At times, I imagined Petra poised at the edge of an abyss into which she feared I had already fallen and that I was hiding this fact from her.

The case of Petra specifically relates to the ways in which the field is erotic[9] and particularly from within the maternal transferences. The following essays also relate to this clinical material along with relevant theoretical discussions: Essay 20, *From foreclosed void to usable space*, where I discuss Petra's dread of the "pit in her stomach" and her fear that she may pass this on to me; Essay 21, *The fate of feminine signifiers* where I discuss the various ways in which maternal symbols have historically been held as demeaned and degraded; Essay 22, *Identificatory love and object love* where I discuss the resolution of unstable and persecutory introjective processes through identificatory love; and Essay 23, *Le visage de la mère* where I discuss the the differences between passivity and receptivity among other related themes.

Notes

1 A version of this paper was presented at *The International Psychoanalytic Association*, Vancouver, British Columbia, July, 2021 on a panel with Stan Coen and Mary Brady. Parts of this paper were also presented as an Invited Address at the *Societa' Psicoanalitica Italiana*, Genova, Italy, November, 2021.
2 See Essay 5, *Safety, danger, couch, chair* (this volume).
3 Active receptivity is similar to the meaning of *passivation* to which Green (1986) refers, not to be confused with passivity, however.
4 See Essay 22, *Identificatory love and object love*, (this volume).
5 For an elaborated discussion on Kristeva's theorizing on maternal eroticism, see Celenza (2022a).
6 (1989, p 133, quoted in Perelberg, 2018b).
7 See, for example, Fonagy, (2008).
8 See Essay 20, *From foreclosed void to usable space* and Essay 21, *The fate of feminine signifiers* for more discussion of the distinctions among internalization processes.
9 See Essay 18, *The erotic field* (this volume).

Chapter 20

From a foreclosed void to usable space[1]

When is an abyss a threatening void and how to convert this void into usable, potential space? Britton's (2004) triangular space allows the child to take an observing position, the observer of the parental couple and thereby develop the capacity symbolize a relationship in which the child does not participate. Triangular space also allows the experience of being an object for others, a third, where one is observed from a distance participating in a relationship. This is space that is usable by the child, an experience of re-cognition by a separate other, in contrast to the space that must be filled in because it is intolerable in experience.

The abyss or dreaded void is distinct from Britton's triangular space and more in line with the negative pole of Green's (1986) *absence* and *the work of the negative.* The threatening void discussed here is made up of non-usable ruptures that foreclose potential space. Britton's space is bounded by three and perhaps thereby usable because of the binding and potential metabo-lizing presence of others. In contrast, the empty void threatens the child with intolerable loss, unresolvable enigmas and confusions; it is the unthought known like a dread or haunting. It is preoedipal, nonverbal and unbounded, harboring ghosts that echo annihilatory chants.

An apt theoretical comparison is Laplanche's (1989, 1997) notion of the *hollowed-out transference,* a space inhabited by the unresolved enigmas in the original maternal/child experience. Through the analytic process, this space is opened up in order to be expressed and thereby potentially resolved and retranscribed as it is actualized, *après coup,* in the treatment.

In many essays included in this volume,[2] I have discussed the theoretical distinctions among internalization processes, especially in relation to those that do not necessitate the repudiation of the associated (usually feminine) signifiers. Identification, being a healthy form of internalization, is a major source of adaptation to loss. As discussed in more detail in the next essay,[3] a repudiated signifier is, by definition, not an identification but an introject where foreclosure, eradication, repression or especially degradation are im-plicated in such internalizing processes (as in incorporation and introjection).[4] In contrast, repudiation is not associated with identificatory processes.

DOI: 10.4324/9781003264095-23

How do we make the shift from incorporation or introjection to identi-fication, i.e., from a void to usable space? In a subsequent essay,[5] I suggest the term *le visage de la mère* to represent the analyst's (and the baby's) nonverbal experience of a benign and helpful maternal or primary care-giver's presence. This is an internalization that aids in the process of me-tabolization of noxious stimuli. The experience of the maternal figure surviving the infant's attacks, for example, without retaliation but instead, with understanding and containment, will provide the infant with the ne-cessary imagery to internalize a benign maternal presence transforming dysphoric affect and experience. This may require the enlargement of the analyst's containing capacities.

The clinical illustration of Petra demonstrates this process. Petra[6] re-members her early childhood as surrounded by her mother's presence and care, physically affectionate and empathic to her emotional well-being. This idealized picture is linked to memories of sitting on her mother's lap, hugs abounding, with lots of touching. In later life, Petra's mother contracted a blood disorder and Petra witnessed a long deterioration in her physical and emotional well-being. Zeavin (2019) makes a useful distinction between an internal good mother and an internal idealized mother, the latter implying an active, unconscious need to *keep the mother good*, evidence that some-thing bad threatens to mar the maternal imago. This internalized scene is indicated by Petra's constant and anxious attentiveness to my well-being. She often asks if I am ill, if my family is ill, whether I can pay sufficient attention to her, etc. I understand these worries as her attempts to reassure herself that she has not harmed me, that I am unblemished and that I will not harm her.

In a later phase of her analysis, a shift occurred in Petra's internal world as she remembered an incident of physical trauma by an intruder (a neighbor who was known to the family). This was not a new memory, but in the *après coup* of the analytic process, the memory now reflects a retran-scription of linked images of her mother, unmasking the idealized maternal introjects and re-elaborating her memories of her mother as sometimes *not* present, even failing her. After Petra's mother allowed the intruder to enter their home, he began taunting her brother, a teasing which ended in a ser-ious physical altercation. When her brother was badly beaten and rendered helpless, the intruder left of his own accord, with Petra's mother and herself standing by, paralyzed and in shock. The intruder was never confronted nor did Petra or her mother tell her father or the police. Worse, her mother implied that Petra may have been the reason the neighbor wanted to visit, a comment that implied something about Petra's sexuality. Petra remains confused by the imbalanced reckoning of this incident.

As a child, Petra was surrounded by maternal figures. She became at-tached to her mother's sister who was smart and attentive, a loving, bountiful figure. I suspect that as Petra turned to her aunt, the internal representation of her own mother was traumatically de-idealized and was internalized as a contaminated other, paralyzed and diseased, perhaps also envious of Petra's vitality. In Petra's constant worry about my well-being (and by interpretation, her worry about whether she has harmed me), I sensed in Petra an internal, representation of an envious, paralyzed mother who attacks her from within and for which I would be recruited to contain or enact. This symptom also encapsulates Petra's frustration and hatred of the unprotective mother (the de-idealized side of her mother) by expressing her guilt-ridden wish to harm me.

It was during this time that my own mother became ill, a long process of decline after which she eventually died. Cancerous tumors had broken through her skin and, at times, would bleed profusely. I ministered to her, mingling my being with her blood, cleaning her up, reassuring her that she did not smell, and comforting her with surrounding, tearful embraces in these last months of her life. We achieved an emotional union that we never had before.

When I returned to our sessions, Petra brought in some objects that she wanted me to hold for a few minutes, transmitting (in her mind) my psychically soothing capacities to the objects she had brought, soon to be transformed and capable of soothing her. I did not hesitate to hold these objects (a stone and a small wooden box), holding them firmly in my hands. Then she brought out a shawl and I placed it around my shoulders. I left it there for about twenty seconds. Petra was stunned that I would so easily let her things touch me. She watched me welcome her presence, through the shawl and my body, as our beings intermingled. I believe this was not simply "putting on a shawl" and the various holding functions that act might symbolize. This was a moment when Petra experienced me willing to risk death and, more particularly, to risk closeness with her destructiveness and murderous capabilities.

I believe my actions conveyed a message from within the maternal erotic transferences: "I will endure what you give me, no matter the shape or form, and you do not need to fear what is inside you." I believe my lack of hesitation put our bodies in touch with each other, a nonverbal communication without mediation, emphasizing the bodily based nature of the interaction. Though we talked about the meaning of these actions many times over the course of the analysis, I believe the absence of hesitation in the moment was a nonverbal communication of my sturdiness and lack of fear, detoxifying her feared internal potentials.

In a concordant way, Petra was able to address ways in which her mother was physically present but psychically absent and even bad (e.g., unprotective, accusatory, persecuting). My conjecture is that changes in me (through the parallel process of my own mother dying while remarkably and for the first time, coming alive to me), enlarged my receptivity to Petra's retranscription of her own memories of her mother.

At least three components of the analytic process, *patience/receptivity, endurance/survival and re-transcription*, serve to offer the analysand alternative channels and attributes for healthy identification. The analyst's ability to hold, endure, sustain and survive projected attacks has this transformative power – as if to convey that maternal/analytic endurance and sustenance can withstand and overcome the toxic effects of destructive attacks. As repudiated, phobically avoided representatives of my maternality (germs, touch, gaze) become endowed with love and care, they are detoxified and transformed into identificatory inner presences. These, then become identifications with the vitalizing components of maternal eroticism, transforming the phenomenal psychic experience of threat, diminishing their fantasied destructive power in both phenomenal and intrapsychically structuring ways. Through these vitalizing effects, the capacity for affect tolerance is enlarged and deepened.

The potential space between Petra and me had transformed from a void to a fertile space, enlarged by virtue of the positive maternal identifications and actual experiences I was suffering, expanding my ability to contain Petra's experiences. I was not afraid of touching my mother, the moments of fluid exchange – blood, tears and love. I believe this message was unconsciously transmitted to Petra in a way that made the containment of her longings to touch me detoxified and uncontaminated. These were not abstract experiences, but highly personal, passionate and embodied, what Wilson (2014) artfully names "that place of the flesh" (p. 103). My memories of this experience with my mother were directly translated into a capacity to offer the same to Petra.

In this way, a void or disavowed, foreclosed area in Petra's psyche became a usable space, first within me, through the enlargement of my containing receptivity and focused penetration (in the sense of targeted curiosity). I believe my receptivity to my diseased mother, my willingness to risk and survive being infected with my own mother's contaminated femininity enlarged my receptivity to Petra's fears and fantasied destructiveness toward me. My willingness to be changed in these ways opened up a space in me that enlarged the erotic field between Petra and me. My capacity to contain what Petra was enduring grew from an erotic rapprochement (Perelberg, 2018b) between my mother and me that I could now offer as mother/analyst to Petra, enabling a nonrepudiated feminine identification.

Green (1986) has offered us the concept of the negative which has a double meaning and within which we can transform our patient's psychic life. It begins with a void and becomes space, a *choiceless beach*[7] upon which something is first allowed to emerge and then can grow.

I now see Petra's worry about contaminating me as an erotic move. Longing for identification had brought with it a fear that she would destroy me.

Seeing, having, touching and knowing were all forbidden as the assault on her brother had contaminated her and, connected to that experience, the traumatically disappointing maternal response. Experiencing me as surviving her psychic attacks – the talk of blood and death – all of these were received by me through my disciplined receptivity of the analytic space.

In this essay, I have connected the wish to know the other with the psychic transformation that begins with a void and becomes usable space. This transformation often requires a shift in the analyst where new, usable space is created first within the analyst, becoming a site for the metabolization of fantasied destructive introjects which are then transformed into (in this case, feminine and maternal) symbols of potential identification for the analysand. It is through the analyst's capacity to receive and be curious about (in a focused, targeted way) the unknown (mysterious and potentially destructive) aspects of the analysand that offers the analysand an experience of receptivity to these hostile and condemning introjects, a space in the analyst for parts of the analysand otherwise disavowed and repudiated.

Notes

1 A longer version of this paper was originally presented at *The Chicago Center for Psychoanalysis* in February, 2020 and *Confer*, Autumn Program in 2020.
2 See Essay 21, *The fate of feminine signifiers*; Essay 22, *Identificatory love and object love*; Essay 23, *Le visage de la mère* (all in this volume).
3 See Essay 21, *The fate of feminine signifiers*, (this volume).
4 In contrast, the psychoanalytic definition of identification is, "Psychological process whereby the subject assimilates an aspect, property or attribute of the other and is transformed, wholly or partially, after the model the other provides. It is by means of a series of identifications that the personality is constituted and specified." (Laplanche and Pontalis, 1973, p. 205)
5 See Essay 23, *Le visage de la mère*, (this volume).
6 See also Essay 19, *The maternal erotic transferences* (this volume) for an elaboration of Petra's early experience in analysis. See also Celenza (2022a) for an elaboration of the case of Petra.
7 See Essay 23, *Le visage de la mère* (this volume).

Chapter 21

The fate of feminine signifiers [1]

Lombardi (2016) speaks of a vertical axis wherein the first condition of life is somatosensory, a corporeal condition where concrete somatic sensations precede introjective processes. This domain revolves around the subjective experience of being a body and the infant's relation to it. In the horizontal axis, the primary caregiver ministers to the baby and aids in the experience of safely dwelling within one's own body.[2] From an intersubjective perspective, I will be developing the idea of *the first signifier*[3] *of the erotic* as a *body-based feminine.* This is derived from the infant's experience of its body as held, soothed and stimulated by the maternal[4] figure, i.e., the experience of the mother with her infant. This includes, of course, the breast, and raises the theoretical problem that this breast is generally discussed as *a de-eroticized breast,* good or bad, but not erotic.[5] Yet, it remains that through body-based ministrations and the primary caregiver's empathic recognition and love, the maternal figure initiates and for a time, comprises the baby's entire relation to the world. The primary caregiver comes to represent, thereby, the first signifier of the infant's vitalized relation to its body.

In a more specific way and through a nonsexed, nongendered lens, [women do not own the feminine (Kristeva, 2019)], the primal and originary experience with a primary caregiver develops the first signifier of the erotic. This experience comes to represent what we call the *feminine,* (to speak of one pole of the traditional gender binary) through the breast or nipple-bottle-breast.[6] Most importantly, this occurs within the relationship between the primary caregiver and infant, because it is when the infant is receptively helpless to the ministrations of the primary object, when our *taking in* of the world is wholly dependent on the satisfying and frustrating primary caregiver, i.e., the good and bad signifier of the nipple-bottle-breast.

If women no longer own the feminine, then what I mean to convey is the way in which the infant experiences the primary caregiver's ministrations, probing and receptive to the infant's needs. These come to represent the signifiers of the nipple-bottle-breast, the first signifiers of the *body-based feminine.*[7]

Though not a theoretically settled issue (see Birksted-Breen, 1996), many psychoanalytic authors believe that ideas about a *core* or *primary* femininity

DOI: 10.4324/9781003264095-24

(especially as these ideas are linked to anatomical metaphors) have been superseded in favor of a psychic bi- or multi-sexuality (see, for example, Harris, 2005, Celenza, 2014 and Perelberg, 2018a). Whether or not one accepts the idea of a primary femininity, the tendency to split representations of the feminine (or to polarize the feminine and masculine) continues to be found in analytic work. Splitting or polarization is the first step in a defensive process of the many forms of disavowal, the next step being degradation of the disavowed side. For example, intense longings for closeness or dependency can be held in mind as "feminine" *and thereby weak*. Problems with assertiveness can likewise be associated with "feminine" submissiveness, and thus devalued. Such significations serve to defensively split psychic capacities, relegating certain personality characteristics to disavowed, dissociated or repressed self-states.[8]

Internalization processes, especially as a response to absence or loss, comprise the ways in which the psyche constitutes itself, i.e., the structures of subjectivity. These structures differ to varying degrees, especially in the extent to which they are more or less ego-syntonic versus those that are repressed, disavowed or otherwise foreclosed.[9] Identification represents the harmonious form of internalization in contrast to incorporation and introjection (Schafer, 1968; Laplanche and Pontalis, 1973; Akhtar, 2009). Indeed, we can say that one way in which processes of internalization are distinguished relates to the degree of harmony and ego-syntonicity that define and differentiate them.

To be specific, the psychoanalytic definition of identification is:

> Psychological process whereby the subject assimilates an aspect, property or attribute of the other and is transformed, wholly or partially, after the model the other provides. It is by means of a series of identifications that the personality is constituted and specified. (Laplanche and Pontalis, 1973, p. 205)

Through this definition and the distinctions among internalization processes, it is possible to see that identification as the central unconscious process for coping with loss (and for the constitution of identity) does not require a repudiation of the characteristics thereby assimilated. Rather, a repudiated signifier is, by definition, not an identification but an introject. Here, foreclosure, eradication, repression and/or degradation are implicated in internalizing processes (as in incorporation and introjection).

In contrast to identification, introjection (and its end-product, introject) are defined by:

> The organized cluster of memory traces … remain[ing] unassimilated in the total self image … Identifications, unlike introjects, do not feel like a

'foreign body' in the self and are more likely to be ego-syntonic and in harmony with the individual's self-image. (Akhtar, 2009, p. 150)

It is reasonable to conclude that repudiated (in this case, gendered) signifiers are *internalized as pathological introjects*, a site of conflict, dystonicity and disavowal where the individual is in some measure at war with herself. The analyst, in contrast, offers an opportunity for identification through identificatory love (albeit, a love that is not to be had) *without repudiation* in the sense of condemnation or degradation. Due to the analyst's ability to contain the projected attacks, these internalizations become usable modes of being that transform the inner psychic presences to a more benign presence.

As Lew Aron has elaborated (2012), castration and the repudiation of femininity took on a central role in Freudian clinical theory and practice.[10] Occupying one side of a series of binarial oppositions, vulnerability, passivity, emotionality and primitivity all comprise the degraded pole of a gendered developmental binary. Stated in later papers, Freud (1937) theorized that both males and females had to repudiate feminine identifications, i.e., the qualities and characteristics experienced consciously and unconsciously as associated with the maternal or primary caregiver. As Aron (2012) states, "To be primitive is to be subject to domination and penetration – embodied and hence vulnerable... the dark, feminine unconscious" (p. 6).

Many feminist psychoanalytic writers have written eloquently about the "recuperation" or "reconciliation" of gender-based identifications as the child attempts to integrate aspects of otherwise disavowed gendered representations (see, for example, Bassin, 1996; Benjamin, 1995, 1998; Celenza, 2014, 2022a; Dimen, 1991; Goldner, 1991; Harris, 2005; Perelberg, 2018a, Atlas, 2016). In particular, Perelberg (2018a) discusses the repudiation of femininity as the repudiation of passivity or dependency, the universal signifier of lack or incompleteness. She goes on to speculate that these ideas are ways in which societies have tried to control fears of the all-powerful woman through the universal subordination of women (p. 36).

Derived from classical theorizing, these conceptions linger. In his paper on *Female Sexuality*, Freud (1931) discusses the preoedipal relation to the mother and the "universal inevitability and durability of *every* child's reproaches against her" (Orgel, 1996, p. 48, *italics in original*). For Freud, the girl's strongest reproach against her mother revolves around her mother "not giving her a proper penis" (Freud, 1931, p. 234). For boys, the reproach revolves around the fear of submission to the mother and thereby, the fear of relinquishing his penis (Orgel, 1996). Freud further speculates that behind each of these universals is a more basic reproach, "[T]he real fact is that the attachment to the mother is bound to perish precisely because it was the first and was so intense" (Freud, 1931, p. 234).

Through a totalistic conception of erotic desire,[11] it can be more usefully stated that the *repudiation* of femininity in the move from dyadic to triadic relations is unnecessary, especially repudiation in the sense of *rejection with disapproval and condemnation*. In addition, repudiation need not be linked to associations of femininity as passivity, submission or other aspects of a devalued, alien self, eventuating in the splitting of the ego-ideal, especially for girls.

It is necessary to resist this divisive impulse, enlarging the analyst's capacity to experience our patients and the analytic process with the full range of affectivity at our disposal. The recognition of a multi-gendered and multi-sexual potential within ourselves will resonate and nurture these identifications within our patients. This is facilitated by transcending the false binarial constructions of femininity and masculinity as well as the feminine ideal and repudiated signifiers of the feminine.

Notes

1 A longer version of this paper was originally presented at *The Chicago Center for Psychoanalysis* in February, 2020 and *Confer*, Autumn Program in 2020.
2 See Essay 26, *Embodied countertransference*, (this volume).
3 I have selected the term *signifier* to connote *carrier of (conscious or unconscious) meaning*. I do not use the term in the context of Lacanian theorizing, but prefer the term *signifier* to symbol, imago, representation and various types of internalization because signifier is general in its connotation and does not specify a form (i.e., verbal, nonverbal, unrepresented) or mode of internalization.
4 I use the term *maternal* and *feminine* to describe the primary caregiver, whom we know is not necessarily a woman. Similarly, I use the term paternal to describe the third person in the family who is not necessarily a man or even a person but may represent the outside world or the third position.
5 One exception is Hilferding (1911/1974) who wrote about the erogenous breast.
6 I use the phrase nipple-bottle-breast in order to depict maternal ministrations, inclusive of mothers who are not women.
7 In a similar vein, the Oedipal complex has to be reformulated through a non-gendered lens, conveying the crucial developmental challenge for the toddler to cope with the move from dyadic to triangular relations – better referred to as the move from two to three than from female (mother) to male (father). See also Essay 22, *Identificatory love and object love* (this volume) for further elaboration of these ideas.
8 See Essay 20, *From foreclosed void to usable space* (this volume) for a clinical application of these ideas.
9 See, for example, Butler (1995) for a description of the daughter's incorporative identification as a disavowed homosexual attachment to the mother. (I disagree, however, with Butler's use of the term identification in this context.)
10 "The repudiation of femininity can be nothing else than a biological fact, a part of the great riddle of sex" (Freud, 1937, p. 252).
11 See Essay 18, *The erotic field* (this volume).

Chapter 22

Identificatory love and object love

Freud's (1905) division of identificatory love (to be) and object love (to have) was his attempt to explain the child's navigation of sexual difference and ultimately the development of gender identity and sexual orientation. In the following, I aim to elaborate the separation of identificatory love and object love as a false dichotomy.

Freud, in his heteronormative construction of the Oedipus complex, splits identificatory love and object love in his attempt to account for gender identification and sexual orientation – unfortunately degrading the "negative" oedipal position along the way.

Perhaps in a move toward a totalistic view of erotic and sexual love, Freud himself later theorized the relationship between identification and object love in a more combinatory way, establishing identification as *an initial stage* of object choice.

> Preliminary stages of love emerge ... [in] the first of these aims, we recognize the phase of incorporating or devouring – a type of love which is consistent with abolishing the object's separate existence. (1915b, p. 138)

And then again, in a later paper,

> [I]dentification is a *preliminary stage* of object-choice, that it is the first way – and one that is expressed in an ambivalent fashion – in which the ego picks out an object. The ego wants to incorporate this object into itself, and, in accordance with the oral or cannibalistic phase of libidinal development in which it is, it was to do so by devouring it. (Freud, 1917, p. 249–50, *italics added*)

In these excerpts, it appears Freud was attempting to contend with the threat associated with object choice (and the ego's attempt to omnipotently control the object of desire by devouring it). However, his early views on identification and object love as separable and as necessarily split in the later

DOI: 10.4324/9781003264095-25

oedipal phase have remained in the fundamental canon of classical theorizing. In 1937, Freud also stated that a successful resolution of the oedipal complex, the move from two to three or from dyadic to triadic relations, requires a *repudiation of femininity* for both sexes.[1] In contrast, contemporary theorizing[2] regards this view of the Oedipal Complex as only one version of the child's negotiation of the challenge to incorporate a third and one which may arise in the fantasy elaborations of a *traumatized* little boy.

Identificatory love aids in the move from the maternal-child dyadic to triadic relations beginning when the child experiences and copes with the mother's absence, but also later, when the child begins to take in the third of the paternal presence. As the first signifier of the erotic is "feminine," through the nipple-bottle-breast[3] and within the relationship between the primary caregiver and infant, the optimal circumstance challenges the infant to cope with the periodic unavailability of the mother through identification, the ability to conjure the mother's presence (in her absence). Later, the oedipal child's move to incorporate the paternal figure or third necessitates the child to cope with the loss of the maternal figure in three ways: as the *only one*, as a loss of omnipotence and as the loss of the preoedipal fantasy of union with the primary object. These losses and the mourning associated with each are also ameliorated through identificatory love.

The split between identificatory love and object love constructs a binary between *being* and *having*, an unfortunate and unnecessary bifurcation (Benjamin, 1995; 1998). This bifurcation creates a division between object love and identificatory love, setting up what I believe to be a false dichotomy. Many contemporary theorists and especially feminist writers have addressed this issue (see, for example, Layton, 2004; Benjamin, 1995, 1998). These theorists argue that the bifurcation of identificatory love and object love represents a *pathological splitting*, a move necessary for the *traumatized* child to *separate and repudiate* forms of desire from those that rest in the psyche in more harmonious and ego-syntonic ways.

Some theorizing elaborated various mechanisms of internalization, including those from a developmental perspective. These retained the idea of separate mechanisms at different points on the developmental ladder. Gaddini (1969), for example, distinguished between early imitations (associated with omnipotent fantasies in line with the pleasure principle) and early identifications (or introjections, more in line with the reality principle) as the young child struggles with becoming or *to be* versus *to have*.

All of these internalization processes address frustrations with separation and loss. Many other theorists had earlier written about these distinctions in various ways (cf. Federn (1952), Fenichel (1937), Ferenczi (1932a,b), Deutsch (1942), Greenacre (1958), Greenson (1966), Stoller (1966), Ritvo and Provence (1953), and Eidelberg (1948). Though many of these writers aim to distinguish among internalization processes, later developmental stages are characterized by a blending of imitation, introjection and identification as the distinction between being and having seems to fall away in later years.

Since Karen Horney's writings (1926), it has been argued that Freud's (1937) view of the Oedipal complex and the necessity of the repudiation of femininity (especially as associated with passivity) is the fantasy of the little boy and/or the father's search for a passive object, both of which inspire an outdated cultural norm of femininity as passive, submissive and otherwise devalued (Benjamin, 1995, 1998). Benjamin (1995) writes,

> Object love, which has sometimes been seen as opposed to, exclusive of, or replaced by identification, may also be seen as *growing out of* identificatory love ... Sustaining identificatory tendencies alongside object love creates a different kind of complementarity, and a different stance toward oppositional differences...Sustaining the tension between contrasting elements ... remain[s] potentially available rather than forbidden and the oscillation between them can then be pleasurable rather than dangerous. (p. 73)

And, in a different source (Benjamin, 1998),

> Failure to represent the umbilicus, which is both the link and the separation from mother, ... sets up the phallus to represent what [the umbilicus] does not (reunion/separation), making of it a defense. .... [I suggest the formulation of] a different kind of complementarity ... bridging rather than splitting opposites. (p. 33)

To state it succinctly, loving always entails both identifications and ideal-driven longings (eventually constituting the ego-ideal, as in the name of the father) and prohibitory superego representations (constituting the superego, i.e., the *no* of the father – in Lacanian terminology, the double meaning of *le nom du père*).

To have and to hold is to desire and to be in such a way that object love and identificatory love intermingle, are two sides of the same coin as it is recognized that identificatory love is the first emotional tie to the object and is not necessarily lost (Benjamin, 1998). Indeed, it might be said that identificatory love is taking in, which implies to have *and* to hold, to have *and* to be. Thereby, all loving is totalistic; to have, to hold and to be are combined in loving and desiring. Just as seeing is having, knowing is owning, wanting is touching. A totalistic view of erotic desire encompasses all of these longings, where no form of love leans on another. Identificatory love aids the process of separation for both sexes, including the move from the maternal/feminine to the paternal object and function (Laplanche, 1997; Benjamin, 1995, 1998).

Notes

1 "The repudiation of femininity can be nothing else than a biological fact, a part of the great riddle of sex" (p. 252). See also Essay 21, *The fate of feminine signifiers* (this volume).
2 Among relational authors, see Benjamin, (1995); neo-Freudian authors, see Birksted-Breen (1996); Chodorow (2011).
3 I refer to nipple-bottle-breast to allow for primary caregivers who are not female.

Chapter 23

Le visage de la mère[1]

In this essay, I attempt to offer a visual image, *le visage de la mère (the face of the mother)*[2] as a nonverbal symbol of the healthy internalization of aspects of the maternal figure. The result of an internalizing process, *the face of the mother* is proposed as a healthy alternative to maternal symbols (verbal or nonverbal) that indicate a repudiated signifier of femininity.[3] The representations of the primary caregiver have long been held within psychoanalytic theorizing in a repudiated manner as a necessary consequence and end-product of the child's coping with the loss of the maternal figure. In classical theorizing, these representations of the primary caregiver were thought to be necessarily repudiated by both daughters and sons as each attempts to cope with different kinds of losses of the primary caregiver (Freud, 1937). I suggest *le visage de la mère* as an alternative to repudiated signifiers and specifically, as a nonrepudiated symbol.

There are many kinds of losses of the primary caregiver ushered in as the infant and child face several kinds of developmental challenges. One example is the confrontation with the periodic unavailability of the maternal figure, i.e., the bad or frustrating object. Another occurs later when the child has to cope with the primary object as a rival who competes for the father's attention. Similar is the developmental challenge of turning to the world in contrast to attending to the primary caregiver. I am suggesting that in none of these necessary developmental challenges does the turn away from the maternal figure need to be freighted with repudiation, in the sense of rejection or condemnation. Further, I suggest that when attempts at coping include some measure of degradation, resulting in introjections that rest in the psyche in a less assimilated fashion, these internalization processes will have occurred under the influence of trauma.

As noted in previous essays,[4] internalization processes differ in the extent to which the end-product is held in an ego-syntonic manner or with varying degrees of ego-dystonicity.[5] Identificatory mechanisms are, by definition, harmonious and ego-syntonic. By contrast, a repudiated signifier, e.g., an introject, is indicative of *pathological splitting*. With regard to maternal signifiers, the *condemnation* of the primary caregiver's containing and

DOI: 10.4324/9781003264095-26

nurturant activity is the result of a *defensive foreclosure* and is, thus, internalized as an introject. Such a signifier is perhaps resorted to as a compromise or response to unique familial threats in a traumatizing maternal or paternal situation (i.e., not a universal or necessary phenomenon).

Likewise, the infant and child are challenged with the mysterious and unknown aspects of maternal desires. The primary caregiver conveys "enigmatic messages" that reside in the child's unconscious. These messages are translated by the child and become embedded within the structures of subjectivity in nonverbal, imagistic forms. These messages are also internalized with varying degrees of ego-syntonicity.

Receptivity and the containing function of the primary caregiver is the source of maternal signification. Similarly, the analytic process offers the analysand a usable receptivity in the containing function of the analyst as the analyst confronts and survives the patient's attacks (projected self-attacks indicative of conflicted and pathological introjects). The analyst's receptivity and survival counters the self-destructive effects of these attacks. In this way, the analyst offers a benign, "uncontaminated," and thereby usable container that can survive various internal psychic threats. I am calling this *le visage de la mère* (the face of the mother), a term that depicts the infant's nonverbal metabolization of the taking in/receptive experiences of the primary caregiver. Through the development of this signification, the child translates noxious symbols of maternal love and sexuality (e.g., vulnerability, passivity, dependency to name the most common) into a benign internal presence. This is the move from a void to representational (i.e. usable) space and the corresponding move from introjective to identificatory processes.[6,7]

Within the context of the dyad, Green's (1998) concept of the negative can be applied to refer to the containing function of the analyst and the analyst's offer of usable space. Perhaps at the crux of this is the important distinction between inhibited passivity and *disciplined receptivity*, the latter being (I suggest) the *eternal signifier of the feminine*.

Here I am reminded of a passage from Anne Lindbergh:

> But it must not be sought for, or – heaven forbid!—dug for. No, no dredging of the sea bottom here. That would defeat one's purpose. The sea does not reward those who are too anxious, too greedy, too impatient. To dig for treasures shows not only impatience and greed, but lack of faith. Patience, patience, patience, is what the sea teaches. Patience and faith. One should lie empty, open, choiceless as a beach – waiting for a gift from the sea. (1955, p. 11)

I am suggesting that both sons and daughters can internalize an identification with the feminine or move from maternal symbols to paternal symbols without the repudiation of maternal signifiers, i.e., femininity, through the mechanism of identificatory love, the face of the mother or *le visage de la mère*. Crucial to this move will be the nature of the symbol as they are held in the mind of the paternal figure. Each parent has a name, a "no" *and a face*. The "no" of each is required to accept the incest taboo and generational difference, resolved through the name of each set up and constitutive of the ego-ideal, the wished-for future self.

Green (1998) has offered the concept of the negative which has a double meaning and within which we can transform our patient's psychic life. It begins with a void and becomes a space, a choiceless beach upon which something is first allowed to emerge and then can grow.

In this playground of the erotic field, *le visage de la mère* is internalized as the nonrepudiated feminine, a maternal ego-ideal that expands psychic life. Through a totalistic conception of the erotic field based on a series of dialectics among knowing, seeing, having and touching, these come together as erotic moves within the transference/countertransference matrix recuperating the degraded, repudiated feminine signifiers.

In this totalistic view of multiply-gendered erotic life, a combined identificatory love and object love constitute the structures of subjectivity in some amalgamation of femininity and masculinity, gender binaries transcended, a psychic multi-sexuality where ultimately no gendered form is repudiated, devalued or condemned. *Taking in* or *disciplined receptivity* (the eternal signifier of the feminine) comprises one component of a dialectic (receptivity/penetration), together which forms an inclusive and totalistic view of erotic life. Such a dialectic allows the patient to transcend gender binaries and embrace a psychic multi-sexuality where ultimately no gendered form is repudiated, devalued or condemned.

It is through the analyst's capacity to receive and be curious about the unknown (mysterious and potentially destructive) aspects of the analysand that offers the analysand an experience of *disciplined receptivity* to hostile and condemning introjects. This is a space in the analyst for parts of the analysand that are otherwise disavowed and repudiated and may be associated with a gendered signifier (in this case, "feminine"). The analyst offers the analysand a space that is both open to and curious about a heretofore foreclosed space within herself and the analysand.

I propose a link drawn between negativity and femininity but not in the sense of a degradation – rather in the sense of an *absence with potentiality* – a space that allows a flourishing, a fertile space awaiting a gift from the sea, receptive like a choiceless beach.

Notes

1 A longer version of this paper was originally presented at *The Chicago Center for Psychoanalysis* in February, 2020 and *Confer*, Autumn Program in 2020.
2 A purposeful riff on Lacan's *le nom du père*.

3 See Essay 21, *The fate of feminine signifiers* (this volume).
4 See Essay 21, *The fate of feminine signifiers* (this volume) and Essay 22, *Identificatory love and object love.*
5 This distinction among processes of internalization draws on the theorizing of Schafer (1968), Green (1998), Perelberg (2018a,b) and Zeavin (2019).
6 In Winnicott's (1971) terminology, the move from identification to object relating.
7 For a case illustration, see Essay 20, *From a foreclosed void to usable space* (this volume).

Chapter 24

The promise that seduces desire

One of the most vexing, persistent and painful sequelae of the particular post-traumatic stress syndrome associated with sexual boundary violations is directly derived from the corruption of the asymmetric structure of the treatment. The treatment contract is comprised of a promise by the analyst to maintain asymmetry (the asymmetric distribution of attention paid). When the asymmetry is corrupted, the betrayal is not the sex, or even the love itself, but *the lie*, the use of the treatment (perversely) *for the analyst,* when the contract (and promise) is for the patient. The problem is not the love, unhealthy, incestuous and asymmetric as it is, but the broken promise upon which the treatment now rests. This, then, challenges the patient-victim with an impossible task – *to believe in a love that rests upon a broken covenant.* The aftermath of sexual boundary violations revolves around this fractured foundation, where patient-victims are tortured by a lingering, persistent and profound inner doubt of the verity and realness of love.

For the patient-victim, this then becomes a pervasive doubt – transformed into a seemingly unresolvable question, "Did he *really* love me?" Despite clear memories of having been told, in both words and deed, that she is loved ("But he said he loved me, why can't I believe it?"), there is always a profound inner doubt that lingers in their mind. Paradoxically, it is usually the doubt about her lovability that formed a conscious rationale for the transgression in the first place. Indeed, often enough it was the analyst's conscious purpose, in violating boundaries, to show her once and for all that she is *really* loved. And of course, this was usually the reason for her seeking treatment.

This persistent doubt about whether the transgressor *really* loved the patient-victim is based on two conceptual problems, the first being confusion over the essential nature of love in the analytic setting and its quality of realness, as discussed in the first essay of this volume.[1] The second conceptual problem is the question of what exactly is the nature of the betrayal in sexual boundary transgressions. Is it the sexual exploitation? Is it indeed the sex? I am suggesting that the fundamental violation, and the most painful disillusionment, is this *particular lie*, inherent in the violation itself

DOI: 10.4324/9781003264095-27

and sometimes stated explicitly, *"This is for you."* Every sexual boundary violation includes such a lie as part of the perversion of the asymmetric treatment contract, though the analyst may deny, rationalize or justify such a means/end reversal.[2]

The treatment contract revolves around a promise to preserve the analytic presymbolic space for the work of expanding meaning construction. This promise is actualized through the roles each member plays, most importantly by the analyst in maintaining the asymmetric distribution of attention, focus and care. In the case of sexual boundary violations, however, it is through this broken promise that the analyst conveys her or his capacity to lie, to have made a promise that is not kept, and perhaps was never meant. Having done this, nothing built on top of this lie will ring true.

For those transferences that arise from within the analytic setting, the promise is to analyze and thereby foster understanding, especially from a psychoanalytic perspective, and to do that *and only that*. For this reason, transferences emerge with great intensity, having been invited and seduced by the promise of maintaining the structure and safety of the setting. Morris (2012) refers to this as, "the enabling *constitutive disavowal* of the analytic setting, i.e., the promise to maintain an illusory separation between analysis and external life."

By virtue of having made this promise, our patients take more risks revealing their desires in bald and undefended form. Through the embodiment of our role, we continually assert, "You are not obliged to me." This is why the exploitation of these revelations for the analyst's own purposes is particularly perverse.

As analysts, we continually make this commitment in a self-state that is restrained in terms of our separate desires and needs. Because of this promise, to restrain our own desire, we invite the emergence of unrestrained, relatively undefended desires of the patient. We are particularly inviting of presymbolic, unmetabolized affects and desires, the unknown, secret, perhaps shame-inducing aspects of the other's longings that have yet to be symbolized. It is in this context of the promise, the commitment to asymmetry, that the invitation to desire and the desire itself is intensified, a promise of presence without repercussion, obligation or consequence. The promise seduces desire to intensify, to express itself in its fullest passion and complexity. We promise and thereby evoke faith, trust and belief in our strength and integrity, that we will maintain our awareness of separateness and inhibition of our own desires and needs; in short, that we will keep our word.

There are also two conditions that can collude in creating a (usually sexualized) role reversal and eventual boundary transgression. One is the empathic (and perhaps overly compliant) patient who has been socialized to meet the needs of others. This is a characterological condition of many (mostly female) patients and often forms the nexus for which they seek treatment. The second condition is the depleted, narcissistically fragile analyst who can no longer restrain her or his desires and needs. We might, paradoxically, rewrite a famous quote from F. Robert Rodman, from the Preface to Winnicott's *Playing and Reality* (1971), "The mother [read patient] provides what the baby [read the depleted analyst] is ready to imagine and in so doing she facilitates the baby's pleasure in a world that fosters its sense of omnipotence" (p. xii). Saketopoulou (2020) writes of the ways in which the psychoanalytic situation can arouse the analyst's rogue eroticism, what she calls the *infantile erotic countertransference*.

Therefore, the question is not, Did he *really* love me (or was he lying about loving me)? but, Is this love healthy and growth-promoting (or an unhealthy repetition of past imbalanced loves)? A healthy love includes a mutual, symmetrical love where power imbalances are negotiable. This is in direct contrast to the asymmetrical love evoked in the analytic setting which is, by definition, based on a variety of structured (and thereby non-negotiable) power imbalances, as in oedipal transferences. Further, it is an unhealthy love because it is rooted in a broken covenant and thereby has sown the seeds of mistrust.

Notes

1 See Essay 1, *Transference, real or unreal* (this volume).
2 See Essay 31, *Perversion and its qualities of being*, (this volume) for a discussion of perversion in this context.

Chapter 25

The phenomenal experience of touch

The act of touching reminds us that we are embodied; any kind of physical contact is body to body. And yet, when we touch another person, we do not touch their body, we touch their *being*. It is true that touch puts us in contact with another body, yet we do not touch another person as solely a concrete act or in the abstract. When we touch, we physically make contact with the being of another person *and vice versa*; indeed, bodies and beings are inseparable (Abram, 1996; Merleau-Ponty, 1962). These two levels of experience, our being and our body, are always one, there is no separateness between the experience and expression of being as well as its containment in one's body (see e.g., Merleau-Ponty, 1962; Foehl, 2009; and Folkmarson Kall, 2009). Even without actual touching, we present ourselves to others through our embodiment. In this way, *"The body is the very means of entering into a relation with all things"* (Abram, 1996, p. 47).

How easy it would be if we could know a person by tracing the outline of their body with our hand, to run our fingers along their face, arm or leg and in this way know a being, to experience a presence through the surface of a body. But how do you touch an absence, especially if you do not know where or what that absence is? The longing to touch and to be touched derives from the awareness of the presence of something else, usually outside reach.

Words cannot fully capture these inner contours. Words cannot touch the ineffable nor formulate where experience is unrepresented and un-represent*able*. These are parts of ourselves outside discourse yet they are precisely what needs to be known and seen. Perhaps a massage will find it – a kind of fumbling in the dark. Perhaps sex will cure the ache.

On a concrete level, we cannot avoid registering the feel of the other's skin, the scent of their body and the warmth (or coldness) of their touch. But the experience of touching someone is more than a feeling of pressure, it is an encounter with another person's being and her or his nature. It is, therefore, an intimate form of engagement, however brief, conventional or ritualized.

DOI: 10.4324/9781003264095-28

In all these ways, the phenomenal experience of touching confronts us with the *reciprocal nature of tactility*. It is not possible to touch without *being touched* and by virtue of this essential fact, discussing the prospect of touching in therapy brings up the mutual aspects of the therapeutic endeavor as a whole. In contradistinction to the simultaneous asymmetric aspects of the frame (e.g., the unequal distribution of attention paid, a defining feature of the analytic set-up as the sole focus on the patient), there are reciprocal dimensions of the analytic frame. Touching, if permitted in whatever form, falls into this category.

Like the relational structure of the therapeutic encounter itself, touch is reciprocal *and participatory*. It is an example of the transitivity of direct perception. To touch is also to feel oneself being touched, just as to see is also to feel oneself being seen (Abram, 1996, p. 69). In its mutuality, touch, thereby, carries with it a responsibility. Because it is participatory, there is a responsibility to clarify the boundaries and meaning. Yet, it is not always possible to know or verbalize what is conveyed in the act of touch. It is ambiguous and plastic, yet concrete and circumscribed at the same time.

Because touch is reciprocal and because we participate in it, there is the possibility of disclaiming one aspect or another of this complex interchange. We can focus on our own meanings or intentions while disclaiming or neglecting those of the other. Often, I have heard, "That hug was not erotic, I had no intention of crossing that line" or, "I am very clear on the boundaries... I hugged her in a platonic way." In these expressions, there is revealed a neglect of the other person's experience or intent, including how she or he might attribute a different meaning to the very same action. Because of the essential reciprocity in touch, the analyst or therapist must account for one's own *and the other's potential experience*. It is not enough to be clear (at least consciously) about one's own intent; there is, therefore, a simultaneous responsibility to refrain from engaging in actions that might be misconstrued. The paradox of touch means that it crosses the border between one person and the other. To touch is to give and receive sensation at once and we cannot deny one aspect of the process in order to rationalize or justify our own participation.

I have touched a few patients. Two were dying of a terminal illness and I visited them each several days before they passed away. One was lying in bed, his body leaden with morphine and unable to move. I stroked his face and told him what he had meant to me in a very personal revelation. The other had just been diagnosed with cancer and had been told he had only a few months to live. We hugged at the end of that session and indeed he died a few months later. Unlike Dr. Aaron Green (Janet Malcolm's, [1980] infamous and rigid protagonist/analyst) who failed to utter a word when his patient expressed her distress over her child's illness, I believe (as I'm sure we all do) it is inhumane to withhold a loving gesture of care in dire circumstances. Touch might be one such gesture.

I am certain these kinds of interactions have happened with us all. Still, the question might be asked, "Why would touching be permissible in this circumstance?" In these final moments of life, the boundaries of analysis or therapy have rightfully dissolved. With the awareness of death approaching, we face the existential bareness of our beings and engage with each other in more simple, human terms. Person to person, we want a moment of intimacy in an unfettered and unconstrained manner, to make contact with a person's being without deprivation in the poignancy of these very human experiences.

More problematically, however, are patients who want me to touch them at some point in the course of regular treatment. They want me to touch them (requesting a hug, a handshake or a kiss) as a symbol that I care for them in a personal way, beyond my professional role and beyond their being my patient. "I need something concrete to let me know you really care for me," they say in one way or another. Perhaps it is a cup of coffee outside the office; perhaps it is a hug at the end of the hour. In the same vein, there are patients who want to be told how I feel about them (especially, whether I love them or desire them sexually) and though I have little doubt in my own mind how I feel (usually in the positive direction), they want me to put these sentiments into words. The fantasy about the spoken word is that it will feel more concrete, will *touch* them in a more palpable and lasting way than their silent speculations might. But words have their own ambiguity and often do not last beyond their utterance.

I usually do not reciprocate a request for such signs of my caring, whether it be a hug, handshake or loving phrase but instead make it the very subject of a detailed analysis. First, I agree with them, i.e., "Yes, indeed you need a hug." (And hugs should abound for all of us in our external lives!) But with me, the question arises, Why do they need such an overt sign of my affection? Why is their ability to detect what I feel for them, in a personal, authentic way (not beyond my professional role but embedded within it) not sufficient? Our focus becomes their overreliance on the concrete level of experience, overt expressions that indeed include words, in an effort to obtain a presumably permanent reassurance that they are loved, desired or appreciated in a lasting way.

At such times, I remind my patients that any concrete sign or gesture will fall flat in the absence of an internal, emotional resonance with what they *already experience* within our relationship. I remind them that words are at once ephemeral and ambiguous too, that persons can lie with words in a way they cannot with feelings. I encourage my patients to explore what they already know *based on what they feel* is between us so that words become less necessary, even thin compared to the depth of attachment between us. It is as if the treatment is designed to hone their radar or antennae, directed at their own feelingful experience of the relationship, including and especially, what they *sense* I feel about them.

Earlier in my career, I put how I felt about a patient into words and I regret it. This was a male patient referred to me during my internship year. He spent the first year or two letting me know directly and vociferously that he had no use for me, that I was not helping him and that he was intellectually (and in all other ways) superior to me. I hung in there through this grueling year and did not let on that I actually (silently) agreed with him. He made me feel incompetent, unhelpful and painfully inexperienced as well as doubtful that I had any natural talent for this line of work. At the same time, he never missed a session. And he got better, progressing in his career, social relations and becoming more personally appealing. He had a sharp sense of humor and endeared himself to me despite his constant devaluing. He also paid me an unreasonably low fee and I colluded with this arrangement beyond his financial need for fear of unleashing a torrent of abuse about how I did not deserve a penny higher.

After a few years, I mustered the confidence to broach the subject of raising his fee. Through a discussion with a well-meaning supervisor, we speculated that there was a strong, mutual attachment (I think I unconsciously refrained from writing attraction) despite all this angry tension on the surface. With the supervisor's prompting, I said to my patient, "Because of the love that there is there between us (or some such awkward phrasing), I've neglected to raise your fee and I think we should talk about it." Well, the fee became a side issue very quickly, because all he heard was that four-letter word. He came to his next session dressed in a suit and high with expectations that we would begin dating. It was painful for both of us to come to terms with that.

It is probably not a coincidence that the patient for whom I had felt the most intense desire to touch, to stroke his arm in a comforting and reassuring gesture that I hoped would convey, "You'll be all right," was a therapist whose license had been suspended for becoming sexually involved with a patient. Surprisingly, for me at the time, he was a most compassionate man who was relentlessly self-critical over what he had done, especially the extent to which he had harmed his patient, a woman with whom he had thought he was in love. He cried for six months in the treatment, believing he had irreparably damaged her. He believed he deserved to be punished in every way and more. But the intriguing aspect of this phase of treatment, from my point of view, was the intensity with which I felt a desire to *touch* him, to reassure him that he was all right, that he would survive and that he was good. I did not touch him but used this urge to understand the almost bottomless longing he felt to be loved, manifested in my countertransference through the wish to provide him with a concrete gesture of my caring. Upon reflection, I surmised that my desire to touch him arose from a projective identification, where he disclaimed his intense neediness and its conversion to a concrete sign, as he had done with his patient. I apparently introjected this tendency through my empathic relation to him.

Psychoanalysis is the science of hermeneutics – the examination and explication of meanings. Touch is nonverbal; it is a mute action. At best, touch fails to reveal meaning and at worst, obfuscates. We make contact without explicating what we intend to convey. In this sense, it is anti-analytic by itself. Perhaps we touch when we want to avoid saying something disappointing, to bypass a feeling or another particular meaning. A hug can be coercive as well as seductive, circumventing the opportunity to make meanings explicit, especially with the arousal of tension or negative affect.[1]

Note

1 For discussions of touching and other forms of physical contact in order to circumvent negative transference, see Celenza (2007).

Chapter 26

Embodied countertransference[1]

A focus on mind-body integration is often associated with the most primitive patients, those with difficulty speaking of their inner lives and affectively-based experience as grounded in their body. Deadness, a sense of falling and areas of paralysis are typical of such faulty integration and these states are usually unrepresented and unsymbolized. Somatic eruptions in body-based symptomatology may be the only indication of their indwelling. These can often involve sexual dysfunctions. Even when patients are otherwise high-functioning, there is a psychotic part of the personality where the body is implicated in containing unspeakable secrets. A focus on mind-body integration, including the analyst's embodied countertransference, presents an avenue of access for these primitive parts, where such an approach is not solely reserved for very primitive patients.

Corporeality is the first condition of life, where the mind begins to form by linking up early sensations and perceptions with felt bodily experience. These perceptions are based on concrete, somatic sensations, unrelated to the world and introjective processes (Lombardi, 2016). Ferrari (2004) and Lombardi (2002) refer to this body-based experience as the Concrete Original Object (COO). This coincides with Merleau-Ponty's (1962) reflection that we are always embodied, we do not experience the world or our lives within it except through our bodies. Lombardi (2002) distinguishes the baby's transference to the body as the first psychic experience, creating the mind in the vertical dimension, preceding the background horizontal experiencing of the other.

The aspects of the mind that are intersubjective (the horizontal dimension) occur later and can cause splits as the individual struggles with psychic traumas that threaten to overwhelm with the arousal of primitive anxieties. Psychic numbing and other forms of depersonalization can be encapsulated in areas of bodily functioning resultant from later intersubjective and object-relational dynamics which can displace or disorganize the baby's relation to its own body. Sexuality is often implicated since the arousal of sexual desire can threaten to overwhelm the sense of safely dwelling within one's body.

As analysts, we are the objects that will not be had, upholding the incest

DOI: 10.4324/9781003264095-29

taboo and thereby cultivating a setting where early forms of desire can safely emerge. We must have the full range of affectivity at our disposal, but we must also help our patients reckon with, interpret and be unafraid, in Lombardi's (2016) phrasing, to experience the excitements and mysteries within themselves (the vertical dimension) and in relation to the unknown other (the horizontal dimension). The body can be a sanctuary or a grave for signification (Lombardi, 2008).

Thomas was in analysis with me for four and a half years. His childhood was rife with trauma, his mother being a rageful alcoholic and Thomas, an only child. He remembers curling up in a fetal position in his bed, shaking with anxiety when his parents would fight. They divorced when he was only 6 years old, leaving Thomas alone with his mother. She continued drinking as he grew up. There were sadistic scenes, one including a breakfast incident when his mother forced him to eat oatmeal. He was a nervous child, never hungry in the morning, but under her forceful hand, he gulped it down. He then vomited the oatmeal and she made him eat that too. This happened twice.

Thomas' mother's body was a site of alienation and danger (Lemma, 2015) where, as Benjamin states, "The inability to represent that first relation and the separation from it makes of a woman a dangerous hole into which the individual may disappear" (1995, p. 85). During his analysis, dramatic maternal images developed in Thomas' dreams and reveries, alternating between a sucking, bottomless pit, needy woman/vagina to a sadistic, biting, castrating vagina. Thomas described a dream where a *cock*er spaniel was limping, bleeding, after having been attacked – perhaps by another animal. When I asked him for his thoughts about the dream, he said the puppy was bleeding and he felt so sad for it. He then added (literally), "I think I got hurt." My throat constricted at hearing Thomas' cognitive slip – a bodily response I had often when hearing of Thomas' traumatic stories. I responded tenderly toward him, saying "The little puppy, so vulnerable ..." and I wondered if he would feel afraid I might hurt him. Thomas often wondered how long the analysis would take, worrying about money and the time away from his family. I wondered if he unconsciously experienced me as capable of sucking him into a long, protracted analysis from which he couldn't escape.

Thomas complained of lifelong premature ejaculation. I linked this bodily symptom with Thomas' need to *"pull out of a woman"* or ways in which he *"didn't want to be inside."* In my view, this was Thomas' experience of his embodied mother and shaped the unconscious fears he had of women, their bodies, their insides and his own body. I told him he had a hatred of a needy body and a fear of a dangerous body within him and in me as well.

Safety concerns were paramount in the early stages of the analysis. Thomas expressed his need to feel securely held in my office and as he was able to feel safe *"in my hands"* (his idiom), I developed an intense but pleasing feeling of enveloping him, cradling him as he lay on the couch, a feeling of securely holding him in my office. This reverie first came to me when he spoke of curling up in his bed as a little boy, shaking. I could feel his shaking and pictured myself calming him, shaking becoming a rhythmic rocking and then, with our bodies together, a kind of warm calm. There is a side by side kind of holding between lovers where each faces in the same direction. We call this *spooning* and this loving action is holding, perhaps representing a mutual containment, and it is also erotic.

This reverie came to me often while I was treating Thomas. I would imagine lying on the couch, my body cradling his, rocking side by side (but facing away) and my hands stroking his back and side. The scenario includes me whispering into his ear, but I don't hear words – instead, there is a feeling, *as if* I am saying to him, "It's all right, you will be all right." In one session, as Thomas spoke of lying in the fetal position on his bed and I had this now-familiar spooning reverie, I told Thomas that I thought he was hugging himself at a time when no one was there to hold him. For me, this reverie often included me as a little boy, holding him and stroking the back of his neck. (I have wondered if Thomas evoked the little boy in me, mirroring him. I also remembered my brother as a little boy when I would lovingly stroke the indentation in the back of his neck.)

The analyst's reverie is an extension of the analytic field, the erotic analytic field and this includes the spiral work of *après coup* on the analyst's part as well. What was once degraded as contaminated, emotional (and thereby irrational and feminine) is now a focus of intense interest as analysts understand countertransference experience as an important contributor to the intersubjective analytic process. We must not be afraid to let our bodies experience the analytic process, to be present to our patients in our totality, including allowing sexual desire to be present in our countertransference. As Coen (2019) says, the more we can acknowledge what we feel at work with our patients, the better we do. But this does not necessarily refer to explicit statements about what we are feeling, it is an acknowledgment to ourselves of what is in the erotic field. Searles (1959), Loewald (1970), Schaverien (1995), Scarfone (2008), Bolognini (2011a), Coen (2019), Reis (2020) and myself (Celenza, 2010b, 2014) among others have all noted the beneficial effects to the treatment when the analyst can admit their loving feelings into the field of play.

In writing this essay, I realized that I was treating Thomas at a time in my life when I was learning to play soccer. As a forward, I would have periods where I considered myself in a slump – I couldn't finish properly, I shot too soon, my aim was off and I would miss the goal. The more I focused on it, the more inhibited I became. Had I contracted Thomas' illness during these times? I now remember my playing differently (both soccer and the play in the erotic field with Thomas) with this possibility in mind.

Responsivity in the countertransference can be an important source of transformation in relation to the analysand's sexuality. The framing structure as the imprint of the mother's arms (Green, 2008) defines the erotic field and the analyst's willingness to flex within this structure is a concretized representation of the responsivity within the analyst's containment.

Thomas requested to sit up, sensing that he would not be able to release "a knot in my chest" lying down. He could not say more than this, except that he did not want to face me – he preferred the freedom of looking away as when lying on the couch. I suggested he sit in a chair in front of mine but facing away. We rearranged the furniture in the room such that he and I were sitting in a column, both facing the same direction. We talked this way for the next several months.

Looking back on this phase of the treatment, the termination phase, I think my accommodation of the framing structure (Green, 2008) helped Thomas access and perhaps constitute for the first time the affects that spiraled through that knot in his upper chest. Perhaps he was afraid he might choke on whatever came up, thus needing to sit up. I too anticipated another "choking up," perhaps a tearful response to something he might say.

As I have noted, I had images of lying on the couch with Thomas throughout his analysis, a holding, maternal erotic countertransference that used my whole body rather than only my arms. As I sat behind him, he and I in the same postural position, I noticed the back of his neck and thought we were enacting the spooning fantasy by virtue of our bodies being aligned symmetrically, yet facing away.

It was during this time that Thomas began to talk and intensely long for his father, an absent figure whose silence was loud. He wondered had his father been present, would he have prevented his mother from making him eat his own vomit. Thomas' fury about this in particular seemed to loosen the knot in his chest. It was also during this time that Thomas' premature ejaculation resolved.

Note

1 A longer version of this paper was originally presented at *The International Psychoanalytic Association*, London, England, July, 2019 on a panel with Stan Coen, Alessandra Lemma and Ricardo Lombardi.

Chapter 27

What, where is home?[1]

I received a card in the mail one day. It came in the usual rectangular white envelope and the return address indicated that a good friend had been thinking of me. A portrait of the Madonna and child was painted on the front of the card and on the inside, the card read, "Home is in your mother's eyes." Really, I thought. Despite that I have never held Hallmark as my erstwhile mentor, I found myself wondering, Is that what home is? A gaze? And in particular, the feeling, the warmth and security of the maternal gaze? Is this what happens the moment I open the door to my waiting room and say, "Come in"?

I am reminded of the first line of T.S. Eliot's (1943) poem *East Coker* invoked by Winnicott for his 1986 book: "*Home Is Where One Starts From*." This reminds me of an interaction that occurred recently at a conference, an experience that I know happens to all of us frequently. I was giving a paper and at the end of the Q&A, one of the members of the audience came up to me and asked, "So where in New York are you from?" I chuckled. "What did I say that gave it away?" I asked. She said, "You said 'tawk'" (To this day, I cannot pronounce that word without the familiar New York-ese.) I told her I was from the North Shore of Long Island, a town called Brookville. She responded, "Oh, I know someone from the North Shore! Do you know....?" That eternal search for connection and familiarity – a way to make any part of the world contain some remnant of home.

As Sarah Mares (2010) noted, "We first exist in imagination, then have a home in our mother's bodies and, if we are lucky, we are then able to move to finding a home within our parents' minds and eventually within ourselves as well as in the world" (p. 221). This is a more elaborated understanding of that maternal gaze. Home is intersubjective – it is the relationship and the eternal search for that relationship, a feeling of mutually gazing and being gazed upon, held in mind, recognized and seen. In effect, a state of minds.

In this essay, I consider the many ways in which home, intrapsychically and intersubjectively, has been psychoanalytically conceived. All of the facets I will discuss have been written from different, usually developmental perspectives (e.g., Fonagy, 2008), but rarely have psychoanalytic writings

DOI: 10.4324/9781003264095-30

collected these elements into an integrated whole and denoted the matrix as *home*. I don't know why the literature has neglected this topic given that our homes and especially our childhood homes are the stuff of what we examine and deconstruct. Perhaps the concept has too colloquial a ring... like a Hallmark card. We like our conceptions more sophisticated. And yet, as Lorrie Moore (1998) intimates, "There was nothing as complex in the world—No flower or stone—as a single hello from a human being" (1998, p. 36).

In my analysis of the meaning of home, I hope to demonstrate how complex, deep and elusive the experience of home is, despite our universal and lifelong search to re-find it. In this effort, I will be discussing the following facets of home and in particular, a good enough home: *holding, reflecting, containment, cross-spatiality, metabolization, familiarity and cross-temporality*. Each of these facets is reciprocal, though not necessarily symmetric, much like the analytic frame – that paradoxical dialectic of mutuality and asymmetry (Aron, 1996). In these ways, I aim to illustrate how a good enough home can be conceived as the heart of intersubjectivity.

Home is the place where one is *held in mind*; relationships where *others symbolize you*. In a good enough home, this place of holding is a relationship that mirrors and reflects back a sense of worth and agency. Home is a vehicle for the externalization of parts of our self-representation that are continuous with self-states held in positive regard. It is also a relationship where we can mentalize others, that is, have a conception of others' intentions in a continuous way. The holding function includes a signification of meaning embedded in a network of others with shared meanings. Our ability to signify others' intentions makes home predictable and relatively safe.

A few sessions ago, a patient of mine elaborated this concept of holding, (we can have no question about the social constructivist nature of experience – she, talking about home just when I was writing a paper about the topic). She said, "I would rather be here all day. It's our relationship. Something about my experience, talking about my feelings and thoughts. It makes myself *be. It is.* Powerful words, two little words. *I am.* It makes me real." To me, this patient is describing the holding function. The way I reflect her experience and help her sustain it, a function she has particular difficulty with, given a constant barrage of unconscious, punitive and annihilating self-criticism.

When others hold us in mind, they also *reflect back* to us their internalized conception of our mental states. Early in life, caregivers provide this self-reflecting function before we have developed the capacity to do so. But this does not mean we lack an internal conception of them, again reflecting that home is a reciprocal, intersubjective self-state. These reflections evolve into expectations of familiar patternings so that we may build up a sense of the world as stable, predictable and meaningful. In this way, we experience ourselves and others as continuous, agentic (authored), intentional and purposeful. Home is where our internal self-states are recognized and reflected back to us (our subjectivity) and where we, in turn, recognize others who are recognizing us (the mutuality of intersubjectivity). Note the crossing of boundaries in this engagement; relationships where the demarcations around self and other may be blurred, depending on each person's capacity for the articulation, elaboration and ownership of self-states. In other words, one's dreams may be held in mind as one's own, held by the other as dreams *for you* in contrast to a more appropriating engagement where one's own dreams become the other's. Dreams can coincide without a blurring of boundaries as well.

Containment occurs when others develop a symbolic representation of our internal experience and this is subjectivized. Paraphrasing Jessica Benjamin (1998), it is the caregiver who not only knows, but who knows *me*, my wishes, my internal states, my subjectivity and holds these in mind in an affective way. Again, this containment is mutual but not necessarily symmetric; we are in this together differently. Affective containment occurs in relational configurations that maintain contact with multiple (especially vulnerable) self-states and facilitate an integrated, coherent sense of self. In a good enough home, this containment has a positive valence and does some important psychic work, that of metabolizing toxic or dysphoric states rendering them benign and tolerable.

Thus far, many facets of home have emerged: holding, reflecting and containment, all of which foster feelings of stability, predictability, continuity and, in good enough homes, all manner of positive regard. Here I want to take a step back and consider what is not home.

Home is not a location or place in the sense of geography but a relationship, maternal or maternal-like, it *crosses spatial bounds*. Still, the question of finding home can often be played out geographically (Harlem, 2010). Space and place are ready containers for dissociated wishes; *here* versus *there* where each location secures a pole of a dialectic.

Disparate countries, cities or towns often choreograph one's desires and fears in a more orderly fashion than the chaotic and conflicted morass of unconscious desire. Geography is a useful and malleable container for unacceptable wishes; serving as a ready receptacle, countries, cities and concrete places can draw out or prompt projections that represent dissociated sides of ambivalence.

This is a familiar need in us all. I remember being obsessed with New York after I left it, my home which I hated when I lived there. Now it became a place where everything exciting was happening. One day, I overheard a young man talking about Los Angeles as the only place worth living in and as the center of the universe (he felt). I thought, "Doesn't he know it's New York?" Somewhere else is the best place (yet I don't go there) in contrast to here (the worst place), where I am and will stay. I do not mean to emphasize only the defensive uses of home. In a more positive sense, houses, the concrete bricks and mortar of a house, become imbued with the sense of rootedness and community, that deeply felt and embodied experience of belonging *there*, turning a house into a home.

The question is not, should one go or should one stay but what does going there or staying here mean and what is it that continues to situate psychic home in one place versus another. Adrienne Harris (2009) in a beautifully written and trenchant paper on impasse, change, *nachtraglichkeit* (after-wardsness, or "the backward action of the present upon the past") and mourning (to name a few topics covered), refers to home as "a location nostalgically misremembered and fiercely reacted against" (p. 2). *There* is the best place (yet I don't go there) in contrast to *here* (the worst place), where I am and will stay.

I am reminded of a joke involving a clinical interview between a psy-chiatrist and a patient on an inpatient unit who had recently transferred from another esteemed hospital. The psychiatrist asked, "So how did you find your stay at MGH, how was the ward?" The patient replied, "Oh, MGH was the best hospital I've ever been in, the ward was great, can't complain." The psychiatrist then asked, "And how was the food?" "Oh, the food – best hospital food I've ever had. Delicious. Can't complain" he re-plied. "Oh, and how was the therapy there?" The patient responded, "The therapy was excellent, I made a lot of progress, my therapist was great, can't complain." The psychiatrist, somewhat puzzled, asked the patient, "So if things were so great at MGH, why did you transfer here?" The patient re-plied, "Because here I can complain!"

It is through containment that a home becomes a good-enough, bene-volent and protective home. But that is one step of a larger process. Home is only that place of comfort and return if it contains significant people, who for the child have a protective function (Mares, 2010). There develops a series of expectations that one will reliably find equilibration at home. In other words, home is where persons facilitate the *metabolization* of the toxic world, interpret forms of arousal and disregulation from which we seek refuge. Home is a place of affect regulation, where the presence of others reflects one's internal state and re-presents it as a manageable image, something that is bearable, acceptable and can be understood. The ability to find meaning in others' actions underlies affect regulation, impulse control, self-monitoring and agency. In other words, a good enough home *helps*.

I am reminded of another story involving an interaction between a revered mentor, Murray Cohen and myself, some years ago. I had called him to ask if he would be the discussant at a case conference. Then I remembered a question about my dissertation, since he was my First Reader. I told him I actually had two reasons for the call and then I remembered another, so I added, "Actually, I have a million reasons to talk to you right now." Suddenly, I became embarrassed, realizing he would see my hysteria. I added, "Oh my god, I'm not that hysterical." Murray responded, "Andrea, just accept it. Hysterics make good therapists." This moment of home reflected the offering of something I vitally needed.

The family or *familiar* aspect of home links to its predictability, reliability and stability. In this way, home has the quality of transcending immediate experience. It exists whether we materially inhabit it or not. I've often thought that marriages are decisions made with partners who feel like family, for good or ill.

A good enough home is one we can leave and find our way back. It includes the ability to depend on a safe place within which we can take risks. Being home and being able to be at home within ourselves and in the world might be about retaining or rediscovering the capacity to play and, in Winnicott's terms, "the capacity for creative living. We are fortunate if we have a home where we are free enough to take some risks" (cited in Mares, 2010, p. 229). In this way, home can contain some amount of disregulation so that it may become a place of growth. In good enough homes, there is an optimal level of disregulation, creative destruction and distinction within the familiar. Here, Adrienne's work is again relevant (Harris, 2009), where she describes the analytic process through chaos theory, a model that can be applied to the experience of home. She describes, "a theory of coevolution of entraining subjectivities...a model for intersubjective engagement of subtle distinctions and overlaps that produce dramatic change and disequilibration" (p. 14). Moments of impasse can occur at home as well as in treatment; those "strange attractors that have the potential to give way to moments of motility and unpredictability" resulting in either closing things down or opening things up (p. 14). We might say that the security of home is in dialectical relation to the capacity for creative destruction and growth, one implying and potentiating the other.

A good enough home transcends both place and time; it has a *cross-temporal* as well as a cross-spatial dimension. By virtue of significant persons having access to one's representational world, a good enough home is one where others have known us through the past, mirror our present and hold as well as project our future. The self is represented not as a static entity, but as an intentional being based on thoughts, beliefs and desires for the future, our psychic future, so to speak (Leowald, 1960).

I realize I am speaking of time in a linear way and we do not experience time thus; rather there is a recursive quality to temporality where the past interpenetrates, structures and thereby shapes the present, a process we know well as transference. The vision of the future is a process that points both forward and reflects back; the present, structured and given meaning by the past constructs and reconstructs both the past and our psychic future in ongoing, retrogressive and progressive ways. This cyclical process in which our present and our conception of the future rewrite the past (and is rewritten by it), is the phenomenon of *nachtraglichkeit,* afterwardsness. We need a term for the ways the past-infused-present structures the future, perhaps *tagtraglichkeit* or beforehandedness, like a premonition refracted through the lens of the past/present.

To some extent, significant others in our mental homes share or recognize these meanings, backward and forward, and have their own version of it. This is the depth in which we experience living and are held in mind. In a good enough home, others hold in mind our psychic future as it is currently conceived and shaped by our desires, always refracted from within the past and present. These significant others also help to *promote* our psychic future. When all goes well, we are born into such a home and then the capacity to feel at home in the world is more easily achieved because "in the world" really means "in our internal world," well populated by these significant others.

I believe all of the qualities of engagement I have described as aspects of home, existing in an optimal way and with a positive valence, are deconstructed ways of describing love. The willingness of one to *take in and hold* another is a generous intimacy and we have an infinite capacity for this. I think empathic resonances and disjunctions (the ongoing trials of negotiating sameness and difference) promote this process and it is what we do as psychoanalysts and psychoanalytic therapists. In short, we make a home for our patients and invite them in.

Note

1 A longer version of this paper was originally presented at Division 39 Spring Meeting, American Psychological Association, Boston, MA, April, 2013, on a panel with Andy Harlem and Adrienne Harris.

Part III

Being

Chapter 28

The unbearable multiplicity of experience

We are beings for whom *being* is an issue. Time was, *being* was parsed ... to understand, to control, to reduce a sense of dread and threat. This is a time of synthesis – no longer *either/or* yet at the same time, beyond *both/and.* A time to capture the universe of affectivity holistically and to conceive of the psychological realm as integral to the physical. A time to mend the Cartesian mind/body duality that structures our thinking. A time to resist the force of various category errors and their sediment of false dichotomies. We do not mistake parts for wholes, pieces for moments, mechanisms for phenomenal experience.

Not so long ago, and most egregiously, we might have reduced phenomenal subjective experience to mechanistic explanatory systems, thereby erasing the particular for the universal, subject for object, I for me ... or worse, *it.* We might have studied the body in a way that considers a body without reference to *whose body that is.* This is a body without subjectivity, without meaning for the individual who enlivens it. Yet we know that when we touch another person, we do not touch their body, we touch their being[1] – partly manifested by the other and partly constructed by ourselves in our apprehension. Neither wholly given nor wholly made, yet both given and made.

Just as transference captures the phenomenology of temporal reality (the telescoping, synchronic experience of past, present and future temporality), so do we embody multiple relations with our patients that have both temporal and spatial dimensions. There is a multiplicity in our relation to our patients and many of these modes of relating contradict each other despite the synchronicity of their emergence (see Celenza [2010a, 2014] for clinical depictions of this multiplicity). For example, we are, at once, a *person* to our patients (reflecting a level of ordinary reality), simultaneously a *woman* (or man), an *analyst* (with attendant expectations of role) and (perhaps) a *parental figure* (depending on the patient's conscious or unconscious experience). These identities and associated modes of relating are undergirded by transferences that may or may not conflict with each other. In addition, they correspond to different levels of reality (Modell, 1990) that represent

DOI: 10.4324/9781003264095-32

multiple lenses through which we can sort out the complex layering of relational engagement at any one time.

Probably most relevant to the patient's experience in analysis are the levels of reality that harken back to early memories, especially painful or traumatic experiences. These are embodied or disembodied states of being, sometimes contradictory, yet paradoxically, simultaneously emergent in the present. The recontextualization of those modes of relating that harken back to self-destructive memory patterning is the primary work of analysis. The analyst must do so without oversimplifying the complex, multiple nature of being.

One fault-line is the emphasis of one particular relational modality (intersubjective and interactive) to the exclusion of others, as if this mode of relating is discontinuous with other self-experiences. For example, to speak to the baby while discounting, ignoring or otherwise neglecting the adult can be regressive and humiliating. A disturbing example is depicted in the book based on the Bean-Bayog case[2] (McNamara, 1994). While I cannot vouch for the accuracy of this rendition of Bean-Bayog's tragic story, the author astutely depicts a plausible unconscious dynamic revolving around Bean-Bayog's ongoing desire for a child. In this speculative rendition of the underlying dynamics of the case, Bean-Bayog treated her patient like the child she wanted, fostering a highly regressive relationship with him that failed to support or foster his more mature capacities. In this way, the analyst was foregrounding her parental role to the child-part of the patient while discounting his other, more adaptive self-experiences to disastrous effect. (The patient ultimately committed suicide.)

The asymmetry definitional of the analytic setting is a crafted imbalance of ordinary, personal and professional modes of relating. The analyst is responsible to reassert the boundaries around the professional modality and to foreground this mode while holding in abeyance personal, ordinary and otherwise desiring modes of relating. In effect, the analyst continually promises, through her or his behavior and ways of embodying her or his professional role, i.e., to be more *analyst* than *woman* or *man*. We promise to forego cultivating, expressing and acting on what we might personally desire in order to maintain the asymmetric focus and thereby remain in our analytic role. But having continually made this promise, the patient and her or his desires and needs emerge in more undefended form than they otherwise might. Archaic patterns, desires, thoughts and memories are given freer expression *due to the promise that there will be no contingencies.* Herein lays the nature of the seduction – an invitation to one-wayness with special accommodations and safeguards tempts the analysand toward more openness, authenticity, baldness and vulnerability.[3]

Given that the analyst embodies multiple self-states in relation to the patient, the associated multiplicity of roles can collapse under the pressure of undue desire or need. The perplexity we often feel when a previously competent, even revered psychoanalyst comes to describe his role in relation to his patient in an oversimplified, justifying manner is shocking both in its distortion of the process, but especially for its *unidimensionality*.

Not only has the analyst truncated a most complex process, but he has also reneged on his superego mandate to hold his personhood, his desiring self, in abeyance. What happened to the integrity of his superego? In these circumstances, I find it helpful to consider, instead of the *superego* of the analyst, the *superegos* (plural) of the analyst. This dovetails with contemporary theorizing on the multiplicity of self-states and also takes into account normal vertical splitting. Just as we are capable of multiple self-states and modes of engagement, some may be recruited for defensive purposes and become foregrounded, substituting for the analytic role.

As I have described elsewhere (Celenza, 2007), my own clinical finding of transgressors includes a vertical split in superego structures. The analyst can, however, under the sway of undue desire or need, engage a more extreme dissociative function in order to relegate perverse behavior to a *not me* self-representation. Within this *not me* self-representation is a *not-me* superego structure that allows gratification in otherwise forbidden contexts. Then, this *not me* self-state can be denied and disclaimed. In this way, I aim to propose a model based on the multiplicity of self-states, each of which contains a superego structure with its own particular set of moral mandates. This superego structure may differ from those of other self-states.

Concordant with this conceptualization is a developmental view of our capacities to uphold ethical standards of conduct. For the classical analyst, the attachment to and identification with ideals of neutrality, anonymity and abstinence can wane over time as aging, mortality and perhaps depleted self-experience become emerging realities. For the relational analyst, the capacity to self-defer, to maintain asymmetry and to put one's own needs in the background can also weaken, as mutual resonances seduce depleted self-states and become foregrounded. Coinciding with such weakening in ego capacities (in either framework) is a transformation in superego mandates, both of which are concordant with an altered, unusual, atypical or long-denied *not me* self-state.

The promise to maintain a frame of non-contingency, absence of obligation and continuous attentional focus on the patient are promises we may not be always able to keep. The uiversal vulnerability to sexual boundary transgressions is easily denied in our current self-state; it is difficult to imagine sometime in the future when mortality looms and we are less capable of tolerating the frustrations inherent in our role.[4] The analysand assumes the promise of asymmetry as inherent in the structure of the setting yet it is a promise that must be continuously asserted by the analyst in her or his professional role as a personal choice. The promises, imbalances, even idealizations and authorities with which we are endowed are structural, i.e., aspects of the setting that we choose to enact and not "charms of [our] person" (Freud, 1915a, p. 160–161).

In these ways, it is not our professional selves only that conveys therapeutic power but the setting itself and the ways in which our patients hold expectations of our professional role. It is our responsibility to maintain our professional commitments and enact (i.e., choose to restrict ourselves) these commitments in an ongoing way. Yet, we are capable of self-deception, especially in relation to our narcissistic investment in ourselves as analysts, the ability to heal others and be admired, appreciated and even idealized by virtue of this capacity. As we get older, seasoned and well-trod, the lure of exceptionalism increases as well. We think we know more because we have experienced more, have more successes under our belt. Yet we also have the approaching terror of death, that encroaching temporal shortening such that exceptionalism can serve as a defensive denial of mortality. This can coincide with a weakening of resolve. Psychoanalysis is a discipline revolving around self-deference, humility and continual focus on our patient's needs (at the expense of our own). While the mutuality inherent in the analytic dyad is inescapable (and requires no effort on our part), the asymmetry is a disciplined commitment to boundary management that must be continually reasserted and renegotiated at every shift in perspective and moment of interaction.

Notes

1 See Essay 25, *The phenomenal experience of touch*, (this volume).
2 This was a case in Boston in the late 1980s where a 28-year-old male patient of a psychiatrist/psychoanalyst Margaret Bean-Bayog was being treated for depression. He ultimately committed suicide, nine months after Bean-Bayog terminated an intense and unorthodox therapy. A series of letters, explicit sexual fantasies, flash cards and notes, all written in Bean-Bayog's hand, were discovered in the patient's apartment. It appeared as though this brilliant young man had been reduced to a state of infantile dependency through Bean-Bayog's attempt to be a symbolic *mom*.
3 See Essay 24, *The promise that seduces desire* (this volume).
4 I have been increasingly impressed, on a clinical level, with the high prevalence of sexual boundary transgressions in senior, highly respected psychoanalysts. To my knowledge, no empirical data or prevalence study has examined age as a differentiating factor beyond the profile of a mid-life career vulnerability (see Schoener et al., 1989; Gabbard and Lester, 1995; Celenza, 2007; and Gabbard, 2016).

Chapter 29

On empathic resonance[1]

Our work requires an exquisite openness to the elements in the field – a willingness to take seriously mysterious processes, unthought knowns (Bollas, 1987), pre-symbolic, unformulated experience (Stern, 1997, 2015) and the varieties of unconscious conveyances we sense and yet, may overlook or dismiss. These are uncanny experiences about which we do not already have a conceptual handle. They may require a willingness to be *thrown about*, to be *at sea* with our patients.

Our psychoanalytic epistemology is one of immersion and embodiment, where there is no separation between ourselves and the function we serve. We know our patient's unconscious not through observation, manipulation or conscious reflection but by dwelling within it, in the words of Merleau-Ponty, "[B]ecause they awaken an echo in our bodies and because the body welcomes them" (1961, p. 355). Likewise, as Winnicott (1958) noted, we experience and live together with the analysand. Or perhaps we can refer to Yeats (1928) and actualize a dance without distinguishing the dancer from the dance.

We are all entraining resonators, this is what we do and each unique forum will reflect new evoked potentials; received, translated, manifested and conveyed invisible signals elegantly crafted by our own capacities for empathic resonance. In our receptivity, we extend the reach of, in Bolognini's (2011b) words, a space of "assisted elaborative containment."

My son, Ethan, recently wrote an essay entitled, *The Bull's Eye is All Around Us: "Do or Do Not. There is no Try" (Yoda)*. In this essay, my son writes on archery,

> One must work *with* the situation, not *at* the situation. For as much as I pull the bow, the bow also pulls on me, and to say that my pulling has a more important purpose is to ignore the smooth, elegant process as a whole.

Then later, on acting, he writes,

DOI: 10.4324/9781003264095-33

To think that one actor is the one pulling the string of the scene, we forget that the scene itself really contains the entire bow, person, environment and target ... We would say that the child is playing with things, were it not equally true that the things were playing with the child ... [I]t is all one process equally important and vivid at every angle. (Embry, 2016)

Our experience is a seamlessness of the person/analyst/role/being and the way in which we embody these self-states in a unified way. This encapsulates an existential given – that we are always embodied and expressive of our personhood even when we make choices about doing this versus that. We are always immersed in a context, our bodies exist somewhere in the world in a field. These are inescapable givens that behoove us to understand well, especially in moments when we might be tempted to segment ourselves or our treatments, parsing the role from the being, feelings from insights or desires from the responsibilities of the profession.

We entrain our receptivity to the analysand's unconscious voice, the way in which the analysand, who cannot speak directly, will communicate through the analyst's subjectivity and countertransference. This is unconscious communication, the mechanisms of which are comprised of introjective and projective identifications. These conveyances call upon the analyst's transformative function as an aspect of metabolizing the analysand's unspoken selves. This is the experience, recognition and understanding of the analysand's voice emergent from within ourselves. Perhaps there is an experience of merger, perhaps we should think about this as *an instinctive resonant capacity* as in the writings of Merleau-Ponty (1961), an unconscious dance whose rhythm we unconsciously sense and feel.

This puts me in mind of a poem – an allegory by Jalaluddin Rumi (Arberry, 1947), the 13th-century Sufi mystic. Rumi spoke of a father who posed a question to his sons, "What if a man cannot be made to say anything? How do you learn his hidden nature?" One son replied:

> I sit in front of him in silence,
> And set up a ladder made of patience,
> And if in his presence a language from beyond joy
> And beyond grief begins to pour from my chest,
> I know that his soul is as deep and bright
> As the star Canopus rising over Yemen.
> And so *when I start speaking a powerful right arm*
> *Of words sweeping down*, I know him *from what I say*,
> And *how I say it*, because there's a window open
> Between us, mixing the night air of our beings.
> [Rumi, ca. 1265, *italics added*]

Our model is also social-constructive, involving the enactment of a co-constructed actualization of the patient's projective identifications as filtered through our inner capacities for resonance. These then anticipate and pre-figure a receptive space for the casting of our patient's transference projections. It is a play space, the co-constructed dreamscape to help our patient continue dreaming. In none of these symbolizations (playing, dreaming or dancing) is there a role for objective reality except insofar as it is filtered and transformed through our inner resonant capacities. This is a pre-symbolic but fertile transitional space where characters emerge or are evoked, cued, enact, convey, recruit and unconsciously prompt again. All involved are changed, deformed and transformed through this mutually influential process.

I notice a feature I have added that evokes a new element. I am saying "*inner* resonant capacities" rather than simply resonant capacities. That is because we are resonators with subjectivity, *subjective resonators*, so to speak. We cannot regard any particular narration as a factual account, but one filtered and co-constructed through personal experience, an awareness of our reveries and our way of embodying and actualizing our patient's transferences. In partnering for the dance, we do the steps within our re-pertoire, a repertoire that is at once limited to and exquisitely sensitized by our own subjectivity (as it is mutually, synchronously entrained). And we may learn new steps through our receptivity to our partners, mirroring, synchronization and unconscious identificatory mechanisms that transform our subjectivity.

Here, I do not mean to refer only to countertransference, but to our *personhood*, our unavoidably present *being*. We each embody our analytic self in unique idiomatic ways. To paraphrase Merleau-Ponty (1961), an *object* resonator is not the same as a *person* resonator, a subject with a point of view that gives the experience a particular meaning. We are more than mirrors that speak (Resnick, 2006, cited in Bonaminio, 2015), we are *receptive mirror-beings* that transform and are transformed by what we ima-gine and actualize according to unconscious meanings, as in Ogden's analytic third (1999).

Ours is a stance of seamlessness, embodiment and immersion. This is the concept of the analyst as "observ***ing***-participant" (Hirsch, 1996), a subtle shift in terminology that has profound philosophical, epistemological and psychoanalytic implications. Hirsch traces the evolution of this term over several decades from

> The concept of the analyst as objective observer … to analyst as subjective, participant-observer, to analyst as observing-participant and more recently, to analyst as mutual enactor (Hirsch, 1996). Each step in this evolution places increased stress on analysts' subjective and idiosyncratic presence. (Hirsch, 2015, p. 2)

There are no lines in nature yet we speak of multiplicity and of certain ways of being in the foreground or background at any one time. This is an attempt to account for the varied selves we know *we are* versus selves we seem *to have*, the latter reflecting our persistent tendency to objectify, distance and concretize our experience, as if we own or possess a self rather than *being selves*. Linear, two-dimensional language tends to objectify. How to speak of the lines that draw distinctions around our different ways of being?

The analyst's subjectivity is a seamless embodiment of the analyst's perspective, the vantage point from which everything flows and is experienced back. We take in and emerge from a place and moment, a space and temporal point. The *piece* of our subjectivity is actually a *moment* in time, situated and emerging from a concretized body that experiences the invisible through our emotional connectedness and tempo.

Ineluctable, irreducible and omnipresent, the limits are defined by the analyst's receptivity. What is to be included as fodder within the analysis, what is to be made explicit, will depend on the analyst's attunement, attentive listening and affective experiencing of the other.

We know, as well, that the field can extend beyond the bounds of concrete reality, crossing spatial and temporal lines to construct experience in other unconscious registers. These entraining signals can extend across oceans and cross time zones. We notice our reveries as they come up, adopting an openness to the nonverbal rhythms of the mother-infant dyad (Stern, 1985; Beebe, Stern & Jaffe, 1979). These rhythms extend beyond our actual presence, as when we think of a friend whom we haven't seen in a long time and then they call. Relationships have a natural rhythm and unconscious tempo, like Benjamin's rhythmic third (2014).

We are in a Pirandello (1921) play – characters in search of an author, feelings in search of representation. And we tend to exclude sexuality. To me, this is an important unconscious attractor, the hot potato that is in need of representation and ownership. We are not simply receptors but have potency, which is to say influence, in the way we write the script, including the characters we cast and *do not* cast.

In my writings, I have highlighted the persistent and almost universal tendency to overlook, repress, dissociate or leave unsymbolized the sexuality inherent in a narrative (Celenza, 2014). Many psychoanalytic authors have similarly noted the pervasive desexualization of psychoanalytic theorizing (Green, 1995; Fonagy, 2008; Dimen, 1999; Chasseguet-Smirgel, 1999). As Green (1995) stated, it is as if psychopathology occurs *before* sexuality or *beyond* sexuality.[2] Psychoanalysis used to be all about sex; now it seems sexuality has to be continually refound. It is no coincidence that I chose the metaphor of a *hot* potato being passed around but not held long enough to metabolize or contain.

In another register where unconscious transferences are at play, we remain close to something far more real and immediate. These are the transferences that structure our patient's realities and give meaning to their experience.[3]

Notes

1 Parts of this paper were originally presented at the Opening Ceremony of *The International Psychoanalytic Association*, Boston, MA, July, 2015 with Vincenzo Bonaminio, Elizabeth Lima da Rocha Barros, and Warren Poland. Other parts of this paper were presented at The Interpersonal Colloquium of the *William Alonson White Institute*, New York, NY, May, 2016 with Irwin Hirsch, Ann D'Ercole and Donnel Stern.
2 See Essay 18, *The erotic field* (this volume).
3 See Essay 1, *Transference, real and unreal* (this volume).

Chapter 30

Embodiment and the perversion of desire

A 30-year-old, exceedingly fit and strikingly beautiful woman came to see me because, as I heard it, "I'm attracted to *my nurse*!" In an acutely anxious state, she went on to describe her attempts to keep her mind off her sexual feelings. She catalogued her rigorous exercise schedule, her writing activities (she was in the middle of writing a play), her television watching (criticizing herself for it as self-indulgent) and other daily activities, all of which were failing to keep her attention from her dreaded sexual desire. I expected to hear about some sports-related injury (given her level of fitness) or body-based pain, both by way of introducing the nurse, but she made no mention of these or of the dreaded nurse. Nor did I understand why she was so anxious about her attraction to the nurse. Perhaps the nurse was partnered or otherwise unavailable, I speculated.

After some time had passed and I did not hear anything about the nurse, I asked her to clarify for me what she had said when she entered my office. It was only then that she repeated, and I correctly heard for the first time, that she was attracted to *minors* … I had misheard *minors* as *my nurse*. While I was re-orienting to this new information, I kept my auditory slip at the back of my mind, wondering about a possible unconscious communication.

When she realized I had just now understood her, Laura quickly added,

> This is why I cannot get married and have children because I have to always be vigilant and make sure I never act on these desires. And I never would. I never want to molest a child or even infants … and I'm attracted to infants too – it's terrible, I cannot be in places where there are kids and I'm now avoiding parks, schools, family gatherings where my cousins might be present .....

She said all this fast-paced while crying. I noted how the future was, in a command-like manner, foreclosed.

Laura told me she had thought she was asexual, but when she was 8 years old, she "felt it." Felt what? I asked and she explained, "Well I didn't then feel much, it's ideas that scare me." Now, she explained, she feels too much.

DOI: 10.4324/9781003264095-34

Since she was 16 or so, she has become aware of sexual attractions, to girls or boys under the age of 8. She masturbates and enjoys it, but is totally horrified that she is intensely aroused by seeing the clitoris or penis of an infant. If this happens, she becomes acutely aroused, does not even have to touch herself to orgasm and then she is totally disgusted with herself. My notes reflect her saying, "I'm attracted from infancy to about 4 years old, when they're nonverbal, before I start talking to people." I think that the last phrase was a slip ("before *I* start talking to people") but I cannot be sure. It is how I wrote it in my notes. Also, she regularly contradicted herself with the ages of when this started and of the ages of children to whom she is attracted. Sometimes the child is under 4 years-old, sometimes 8 and either she was 8 or 16 when the awareness of sexual feelings set in. At the beginning of our work, she reassured me in almost every session, "I am very good at and very serious about impulse control."

Given Laura's acute anxiety, I suggested a twice-weekly treatment and she readily agreed. I asked her about her experiences in romantic and sexual relationships. She said she has had none with the exception of kissing one boy. She has been attracted to others, though rarely, and always these persons had some built-in obstacle, such as they were "too close a friend," or a woman (she does not think she's gay), a cousin ("It would be incest!" she exclaims) or now, with children. I say that her sexual feelings seem to find a way to emerge in just the places where they are prohibited and she agrees, which is why, she tells me, she is so terrified. She dreaded these feelings would never go away. (I noted to myself the way she understood my comment in this early session. She seemed to take it at face value rather than as a suggestion of the operation of defenses. Was she unable to think about the workings of her mind, I wondered?)

Laura told me she was completely unattracted to (and frightened by) men her own age. Of course, I found these clinical facts extremely interesting in light of her attraction to children and when I shared this with her initially, she immediately dismissed my linking of the two, thinking they were only vaguely related. I thought if she could appreciate her mind in conflict and the defenses she might be unconsciously utilizing in order to mediate that conflict (e.g., projection and displacement to manage her fears and wishes) she would be relieved, but in early sessions when I furthered explained these possibilities with her, she was highly suspicious. The immediacy with which she had dismissed these ideas led me to wonder further. I thought she might be experiencing my interpretations as seductions, tempting her to loosen her vigilance on her desire to molest a child. In the early weeks, I did not suggest this to her, for fear of frightening her with a transference interpretation before establishing a sufficient alliance. Weeks later, however, we had the following exchange:

A: You seem afraid of this idea that the two [her fear of dating and her attraction to children] might be related.

L: I am very good at self-control, I think I told you. I would never harm a child.

A: Are you afraid to relax your vigilance, that *I* might be tempting you to relax your vigilance?

L: I know you mean well, you want to help me, but I am afraid of this idea, it's true. I know I would never molest a child. But the feelings are still there, so there are temptations. How would it work if these two ideas are related anyway?

A: Your mind seems to find ways of allowing desire only where there is sufficient, even extreme prohibition. It's with men your own age where you cannot allow yourself to feel anything and there, it would be permissible to act ... maybe that's the real temptation.

L: I don't know – I did kiss a boy once. I felt nothing. But you're making it complicated. Is this possible? I'll have to think about it.

At this point, I noted that Laura was able to consider my comments without becoming suspicious of me, presumably because of the increasing trust between us and a sense of confidence that I was a benevolent person trying to help her. (If this were indeed true, I also knew that our growing alliance would not rule out the possibility of my becoming a seductive, tempting object at some point in the future.)

In subsequent sessions, Laura did report feeling some relief and, though she was by no means convinced that her sexual feelings might be the result of an unconscious defensive transformation, she was willing to consider this as a possibility. She also became interested in the workings of her mind. She requested a third weekly session and expressed interest in my writing, stating, "The titles of your books are so *cool*. What interesting subjects you write about!" I noted that though she thought the titles were "cool" (an interesting choice of word), she did not read anything further nor ask me about my writing. I asked her what aroused her curiosity in particular and she spoke of the title of my first book (*Sexual Boundary Violations*). She then associated to her parents' extreme permissive child-rearing style. Still, I noted the emergence of curiosity about me and about the subject of sexuality in general. I wondered if there was a role for her anxiety now emerging in the transference, but these comments by Laura had an intellectual quality only. The feeling for me was that her interest was *cool*, she did not pursue her curiosity further nor speculate about me. (Only later did I realize that her lack of pursuit might portend other foreclosures as well.)

Laura stated that she comes from a family with an atmosphere and strong ethic of almost unlimited freedom, indeed boundlessness. She felt "everything was permitted" and the only boundaries that existed were self-imposed. Her parents talked to their children about drugs, for instance, but this took the form of sharing their own experiences with them. She took baths with her brother and father (in a small tub, she added) until she touched her father's penis and he realized bathing together was not a good idea. I asked her directly if she remembered other sexual incidents. She stated forthrightly that she had no memory of outright sexual abuse. I had the thought that her symptoms would be consistent with this historical reconstruction, but also noted that the atmosphere in the home (as she described it) might be sufficient to create anxieties about the limits of desire, even if sexual acting out had not occurred.

Laura described her family as guilt-ridden, always speaking of giving back and devoting many hours to charity work. Laura was also preoccupied with doing good works and making something of her life that will make a difference in the world. "Giving is prioritized; taking is forbidden. If you're consuming, you're not doing," she stated succinctly. She said her parents have unconditional love, but she is sure that her attraction to minors is the condition that would break it.

As Laura continued to tell me about her sparse dating history, I noticed that she seemed to eclipse the space between herself and her bodily receptivity to pleasurable feeling so that she could not think about pleasure except to condemn herself. She explained that when she has tried dating, she is quick to tell her prospective date (before they meet) that there will be no chemistry, they will only be friends, she will not feel anything and if he is okay with this, they can move forward. "Sounds like a command," I said and she explained, "I dread hurting him." She was apparently convinced this is the way it would go. She continued, "I become inarticulate when dating. I have overwhelming anxiety to the point of panic. Dating guarantees someone is going to be hurt. I have an infinite capacity to hurt people so I'm looking for a reason to say no."

When it comes to sexual feelings, Laura said she doesn't have a *physiological reaction*, she has an *intellectual longing*. She explained that she "desires to desire an attractive man, but the biggest, most powerful, and horrific thing is to reject somebody. It is soul-crushing." She stated that she does not want to hurt anybody which is why she has no interest in dating, she is convinced she will have no feelings and will have to hurt him. She said she used to be afraid she'd be pressured to have sex on dates; now it's about setting the boy up for disappointment which, in her mind, is immoral. She remembered telling me she is frightened, but could not own her anxiety in these early weeks of treatment. Though she was increasingly curious about herself and able to reflect on her symptoms, she continued to seem intellectualized, affectless and afraid of her feelings.

Laura also told me she has struggled with periodic depressions throughout her life and, interestingly and consistent with her intellectualized presentation, she said the quality of these are not primarily affective. They are dominated by suicidal ideation (she assured me she would never do it) and the fears are existential – that she is not going to continue to be the same person. They occur in transitions – separations and moves – and the thing that has helped is her gradual realization that she will continue to be the same person from one end of the juncture to the next.

Another form her suicidal ideation tends to take is in answer to the question, "Is this enough to want to live?" Her life has been dominated by work and achievement-related activities that she is committed to yet from which she derives little pleasure. Or at least, little enough that it raises the question, "Is this enough to make life worth living?" She is plagued by a growing awareness that the sexual desire she feels toward children and infants is the one thing that might be enough.

As noted, Laura is not completely sexually dormant. She started masturbating compulsively when she was 12 years old, long before she had any crushes. She likes erotica or soft porn, man on woman and prefers stories where a woman is totally taken over, where the woman "has zero control." This might include being given a drug, hypnotized, bound or tied up, or where "a guy age regresses a woman to a child, someone with less boundaries." She considers these situations to comprise "not *non*consent, but reluctant." I noted the truncation of desire and agency in all of these scenarios.

Tentative formulations of Laura's psychic distress can be constructed from various theoretical orientations. Perhaps Laura's symptoms represent an attempt to find the limits to her omnipotent, destructive and voracious fantasies and wishes. From a conflict perspective, her sexual pleasures are freighted with intolerable guilt and fear such that she projects and displaces them onto prohibited objects. From another perspective, she might be viewed as having a self-disorder – fears of annihilation, depersonalization or fragmentation arise when separations loom, intolerance of difference and separateness, the gaps experienced as voids making separateness psychically dangerous. She truncates her potential to think and feel, just as she does when she is about to date and she commands herself (and her date) to have no chemistry. She makes a pact, as it were, not to feel nor leave a space for the uncertainties, mysteries and excesses of her desire. Yet another perspective highlights fears of receptivity, one pole of a dialectic where potency, the *desire to do* good works and accomplishments that would change the world, are privileged over anything associated with *taking in*. Finally, there is the possibility that the infants and children toward whom Laura is attracted unconsciously represent infantile versions of herself, dissociated self-states perhaps secondary to sexual trauma that she does not recall.

Suddenly (to me), my work with Laura was prematurely terminated when she announced she was moving. After only a few months of treatment, she stated she was moving out of the area and presented this move as unavoidable, a career opportunity that she insisted she had told me about in our first session. I think in fact she had. Looking back, I remembered that she had informed me about a pre-existing career commitment she had made (to begin several months hence), thereby artificially circumscribing our treatment to be of short duration, however, I had apparently let myself become absorbed in the work and had forgotten!

I saw Laura's foreclosing the treatment as a possible enactment of her command to prospective dates: "There will be no attraction, no chemistry," i.e., no *felt* relationship, commitment or ongoing attachment. On a reality level, it appeared that her prior commitment was indeed an important career opportunity and I did not want to interfere with this. However, I shared with her that though it seemed necessary for her to leave the area, I could not ignore the possibility that she was truncating our relationship in ways that fit the pattern of forestalling her desire. She did not *feel* the importance of this, but agreed to consider it as a possibility. Since she could see the pattern, she then wondered if I would be willing to continue the treatment remotely. I told her I would think about this.

My private reflections on this question led me to the following considerations. I observed Laura's capacities to increasingly reflect on the workings of her mind, i.e., ways in which she was now able to consider defensive processes, the possible meanings of her fears and anxieties and ways in which her upbringing may have contributed to her inhibitions. The treatment, in other words, was developing her reflective capacities. But this was not where I thought the core of the work might be located. I speculated that Laura's inhibitions revolved more around her capacity *to feel, to be receptive to affective (sexual) experience*, especially in relation to her sexual desires as it was tied to *her own agency (intentionality)*. If this were true, she would need to allow certain fears, anxieties, desires and wishes to emerge within a sufficiently containing and affectively-charged transference experience. I could not be sure if the *embodied presence* of an analyst would be necessary for this to occur, but I suspected it might be.

I also thought it likely that Laura's treatment would require several years of intensive, affectively enlivening work. Though I would have enjoyed continuing to work with her, we had only just begun and after extensive thought on my part, I surmised it would be best for Laura to have an *embodied analyst*. At the risk of enabling a possible transference/countertransference enactment in this nonnegotiable truncation of the treatment, indeed, a truncation of the relationship through a premature termination, I referred her to an excellent analyst near her new home.

Laura is further discussed in the context of theoretical propositions in relation to a contemporary definition of perversion in Essays 31, *Perversion and its qualities of being*; Essay 32, *Transitional perverse scenarios* and Essay 33, *Psychic positions, healthy and perverse*. In these essays, I propose a contemporary definition of perversion that reveals a form of psychic functioning as a quality of being toward others, toward one's body or toward internal objects. This quality of being is contrasted with perversion denoting a specific set of behaviors, as in classical conceptualizations. In particular,

I propose that a perverse internal psychic mode is one where affective, embodied and pre-reflective self-experience is split off or dissociated. I also suggest that perverse modes of relating toward others (primarily through objectification) are more common in males whereas the objectification of one's body is more common in females.

Chapter 31

Perversion and its qualities of being

The concept of perversion has a long and tainted history. In contemporary times, many psychoanalysts refuse to use it, rejecting the heteronormative and phallocentric assumptions that imply the pathologization of non-heteronormative groups. To other analysts, however, the concept conjures meanings that are complex and clinically useful. Contemporary usages can reveal complex dynamics, including (but not limited to): Eiguer's (2007) study of the "intersubjective link," Purcell's (2006) discussion of the analyst's excitement in the analysis of perversion, Jeménez' (2004) phenomenology of perversion, Grossman's (2015) object-preserving function in sadomasochism, my emphasis of libido in sadomasochism (Celenza, 2000a), Josephs' (2003) "perversion of the observing ego," Sanchez-Medina's (2002) hypothesis of "perverse thought," Carignan's (1999) clinical description of a perverse transference, Heusser's revelations on excitement and its shaping of transference and countertransference, my (2022b) discussion of the analyst's suffering in treating perverse scenarios, and Etchegoyen's (1978) thesis of transference perversion. For the purposes of this essay, I aim to build on Parsons' (2000) overview and recasting of sexuality and perversion in object relations terms. In this essay, I aim to clarify the concept of perversion by refracting it through a contemporary lens, especially at the level of epistemology (namely, social constructivist), thereby reclaiming this complex theoretical construct - to destroy it in order to preserve it, as it were.

The classical definition of perversion is complex and multi-layered, differing even from within the arc of Freud's writings[1] and then subsequently in the literature from various early psychoanalytic writers. The following definition is excerpted from Laplanche and Pontalis (1973, pp. 306–309) and will be used to situate the classical ways perversion has been understood in order to contrast this with a more contemporary view. Several dimensions of the classical view of perversion can be identified, including perversion defined as 1) a deviation from a norm (that being coitus with the opposite sex by means of genital penetration; 2) orgasm achieved with other sexual objects (other than a person of the opposite sex); 3) orgasm achieved via

DOI: 10.4324/9781003264095-35

erogenous zones of the body other than genital penetration; 4) where orgasm is subordinated to extrinsic conditions that bring about sexual pleasures.

These elements, taken together, combine to define perversion as aberrant *behavior* underlaid with heteronormative and phallocentric assumptions. My purpose is to find what is still useful in the terminology and discard outdated assumptions no longer held to be true or valid. A contemporary lens focused on healthy sexuality allows for wide-ranging behaviors that are not necessarily tied to a specific erogenous zone or a partner of a particular sex. Further, as noted above, the idea that *behaviors themselves* can be deemed perverse (or not) is a prescriptive orientation that implies or directly identifies ways of behaving, the judgment and prescription of which is pointedly anti-psychoanalytic.

Therefore, the term perversion requires the dismantling of phallocentric and heteronormative assumptions as well as links to pregenital functioning and part-object ties. At the same time, seemingly gendered anxieties often lurk in perverse symptomatology (regardless of how perversion is defined), a clinical fact that cannot be ignored. In the case of Laura,[2] for example, the conflict between the desire for sexual pleasure and the prohibitions and fears against them can be viewed as representing stereotypically gendered anxieties. Laura can be viewed as embattled or trapped within a stereotypically gendered binary where she cannot desire "masculine" penetration for fear of "feminine" receptivity. This parallels some stereotypic ways in which perversion has been characterized in classical literature, through the depiction of exaggerated acting out of "feminine" or "masculine" behaviors. Given the persistence of seemingly gendered concerns in perverse scenarios, it is my contention that the classical literature on perversion may retain relevance in the understanding of perversion today (see, for example, Freud, 1905, 1927; Arlow, 1971, 1987; Sperling and Arlow, 1954).

Further, I suggest that the classical literature on perversion retains clinical utility because *persons engaging in perverse scenarios are attempting to imagine a one-person universe* (albeit wishful, illusory, impossible and fantastically construed). In this view, a perverse mode of being or a perverse mode of functioning is a defensive fantasy construction that constitutes a retreat from interpersonal experiencing (either in relation to internal objects or those in actual reality) and/or certain internal psychic positions in relation to one's body. This is essentially an effort to construct an imagined, (yet impossible), self-contained (in the sense of omnipotent) and constricted one-person universe. Such defenses are unconsciously mobilized in order to defend against a perceived danger, consciously and concretely located either outside the self or from within.

The essential aspects of perverse scenarios (a fantasied construction that constricts modes of being) will be outlined here.[3] At the outset, it is most useful to discard the notion that perversion refers to a set of behaviors. Rather, there are several characteristics that define a perverse quality of being. These include: *constriction and constraint, repetition, objectification, sexualization, desire to harm, means/end reversal and absence of symboliza-tion.* Taken together, a perverse mode of being is where perceived dangers are unconsciously symbolically rendered in some objectified form in order to provide concrete props for an unconscious drama that may be enacted. Sometimes a prop can be a person, sometimes it is a thing. These then set the stage for personally meaningful scenarios that are unconsciously scripted to address a variety of anxieties. These scenarios are unconsciously choreo-graphed to manage and control perceived (interpersonal or internally lo-cated) dangers.

Constriction and constraint. This is the experience of deadness, control and predictability, resultant from a retreat from interpersonal relations, where others are viewed as dangerous external or internal objects. This also in-cludes the relationship to one's own body as a dangerous "other." The de-fensive process employed to manage such dangers (either located externally or internally) is a kind of devitalization or objectification. Such dangers are marked by intra-psychic divisions, often referred to as splits or dissociations, for the purpose of cordoning off affective, embodied modes of experiencing. Undergirding this definition are implied assumptions about healthy modes of being that are worth delineating – as psychoanalysts, we privilege affec-tive aliveness, the capacity to experience the full range of affects, in their intensity and creativity.[4] Perverse modes are the opposite of this. Play is a good example of a creative outlet that can be conscripted for perverse purposes if the play is enacted in a repetitious, constricted and rigidified manner. "When play takes on a compelling, obsessive quality, it is no longer play. It becomes a symptom" (Arlow, 1987, p. 34). It is obvious that Laura is struggling with the feelings of deadness in her body as she describes, for example, being unmoved by potential love objects of her own age. This can be viewed as the result of a defensive process where her body is devitalized in relation to certain others in the external world.

Perverse scenarios are *repetitive.* Repetitious modes of being and experi-encing can be clinically observed. There is a fixed and ritualized quality that evokes associations to trauma and are, often enough, the result of a re-petition compulsion (Arlow, 1987; Stoller, 1986). A perverse scenario can be understood as an attempt to turn passive into active, to triumph over pas-sively endured pain. This, of course, depends on the individual meaning of the perverse scenario. If there is sexualization or other pleasurable aspects to it, there can be a self-reinforcing feedback loop. (This is one reason perverse scenarios are difficult to treat.) The symptom of attraction to minors, as per Laura's report, comprises an unbidden,[5] repetitive experience that pre-occupies her and requires constant vigilance. This symptom can be viewed as a repetitive preoccupation with a prohibited, sexualized other.

In terms of constriction, constraint and repetitiveness, perverse scenarios are much like obsessive rituals. Perverse scenarios differ, however, in their additional qualities (delineated below), especially in terms of harm to oneself or others, a means/end reversal and the lack of symbolization. The lack of symbolization, in particular, is a distinct feature of perverse scenarios (as they differ from obsessions) given that obsessive rituals are often represented in the ideational realm, can be discussed and referenced in the individual's mind.

Perverse modes of being involve *objectification*. Building on Parsons' (2000) view of perversion as a defense against object-relatedness, I suggest that perversion can be viewed as a retreat from interpersonal relatedness and/or the relation to internal objects where *the other* (in external reality or as fantasied from within) is perceived as a threat. Alternatively, these threats may also be experienced as arising from within one's own (affectively experiencing) body. Perverse modes of being transform this threat to a manageable "thing" – in effect to "thing-ify." Examples of this mode of experiencing are reflected in many of Laura's reports: depression as "an idea, not a physiological reaction," "I didn't then feel much, it's ideas that scare me," and the commands to prospective dates, "There will be no chemistry!" Culturally, we refer to self-states in an objectified mode, as in, "Part of me ...." This references a *piece* of the self, concretized and thereby reduced from an experiencing self that is, in contrast, situated in a *moment in time.*

In the clinical setting, I have found the tendency toward objectification to have a different form in women than men where the dangerous affective experience, sense of intention or agency[6] is located within themselves and experienced as a threat. As an example, for many women, it can appear that their own personal desires (arising from within) are experienced as dangerous such that the "other" becomes their own body, especially in its capacity for generating desire, and in this way the body can be objectified and/or fetishized. There is a kind of Cartesian duality, a mind/body split that serves to anesthetize the body and its capacity to arouse desire. For some women, then, it might be more accurate to say that the retreat is not from the experience of interpersonal relatedness but from certain internal psychic experiences, especially in relation to their sense of intentionality or agency and how these intersect with pleasure and the sense of embodiment. A patient of mine recently said, "It's as if I'm holding my head out here, a foot away from my body."

This problem is easily identifiable in Laura where she commands herself and a prospective date that "there will be no chemistry" between them. She complains that her depression is not a feeling state, but an idea. And most notably, she finds herself arousable, that is capable of a feeling state, only in contexts where such feelings are prohibited, contexts she must therefore avoid.

Sexualization is commonly employed to transform a perceived threat into a pleasurable experience. We know that sexual gratification can be experienced alone; somatic, bodily pleasure does not have to be a two-person event.

In perverse scenarios, sexual pleasure (whether or not an actual other person is involved), counters the deadening effects of objectification and the retreat from the experience of interpersonal relatedness or internal affective experiencing. We see here how the body can be either a cradle or a grave for signification (Lombardi, 2008).

In contrast, Grossman (2015) emphasizes the *object preserving* quality of sexual perversion wherein the sadistic tie is characterized as an attempt to control and thereby maintain an attachment to the object. In a previous paper, I also discussed the erotic dimension in sadomasochistic relations as an irreducible, hidden structure that both threatens *and sustains* the destructive attachment (Celenza, 2000a). While these reports can be interpreted as contradictory to the present thesis, I aim to emphasize here the destructive aspects of the perverse scenario to the other's intentionality, agency and personhood such that the other is objectified and thereby (in fantasy) controlled, deadened and thereby destroyed. The same logic can be applied to the experience of affective deadening through an attack on the body's threatening affective vitalizing potential.

Laura's symptomatology was highly sexualized, possibly converting a noxious traumatic repetition or deadening experience into a pleasurable (yet horrifying) experience. She described giving in to the temptation of masturbation only to feel disgusted with herself afterward. She also reported an avoidance of others ("minors") who threaten to arouse her body. As the treatment progressed, she elaborated the experience of suicide as an attempt to kill the desires that came to her from within. These were often accompanied by a sense of depersonalization, a fear that she had lost a sense of continuity and a concomitant feeling of deadness within her body.

Stoller (1986) identified the *desire to harm* as part of a perverse scenario. Objectification itself harms the other or one's own body when perversion is viewed through the lens of a mode of relating or mode of being (respectively). Often the desire to harm represents a desire to exact revenge (and this is surely evident if the unconscious meaning of the perverse scenario is a repetition of a traumatic event). Were Laura to act out her attraction to children, this would comprise a molestation or abuse of a child, causing trauma and harm to the child (as well as horrifying Laura). It is possible that Laura's preoccupation with her attraction to minors (or "her nurse") represented a return of some repressed or dissociated memory of trauma she endured as a child or "minor" and for which she is now unconsciously seeking revenge. On a conscious level, however, she was preoccupied with the attempt to obliterate desire both in actual reality and from within herself.

The most important aspect of the definition of a perverse mode of being is the employment of a *means/end reversal* (Stein, 2005), i.e., *the use of constructive means, tools or processes for destructive ends.* This turns a constructive process on its head, an undermining of the constructive purpose with a destructive goal. In intimate sexual relations, for example, there are components of mutuality, growth enhancement, affection, reciprocity and nurturance. A perversion of loving relations is an engagement with another person in nonreciprocal, non-intimate (objectified), harmful and restrictive ways. Paraphrasing Stoller (1986), perversions of loving are essentially an erotic form of hatred. This is the mechanism that creates various perverse transferences (Richards, 1993; Etchegoyen, 1978; Meltzer, 1973), the ways in which the analytic purpose is subverted and degraded, either by stripping words of affective meaning, engaging in pseudo-dialogues or fetishizing aspects of the process.[7] In a broad way, a perverse scenario, as a means/end reversal, employs the tools of analysis in order to de-vitalize, control, manage and deaden rather than vitalize and deepen affective experience and growth. Laura's ultimate foreclosure of the treatment can be viewed as a retreat, an avoidance of her growing relationship with me. It subverted the treatment as the process was deepening and foreclosed the growth-promoting efforts we had been developing.

In this way, perverse modes of being are on the opposite pole to truth. They are designed to subvert truth. Many writers (see, for example, Kaplan, 1991, 2006; Sanchez-Medina, 2002; Stein, 2005) name *the lie* as its hallmark. In her symptomatology, Laura was upending the potential of a love re-lationship by converting her attraction into a horrifying and unacceptable scenario. She was aware of her potential to harm others (e.g., "rejection is soul-crushing") and therefore used this as a rationale to avoid interpersonal relations altogether. Similarly, her attraction to minors incorporated an inherent aspect of abuse rendering seeking such relations or gratification taboo. In this way, she was attempting to eliminate from the world (her world) these stimulating others.

Finally, in persons struggling with various perverse modes of being, it is possible to see the *absence of symbolization*. Persons engaging in perverse scenarios can appear to be particularly concrete, or if not in general, have a demarcated, concrete way of holding the perverse scenario itself. It is viewed nonpsychologically – *it just is* and can sometimes be experienced in an ex-ternalized, disowned way, i.e., as if the perverse mode of being persecutes oneself. Laura did not think about her preoccupation with minors in psy-chological terms when I began treating her. The potential meanings of her attractions only became thinkable within the process of treatment. Though she initially dismissed my interpretations and my attempts to reveal the defenses she was utilizing (for fear of loosening her vigilance on her beha-vior), she gradually considered these possibilities as the patterns became more and more coherent to her. She reported feeling some relief as she could consider the possible meanings of her symptoms instead of taking them solely at face value. This too had the effect of opening her mind to psy-choanalysis, leading her to request a third hour and eventually to accept the referral to a psychoanalyst near her new home.

Notes

1 See Grossman (2015), for an explication of the changes in Freud's views on sadism and masochism in parallel with the evolution of instinct theory.
2 See Essay 30, *Embodiment and the perversion of desire* (this volume).
3 For further elaboration, see Celenza (2014).
4 It can be argued that these comprise judgmentalisms or moralisms, i.e., where psychoanalysis prescribes *ways to be*. Indeed, we do have values and goals for our patients, what defines healthy modalities and what constitutes liberation from conflict or constraint. However, our prescriptions are in terms of the expansion of growth and capacities, not prescriptions of behavior or choices in how to live.
5 In this sense, unbidden refers to "the emergent quality of our experience…[the] felt sense of the arrival of experience in my mind, of how little my conscious intentions seem to have to do with the whole process" (Stern, 2015, p. 3).
6 Often, in the case of women, the threatening affective experience is associated with desire, appetite (as in eating disorders) or power (see Celenza, 2014).
7 Again, these behaviors are selected as examples because of constriction, constraint and other features of perverse scenarios, not in terms of the manifest behavior itself.

Chapter 32

Transitional perverse scenarios

Not surprisingly, many patients who engage in perverse scenarios report histories of trauma. As I have mentioned, one way a perverse scenario can be identified is in its attempted mastery over some trauma, the wish to turn passively endured pain into an active experience; there may be evidence of an attachment to a destructive object, a desire for revenge; and/or the perverse scenario may function as a drive to remember. I have had patients wonder, "Did this happen or am I imagining it?" or "I think I have done this before." These are motives characteristic of all defensive organizations and coping mechanisms resultant from trauma. Here, I offer the idea of an *attempt to function in a one-person universe* as representing an unconscious and impossible fantasy, due to the quality of relatedness in perverse scenarios where the other is depersonalized (as in objectification) rendering oneself triumphant in a world of nonthreatening (literal) objects, i.e., nonpersons. In the case of trauma that is enacted within oneself or within one's own body, the internal world associated with this type of perverse scenario is highly constricted and rigidified, especially in relation to the capacity for affective vitality, rendering one's own body *a thing*. (The schematics that follow attempt to depict the internal self-experience that is associated with perverse scenarios in such a constricted fashion.)

It is difficult to escape notice how often stereotyped gendered themes (and binarial constructions) are involved in perverse scenarios. Perverse scenarios are often ways of coping with threats to one's gender identity (the question of whether one is male or female) or gender role (confusions surrounding the sense of oneself as "masculine" or "feminine"). These confusions and restrictions can be understood as imbalanced reckonings between the dual capacities of receptivity and potency. Perverse scenarios may choreograph ways to free oneself from a constricting binarial trap where these two capacities are polarized and split. These are usually highly stereotyped notions of masculinity and femininity that are depicted in extreme form, e.g., a woman as a maid, or a man as a master to a slave. Though not inherently gendered, the polarization of the dual capacities of receptivity and potency can be recruited to illusorily delimit the set of challenges that otherwise

DOI: 10.4324/9781003264095-36

would overwhelm the individual as she or he strives to organize gendered and nongendered self-development.

In general, perverse scenarios can be understood as ways to defend against the threatening intentionality or personhood of the other, often defined in a gendered way. As an example, Dunn (2015) makes a compelling argument that the protagonist's anxieties in the movie *Rear Window* (Hitchcock, 1954) are related to gendered threats within the primal scene, i.e., women tyrannize men; men exact bloody revenge on them.

Primal scene fantasies are struggles with triangularity, however anxieties that might form the underlying content of perverse scenarios can be dyadic in nature as well. There can be a fundamental anxiety around separateness. In these cases, the danger associated with the separateness of the other usually revolves around fears of the other's intentionality, i.e., fantasies of what the other might (threateningly) do. Fears associated with difference might play a part in perverse scenarios as well. These may symbolize anxieties about castration, the difference between the sexes or fantasies and fears of the other as alien.

I have found that the effort to *localize the perceived danger* can open up new meanings of perverse scenarios in a helpful way. If the localization of the danger is projected outward and experienced as residing in the outside world, this is the most common mode of perverse scenarios in men where the perceived danger is the personhood or intentionality of the other. In contrast, when the perceived danger is localized within, i.e., within one's own body or as one's own dangerous intentionality or desires, this is a common mode of perverse relating in women. The body is objectified and/or fetishized in these cases.

Representing a British Object Relations point of view, Michael Parsons (2000) describes perversion in a way that makes the necessary shift from viewing perverse scenarios as "a defense against drive derivatives to a defense against object relatedness" (p. 43).[1] Instead of viewing perverse behaviors as a defense against a threatening impulse or affect, he sees it as a defense against object-relatedness. To this, I would add that perverse scenarios can represent a defense against the experience of the other *as a person or center of agency* in their own right. In this way, perverse scenarios can fruitfully be viewed as an attempt to defend against *the personhood or intentionality of the other* or to defend against *a dangerous intentionality or desire within*.

From a narrower perspective, however, viewed from within the confines of the symptomatic picture and solely from the patient's point of view, it can be seen that the nature and form of the perverse scenario is an attempt to create and live in a fantasied, wishful yet impossible one-person universe. In short, the perverse scenario is a defensive attempt to construct a one-person drama, obliterating, *in fantasy*, the intentionality and difference of the other (in actual reality or as internal objects) or the affective experience of the self, arising from within one's own body.

What constitutes a threat in the other? These tend to be the experience of difference and/or separateness. These challenges of difference and separateness are not exactly the same, though often constitute simultaneous and intertwined threats. Difference (otherness) is perceived as dangerous because it is unfamiliar and alien, threatening the unknown. Beyond difference, however, is the other's intentionality or separateness that threatens as well. The other's intentionality can threaten harm if the other is recognized as an enlivened subject. The fantasy of merging, a common feature of perverse scenarios, is often an effort to omnipotently control these threats.

As noted here, perverse modes of relating or qualities of being are pathological because they do destructive things to others and/or to oneself. They are by definition anti-growth promoting, developmentally constricting and repetitively truncated. They cause personal suffering and careful psychoanalytic theorizing can encompass these patterns in a way that problematizes them. This is not to ignore or minimize adaptive aspects to a particular perverse scenario or the way perverse scenarios may represent attempted solutions to pathogenic situations. It is for this reason that I conceive of *levels of perversion*, where at its most extreme, a perverse mode is defined by rigidity, constriction and constraint. At some moderate level, however, perverse scenarios may serve a *transitional function*, where an individual's enactment of a perverse fantasy is reflected upon and in this way, opened up toward a potential for play (see, for examples, Bader, 1993; Corbett, 2013).

I am proposing a category of perverse scenarios that serve a transitional function, as in *transitional perverse scenarios*. This is when there is the capacity to reflect upon the perverse scenario and when the analyst/therapist is allowed to join in on the perverse scenario. Defenses aimed at objectification, constriction and constraint will be aimed at the analyst in an attempt to defend against the arousal and containment of affective experiencing. These defenses also reflect that affective experiencing is a potential possibility. This signals an opening, i.e., the presence of a gap where symbolization is possible, the attempt to play and to find a space in order to allow the presence of the other despite separateness and difference. The presence of the analyst/therapist is necessary so that uncertainty can be tolerated, as one attempts to feel, symbolize and think. This creates a psychological space where meanings can emerge or be constructed, the opening up of psychological mindedness, the potential for affective vitality and the creation of meaning.

These ideas helped me sort through the decision of whether to continue with Laura[2] via some form of telehealth or refer her to another analyst near her new home. I do not want to suggest that virtual modes of treatment can never be helpful. Indeed, they are currently being discussed as serving a transitional function for many schizoid patients, especially when in-person modalities would not be tolerated (see, for example, Lemma and Caparrotta, 2014; Knafo and LoBosco, 2016).[3] For some, a virtual treatment is the only way to begin the process of reflecting on oneself. I also think a virtual treatment might have been successful in Laura's case, given that she already demonstrated capacities to be witnessed in my actual presence, despite that engaging her at an affective level was still elusive. However, I do not think a virtual treatment is ideal in general and if alternative modalities exist, they should be prioritized.

Notes

1 Parsons notes that this theorizing adds "an emphasis on depersonalizing the object but also merging with it … what is unbearable is the relationship to a *person* who has his or her own *otherness*. The *personhood* of the other is avoided by turning the person into a thing while the *otherness* of the other is avoided by the merging." (2000, p. 45, italics in original). I would add to this an important conceptualization of the threatening other (personhood in Parsons' terms) *as a separate and different subject, i.e., center of initiative.*
2 See Essay 30, *Embodiment and the perversion of desire* (this volume).
3 See Essay 4, Changes in the frame (this volume).

Chapter 33

Psychic positions, healthy and perverse

This essay attempts to depict, with graphic illustrations, the phenomenology of conscious psychic positions. The first schematic (Figure 33.1) depicts internal psychic positions over which an individual experiences some measure of conscious control, though each position is undergirded with unconscious factors and elements. This schematic attempts to depict multiple ways of positioning oneself, multiple self-states within the individual's psychic experience and/or in relation to others, internal objects or in relation to one's own body. The use of the term *internal psychic position* is utilized here to denote various internal perspectives within the individual that differentiate and characterize the individual's relation to herself or himself and the various perspectives one can take toward oneself, one's body and others in the external world. In healthy modes of being, these internal psychic positions flexibly interpenetrate and form the basis upon which the individual experiences herself or himself in relation to internal, affective experiencing and in relation to the outside world. This terminology will be further explicated below.

The positions are capacities, ways of perceiving oneself in relation to others or in relation to one's own reflections on oneself. For example, there is a familiar state of mind when one is alone, lost in thought about oneself. This is the position of the Reflective Self or the self that can take oneself as an object for itself. Then there is a shift when one becomes aware of someone watching, engaging the Subjective Object or self for others. In the healthiest case, there is a capacity to flexibly alternate and access the various positions simultaneously or in succession, depending on context, to move from one position to another. None of these capacities are truncated, cut off from affective experience or inaccessible. In a healthy, mature individual, we would expect the capacity to reflect on oneself as well as the capacity to present oneself publicly and to reflect on that.

The center of the diagram depicts *The Embodied Self* (the pre-reflective, experiencing and agentic self, a nonreflective position). Arbitrarily located around the center are other positions, including *The Subjective Object* (the capacity to take oneself as an object for others or "Me"; the public self), *The*

DOI: 10.4324/9781003264095-37

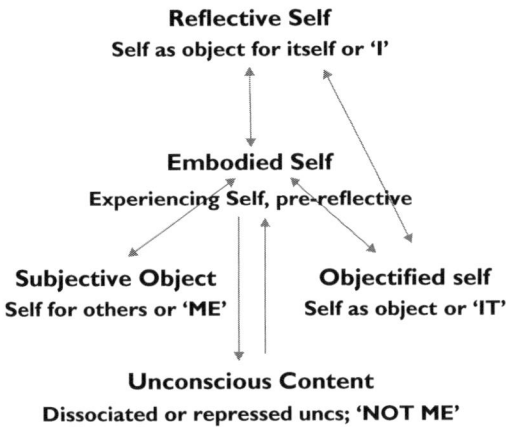

Figure 33.1 Internal psychic positions.

Reflective Self (the self who reflects on itself, i.e., takes itself as an object for itself or "I") and the more dissociated, sometimes pathological self-structure, *The Objectified Self* or "It." These positions are descriptions from the point of view of the experiencer; it is a schematic attempting to depict phenomenal (i.e., conscious) subjective experience that may or may not coincide with an intrapsychic formulation constructed by an outside observer.

All of these internal psychic positions are rooted in and influenced by unconscious processes, defenses and self-states, categorized as "Not Me," which may be comprised of dissociated unconscious images or self-states, repressed unconscious fantasies, either encoded or unencoded, the latter referring to Bollas' (1982) unthought known and/or non-encoded, unformulated yet embodied unconscious and nonconscious processes (as in Stern's (1997, 2015) unformulated experience).

This schematic borrows from the work of many theoreticians who denote some of these positions with slightly different names and I lean heavily on these understandings. The *Subjective Object* includes Bollas' (1982) discussion of the relation to the self as an object, where the individual recreates aspects of the mother's facilitation of his existence. Similarly, Dimen (2008) speaks of subject-as-object, the self as object to itself. Ogden's (1994) ideas of self and the phenomenology of subjectivity also overlap with many of these categories. The *Reflective Self* denotes the position that embodies self-reflexive functioning, as Aron (1998, 2000) discusses. Grotstein (2000) denotes similar ideas in his Phenomenal Subject and the Ineffable Subject of the Unconscious. On Grotstein's Phenomenal Subject, I use the term *Embodied Self* in order to emphasize the conjoint presence of embodiment and sense of self,[1] the experiencing self. In my view, this is the dreamer who dreams the dream. (See Celenza, 2014 for a further elaboration of these positions and other writers on these subjects.)

Several types of links (i.e., the interpenetration of these positions or the capacity to flexibly alternate among them) can be conceived depending on the individual's defensive organization. The links might be depicted as a line with a double arrow or a single arrow at one end or the other. These arrows depict either a reciprocal relation or a one-way relation, displaying the degree of psychic communication that exists between the different positions, especially in relation to affective communication. A single-arrowed line depicts one-wayness, where disowned, repressed, dissociated or disavowed affective states are disclaimed or otherwise banished from consciousness, i.e., not to be experienced or thought. The relationship between the *Embodied Self* and the *Unconscious*, Not Me position (like a repository) might be considered only relatively pathological depending on the individual's functioning, from neurotic to psychotic, a Not Me relation where the function is to expel those proto-mental experiences that must be expelled, with or without symbolization.

In contrast, it is possible to objectify oneself and/or others in the individual's psychic experience. As I have written elsewhere (2014), this appears to be common in female perversions and in the case of Laura² where intolerable anxiety associated with sexual impulses and feelings leads to a defensive deadening of her body and affective experience in certain situations.

Figure 33.2 depicts a perverse relation between the *Embodied Self* (the pre-reflective experiencing self), and the positions of the *Reflective Self* and the *Objectified Self*. I suggest that when Laura is prescribing to a prospective date (and herself) that no emotion or arousal will be felt, she is positioned in a perverse mode of being in relation to her body and the other. There is no link from her *Embodied Self* to all other positions except the *Unconscious*, Not Me position; her phenomenal, affective life is deadened. Rather, in these moments, she engages from the position of an *Objectified Self*, representing a perverse mode of being. This depiction and the absence of *double-headed* arrows may also be viewed as a graphic illustration of attacks on linking (Bion, 1959).

It is also interesting to consider that the *Reflective Self* might still be partially operative, a possibility that demonstrates the limited utility of insight alone in these cases. During my brief treatment of Laura, I repeatedly had the experience that she was taking in (increasingly) my interpretations, especially in relation to the possible defensive transformations that she might be employing, yet these interventions did not yet increase her responsivity and capacity to feel her body at an affective level. This may have been due to the brief nature of the treatment. As Figure 33.2 depicts, she was sufficiently cut off from her affective experience such that she could not allow herself to be receptive to affects at this point in time, despite being able to consider my interpretations at an ideational level. But I suspect that had

Reflective Self
Self as object for itself or 'I'

Embodied Self   mind/body split
Experiencing Self, pre-reflective

Subjective Object ←——→ **Objectified self**
Self for others or 'ME'   Self as object or 'IT'

Unconscious Content
Dissociated or repressed uncs; 'NOT ME'

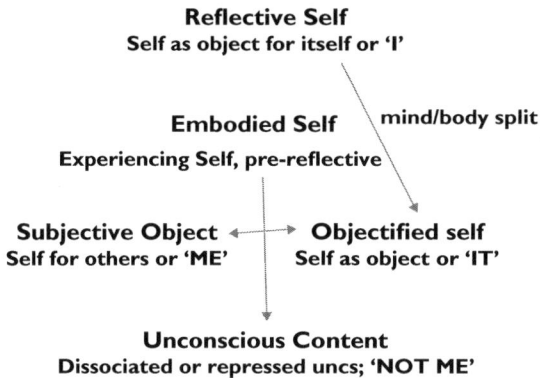

Figure 33.2 Perverse psychic positions.

the treatment continued at a sufficiently intensive frequency, there would have been transformations in her *Embodied* (experiencing) *Self* through transference/countertransference repetitions (of some kind) where she might have gradually and increasingly allowed herself to be more affectively present to our relationship and her experience without foreclosure.

When Laura was suspicious of interventions pointing out the ways in which she truncates the transitional space, cannot think or entertain uncertainties where affective experience might in some way be engaged, I believe she was demonstrating her inability or unwillingness to relate to me in an embodied, affectively vital way. It could be said that she was relating from the positions of an *Objectified Self* and *Reflective Self*, but no arrow would link to her as an *Embodied Self*. Because I viewed her psychic experience in this way, aided in part by the graphic depiction of her psychic capacities as they were foreclosed, I was skeptical of the usefulness of virtual meetings in order to continue the treatment.

In my view, interventions aimed at helping Laura expand her receptivity to pre-reflective affective experiencing were clinically indicated and would establish links to the other positions of her internal psychic states. Questions such as Do you feel that? How do you feel that? Where is it in your body? are aimed at expanding the capacity for pre-reflective experience, Laura's relationship to her body in its affective, sensory modality (the vertical dimension of transference, in Lombardi's (2008) terminology). On the contrary, interventions that expand or primarily engage her *Reflective Self* (those aimed at insight and her capacities to observe herself) would be of limited utility. This was borne out in the early stages of the treatment when I suggested to Laura that her desire seemed to find expression in exactly those places where it was forbidden. This interpretation stimulated greater resistance presumably because she became more anxious about relaxing her vigilance. Insight-oriented interpretations eventually provided short-term relief, offering alternative formulations to her being a "pedophile," such that she gained confidence in continuing the work with her next analyst. Employing the model introduced in this paper, we might say that a person transitions from engaging in a perverse mode of relating to a transitional mode when the *Embodied Self,* i.e., the pre-reflective self is expanded and establishes links to other psychic positions.

Notes

1 Benjamin (2013) comments that the term *embodied subjectivity* should be re-dundant; however, it is not, due to the history of mind/body duality in Western philosophical thought.
2 See Essay 30, *Embodiment and the perversion of desire* (this volume).

Chapter 34

Reverie, countertransference, elasticity [1]

A psychiatrist is sexually exploiting a patient. He came to me for help and knows he violates his ethical code, but does not want to end the relationship. He says he does not love her yet cannot say why he is sexually involved with her while also treating her psychiatrically. He knows he is enacting a self-destructive perverse scenario, one that has driven him to thoughts of suicide as he stands to lose his profession. Yet, he tells me he will quit the treatment with me if I "cannot love and respect him no matter what he does."

He resists exploring the meaning of the relationship with me. He insists talking about it will spoil the excitement. He accuses me of being intrusive, not understanding him and refuses to expose his feelings about her to me. Over time, I become more and more distressed and angry with him. I feel silenced and impotent. I feel bound and gagged, unable to think and wonder if we are creating a "subjugated third" (Ogden, 1994). In my private reverie, I wonder how his behavior is meaningful in relation to me, perhaps a defiance to our work and taunt to my expertise. Or perhaps I am no more than a witness, as he provokes the father (the licensing board? the profession?). I am supposed to watch him destroy the link to the paternal function and see the impotence of the law (Eiguer, 2007).

The night before a session, I dream I have my period, a bloody mess between my legs and I wake up distressed. I think the dream indicates that he is hurting me. He seems to want me to reprimand him (and indeed I feel like I possess a whip, stinging him with my hurtful insights). I then realize that such an image is aggressive, perhaps an attempt to free myself from his tyranny. I want to share this insight with him but I know he will not accept it.

A few days later, I consult a colleague. We realize another meaning of the dream: that he has not impregnated me. I have the fantasy that the impregnation would result in the opposite of the Messiah, instead with Rosemary's Baby.

Through a projective identification, I further elaborate this reverie. I think my patient is trying to rid himself of something self-destructive inside him. He wants to put it in me, perhaps his aggressive, reactive, defensive and vulnerable self. Maybe this is the way the field will contract his illness (Ferro

DOI: 10.4324/9781003264095-38

and Civitarese, 2013). By impregnation, I will have introjected his aggression, his badness, and I will need to find a way to metabolize it, to purify the field. Rosemary's Baby encapsulates this metaphor well, I think.

I recognize there is hate in the countertransference. I think the enactment casts me in the role of the reprimanding parent and I consider sharing this dilemma with my patient. In this way, I hope to join him in his search for a benign, supportive other who will accompany him on his journey. Perhaps I could become that other whom he desperately needs but has bound and gagged. I think of his critical father, who he complains never knew him except to criticize his closeness with his mother. From the vantage point of a paternal transference, I think it is no wonder he wants to prevent me from speaking, expecting condemnation. I see the link with his past in the here and now experience with me.

I suspected my nocturnal dream conveyed meaning for this patient because I was aware of being anxious to see him the next day. Upon waking, I noted my association that he was hurting me and wondered what internalized self- and object-configuration might be emerging through me, especially as this related to his history. His father was critical yet impotent, especially in relation to his highly seductive and more powerful mother, a possible template for the perverse scenario in which he currently engages in a self-destructive, repetitive pattern. I see this pattern both with his patient (being the seductive and powerful mother) and with me, where I embody the condemning paternal figure.

Reverie, countertransference experience and repetition all emerge in the here and now experience (either in the interaction with me or in my private affective/imaginal experience). In this way, my internal unconscious process is realized in the transference/countertransference matrix. Some of my reverie is structured as a relational configuration, manifested in the present and drawing parallels with the historical narrative. I believe my eventual sharing of these reveries, elucidating the pattern in the here and now will aid in liberating him from old and constricting modes of being with me (and others, perhaps even his patient). I hope that this linking from present meanings to the past narrative will be clear to him. At the moment, he cannot look back.

To build on the unconscious communications, I continue to query and co-create inner fantasies of me and him as externalized in the dream field. Of course, I do not expect a clarification – the ambiguity of whether these imaginings reflect truth or fantasy remains ambiguous, indeed a persistent characteristic of the field.[2] Here, meaning production is not relationally pre-figured; the search for unconscious derivatives does not cease as these are continually produced. As I was writing this paper, for example, I imagined holding Rosemary's Baby and, in my reverie, I dropped the baby with a concomitant fantasy that it had bitten me. I thought this represented the difficulty containing my patient's wishes, but then I wondered which patient

I was referring to. Was it my patient's wishes or my patient's patient's wishes that could not be contained? The elastic field expands.

In describing my thought processes and affective experience with the patient in the vignette above, it is apparent that different fantasies were elaborated depending on my mindset, especially in relation to my attentional set,[3] each leading to disparate technical choices depending upon where my attention was directed. In many instances, my attention was directed to the paternal transference where a reprimanding father condemned my patient's current behavior with the seductive and powerful maternal figure (his patient). In a mindset that engaged a more diffuse attentional form, there was a construction of a joint fantasy, based on projective/identificatory mechanisms where the patient was attempting to impregnate me with his devilish Rosemary's Baby self. These then became further elaborated, suggesting Ferenczi's (1928) elastic, relaxed and mutual participation in the field, as I continued to be a character receptive to unconscious projections. The image of the impregnation arose in consultation first with a colleague, then the image of a biting baby came to me (incidentally but meaningfully when I further enlarged the elastic field).

Drawing on the analyst's role as an observing participant (Hirsch, 2015), we can see that the participatory and observational functions are associated with distinct attentional and cognitive sets. The participatory mode engages a diffuse attentional set and a form of thinking associated with analogic, synthetic modes of cognition, globally receptive to affective shifts and emergent experience. This is a receptive mode of attention, especially for visuospatial (pictorial) images and affect-laden forms of processing.[4] I believe this is an evolved example of Ferenczi's elastic, relaxed and mutual participation in the field. The participatory mode contrasts with the observational mode in that the latter engages a more directed, intentional form of thinking, especially as the analyst directs her or his attention to the patient's history or patterns of relating.[5]

In the immersive, participatory experience of the analytic process, the nature of the analyst's attention is relaxed and diffuse. My reverie of Rosemary's Baby came to me in this mode. In contrast, when I became aware of hatred in my countertransference, I directed my attention to the patient's history, creating links between my present relational experience with patterns from his past, a more directed cognitive process. Taken together, these different cognitive and attentional sets enrich the psychoanalytic process as well as dialectically refer back to each other.

Notes

1 A version of this paper was presented as a Plenary Panel at 13th International Sandor *Ferenczi Conference, Ferenczi in Our Time and A Renaissance of Psychoanalysis,* in Florence, Italy, May, 2018 with Chris Lovett and Giuseppe Civitarese.

2 See Levine (2013a) and Stern (2013b) for a discussion of the role of certainty.
3 See Essay 14, *Stance and attentional set in analytic listening,* Essay 15, *Directed attentional set,* Essay 16, *Diffuse attentional set* and Essay 17, *Stance, set, transference* (all this volume).
4 Stern (1990) might refer to this mode as the analyst as conduit, an active receptivity to unconscious communication.
5 Neurophysiological studies (e.g., Damasio, 1994; Schore, 2018) have repeatedly demonstrated that sequential, linear ("analytic") modes of cognition are governed by the dominant hemisphere (in most persons, left-hemisphere) while analogic, synthetic modes of cognition are governed by non-dominant or right hemisphere visuospatial modes of processing. Neither of these modes typically function alone; rather, one mode tends to predominate in particular mental states. This finding dovetails with field theorists' favoring of analogic, metaphoric and pictorial modes of cognition salient in creativity and dreams, a mode of processing associated with the dominant or right-hemisphere visuospatial modes.

Chapter 35

Mutual influence in contemporary film

It has been said that life imitates art. This axiom was famously enacted by Pablo Picasso when he painted a portrait of Gertrude Stein and quipped, "Everybody says that she does not look like it but that does not make any difference, she will." (Stein, 1933, p. 12). Today, we look to films for our reflections, our aspirations, what we *want* to look like and how we should behave. They both reflect the culture and play a part in constructing it. Yet films (like paintings) are created by real persons, so it is impossible to say who is imitating whom or which came first. A conceptual frame that captures this dialectic is the dynamic of mutual influence – there is both a reflection and a pull by each toward the other, one implicating the other's demarcations.

Films have moved beyond entertainment in recent decades as they more seriously take on questions and perplexities of real life. They have deepened their message as audiences have deepened their awareness. Some films even explore bedrock psychoanalytic themes. Who is imitating whom? Are we (psychoanalysts) imposing our understandings on films or are screenwriters reflecting the ways in which they have been influenced by us? Writers *are* us; films reflect our current awareness and this, in turn, is translated by those who write films.

There is a story of a young boy, the son of a psychiatrist, who realizes that he wants to be a psychoanalyst. He asks his father how best to prepare for this profession. His father (not a psychoanalyst) suggests he write to Anna Freud for guidance. He does and she answers, "You ought to be a great reader and become acquainted with the literature of many countries and cultures" (cited in Kohut [1968], p. 552). Apparently, she had in mind that art imitates life.

Contemporary films portray and are infused with the deepening awareness in which we live our lives. That the media have depicted our profession in bizarre and absurd ways is at least in tiny part a function of the ways in which some psychoanalysts actually behave. Granted, taken to a point of caricature, especially in the past, portrayals of analysts still contain a grain of truth – the silent analyst, the authoritarian know-it-all, the perverted

DOI: 10.4324/9781003264095-39

exploiter (unfortunately, he has existed throughout time and beyond our industry – sex always sells). But these depictions are changing and some contemporary films have captured more faithfully what we, as contemporary psychoanalysts, actually do.

Still, there has been a profusion of films that continue to portray therapists, psychiatrists and, in particular, psychoanalysts as absurdly weird, crazy or perverse. A Scandinavian study (Gharaibeh, 2005) examined the various portrayals of psychiatrists/therapists in American movies and found that, overall, the image is not flattering. Almost half are portrayed as obviously incompetent, as violating boundaries or both, close to one quarter violating sexual boundaries. This distortion has always been true and included depictions of therapists as outright insane or perverse (see, e.g., Brian De Palma's, 1980, *Dressed to Kill* and Jonathan Demme's, 1991, *Silence of the Lambs*). What is different now is that there are relatively competent portrayals added to the mix. We will never be rid of Hollywood's affinity for drama, suspense, intrigue, satire and perversion – what we now have, however, are representations that come close to the mark of what we actually do (see, e.g., Robert Redford's, 1980, *Ordinary People;* Norman Jewison's, 1985*, Agnes of God;* Craig Gillespie's, 2007, *Lars and the Real Girl* and Hagai Levi's, 2008 television series, *In Treatment*).

We can quibble with the fine-tuning, but we cannot ignore that contemporary films are getting closer to the real thing, not entirely but certainly here and there. Lorraine Bracco won an award from the American Psychoanalytic Association for her portrayal of a psychiatrist, Dr. Melfi, in *The Sopranos* (Chase, 1999). In her acceptance speech, she noted that much of her method in portraying Dr. Melfi had been derived from her own experience in therapy. Likewise, Hagai Levi recognized the influence of his 17-year psychotherapy experience in his Israeli series *B'Tipul* (on which the American TV series, *In Treatment*, is based). Analysis in real life making its way to the screen could not be stated more explicitly. This should not be surprising: where else is there a forum, an audience, as it were, to listen and help us organize and elaborate our perceptions?

Another influence on the contemporary scene stems from the fact that Hollywood often uses real-life psychiatrists and psychoanalysts to consult with their writers for the screen. Granted, the writers may still opt for a dramatic, satirical or fanciful portrayal, despite the consultant's best efforts to the contrary (Roni Baht, the consultant to the writers on *B'Tipul*, tells of his frustration with certain writers in this regard [personal communication, 2006].

Inevitably, contemporary films depict some general principles that characterize and reflect contemporary psychoanalysis. If the media's portrayal is getting better and deeper at characterizing our profession, perhaps the reason is that *we* are getting better at our craft. To describe this side of the dialectic, what we do (i.e., shifts in technique and stance) is being reflected in films and has changed the way screenwriters experience us. This evolution is not a coincidence. I surmise that there is no greater consumer of psychoanalysis (save psychoanalysts themselves) than literary critics and screenwriters. It makes sense that contemporary psychoanalytic precepts would make their way into the vernacular of the cinema.

In my own work with patients, I frequently refer to scenes from this movie or that TV show as they seem to perfectly reflect what my patient is telling me. Sometimes movie scenes may suggest a way to organize the dynamics in my mind so that they may be better understood. Herein lies the mutual influence, a decidedly contemporary notion of the ways in which we co-construct our experience between people and between the personal and the artistic.

Flawless (Schumacher, 1999), centers on two characters, each embodying a gendered extreme: the hypermasculine war hero, Walt Koontz, who has little patience for human frailty; and a "pre-op" transsexual, Rusty, who is saving money for her sex-change operation. Both characters depict real-life stereotyping: Walt is the prototypical male chauvinist and Rusty wants to be all female, no "he" to be found in his being. By some strange coincidence, they live in the same apartment building in the meat-packing district of Greenwich Village. They hate each other, of course, each personifying the disclaimed aspects of the other's gendered extreme. A cerebral aneurysm bursts their respective bubbles (so to speak) as Walt finds himself unable to speak as a result of a stroke. His doctor suggests that he take singing lessons to regain his ability to articulate. Rusty happens to teach singing. Through their mutual need, each gives the other a priceless gift – Rusty becomes more courageous, more able to stand up steadfastly for what she wants and Walt finds his humanity in all its vulnerability. Through mutual identifications, each gives something vital to the other that crosses the boundaries, at least in this film, of classical gendered dichotomies.

Likewise, the idea of mutual influence has found its way into psychoanalysis and has helped transform our craft from a modern, sterile *doer–done to* (Benjamin, 2014) kind of enterprise to a postmodern, accessible and relational give-and-take. It is part of a transformation in psychoanalysis that recognizes the ways in which we are inextricably tied to each other. Similarly, there is no decontaminated field or objective view apart from what we see through our own particular lens. The "decontaminated transference" used to be defined as a thing apart; now we know that patient and therapist construct it together and each is changed by the other.

Lars and the Real Girl (Gillespie, 2007) is a poignant drama by screenwriter Nancy Oliver (who also wrote *Six Feet Under*). Though the story does not primarily involve the theme of mutual influence, it contributes to the contemporary trend in films that depicts character studies at an increasingly psychologically sophisticated level. The idea that films are better because *we* are better analysts is well exemplified in this gem.

Lars is a troubled and inhibited young man whose mother died giving birth to him. He grew up with his brother and grief-stricken father who recently passed away as the story begins. Lars is afraid of intimate involvement, literally afraid to touch or be touched. He makes expert use of a life-like mannequin, Bianca, a sex doll sold on the Internet. To Lars, she is a personal transitional object on his developmental road to real intimacy. The film mentions everyday object usage as well; his co-workers have their action figures and teddy bears sitting on their desks. But the skillful handling of Lars' psychological well-being is superbly depicted in the character of the small-town psychologist, Dr. Dagmar. She advises Lars' distraught brother and sister-in-law (Gus and Karen) to go along with Lars' delusion and when they balk, she reminds them that they do not really have a choice, a profoundly simple homage to the power of the unconscious.

Gus responds with a worry that people will laugh at Lars, to which Dr. Dagmar calmly suggests that people will laugh at him too, depicting her piercing willingness to face life's problems head-on. She also leaves open other questions: Who is laughing at whom? Are the townspeople going to laugh at the whole family or, more subtly did she mean, "Are you going to laugh at him as well?"

Dr. Dagmar's firm but gentle nudge to Gus and Karen to *do what Lars needs* is the epitome of a corrective emotional experience. She suggests that they go along with what Lars needs until he no longer needs it. When they protest that Bianca is not real, she counters with (again, simply) that she is. Double entendres abound. She is real in a concrete sense. She is also real to Lars. And then Dr. Dagmar wisely suggests that there's a reason Bianca is in town.

In the end, when Lars is ready to let his mannequin "die," Gus and Karen balk again! They protest to Dr. Dagmar, wondering how she could let this happen, displaying their own attachment to the mannequin. Herein is the theme of mutual influence. Dr. Dagmar explains that *she* did not let this happen, it was always orchestrated by Lars. She implies the role of Lars' unconscious in all its manifestations and effects. These exchanges show the astute wisdom of a grounded therapist, firmly planted in the asymmetric and imbalanced relationship with her patient, and one who also understands the meaning of mutuality, that ability to *be there with* the patient in an undemanding but compassionate way.[1]

Note

1 See Essay 36, *To be* "in it with" (this volume) for more film references in connection to contemporary theories.

Chapter 36

To be *in it with...* [1]

A patient tells me he hates to be controlled, yet I sense a certain compliance. He begins a session with his eyes closed. I say he seems to want to be alone, perhaps to immerse himself and suggest he consider the couch. He refuses, saying it would be too submissive. A moment later, he lies down. I recognize this is the conflict he came to examine. I wonder if he felt pushed, if I pushed him. I expect and want to engage in his conflict. I wonder how it was actualized in this moment. I review to myself how I experience him, who he reminds me of, my response, the way I said it, my words and my tone. I remember that I felt dismissed when he closed his eyes. I recognize a familiar conflict in me that no doubt was stirred. How did my response, a reaction to him yet arising from within me, interact with his?

What continues to interest me as I find myself more securely situated in contemporary psychoanalysis is not so much the answers that derive from a postmodern, perspectival awareness but the questions that persist. How do I acknowledge my influence in shaping a particular event without it becoming *about me*? How to focus in a way that is generally useful, beyond us, yet without disclaiming my particular involvement? I know even a spare description of this interaction will reveal and suggest the elements that stand out to me, what I have selected as important and what themes I ask him to consider. What is implied about *his* freedom when the certainty of my *being in it with* him is taken into account? If I cannot read myself out, is there a place for objective reality and can either of us know it? A contemporary perspective translates many of these questions from *whether* or *if* to *yes, but how*.

Eve, from *Three Faces of Eve* (Johnson, 1957) asks her psychoanalyst if it matters that one of the voices she hears is her own. He responds authoritatively that it does not! She wonders why not and of course, he doesn't answer. Rather than getting up and walking out (the more reasonable thing to do), she remains ensconced within her faith in his superior knowledge and wisdom, a wish-driven persistence. She says she believes he knows but is simply not telling her. The presumptuousness of the therapist's authority is outdone only by Eve's willingness to give hers up. Contrast this view of

DOI: 10.4324/9781003264095-40

psychoanalysis with the exchange between the prostitute and her analyst in *Klute* (Pakula, 1967), where the patient is exasperated that her analyst will not give her advice. The analyst asks if she (her patient) assumes she knows the answers and the patient reminds her that *that* is why she pays her.

A patient of mine is frustrated and wishes I could read his mind. A second later, he reconsiders and says, "No, only what I *want* you to know!" These days, it is politically incorrect to want this power. In modern times (before), knowledge was assumed and the unanswered question was interpreted as a purposeful, knowing restraint. But silence too often left the therapist's power unexamined, a posture interpreted by the patient as a way of acting *as if* we knew, leaving the patient wondering or assuming that we do. The *decontaminated transference* was defined as the patient's way of relating to the analyst that took the analyst out of the picture. These were moments when the analyst participated in the illusion of *not being in it with* the patient. Neutrality used to be conceived as an attempt to avoid bias and influence; we now know that the analyst's bias (i.e., perspective) is in itself influential. Even an interpretation suggests a construction that says, "Let's make it so." To recognize my continuous participation is to accept the continuous shaping of my perspective.

A patient begins an hour commenting that in our last session I revealed I did not know what *myocrismus* is. He talked about how unself-conscious I was about my gap in knowledge. He then was critical of his former therapist who was a "know it all," suggesting art galleries in New York he should visit and such. Later in the hour he quoted some advice she had given him. When I called his attention to this contradiction, suggesting that perhaps he *wanted* me to "know it all," he admitted that my gaps in knowledge made him nervous.

"Dr." *Mumford* (Kasdan, 1999) spends most of the film in a posture that pretends he knows what he's doing. He is a con-man posing as a therapist in order to forget his past and carve a new identity. When he sheds the illusion (actually he's found out), he admits he had lied about almost everything except knowing how to do therapy. Even in the end, when he denies all claims to being a therapist, a taxi driver insists on baring his soul. This is the "there" in *Being There* (Ashby, 1980) the innocent, non-authoritative presence that our patients seem to want and not want. The stance encompasses two impossibilities: an unbiased knowing and a non-influential power. Failing these, we have a new humility, not a restrained expression about what the analyst knows, but a willingness to *be there with*, an attitude that includes an expectation of being caught up in a way that implicates our unconscious participation, something we cannot know or predict ahead of time. It's a knowing *that* and a willingness *to*, without knowing *what, when or how,* i.e., an uncertain knowing that derives from the fact that the intrapsychic cannot be divorced from the interactional sphere. We know that there is no apprehension of the external without this structuring, no recognition of the external field without our mutual involvement in it. How the intrapsychic structures the external field by both patient and analyst is the recursive and extended reach of contemporary psychoanalysis.

The pull to know right and wrong *objectively* is driven by a persistent wish: that great panel of judges in the sky ... but then again, only when the verdict is in our favor! Moving away from this inevitable pull requires a constant push toward the realization and disappointment that there is no such jury. Even a cruel but just god is preferable to the devil of infinite uncertainty.

When a patient consulted me about her agitation over Y2K (to the point of stockpiling food and water), part of my attraction to working with her involved the fact that her prediction would soon be tested. Objective reality promised to intrude by virtue of a change in date, arbitrating her vision and determining in black and white whether it was right or wrong. No such arbitration generally exists. Reality conspires to accommodate a wide range of interpretation by virtue of its inherent plasticity.

What this example reflects is the need to bring into some resolution both the need for internal coherence and the need to accommodate reality. Transference is no longer *a* lens through which reality is judged and distorted, it is *the* lens that ascribes meaning to all that is perceived. Transference does not exist alongside the real. Transference defines *what is real*, it is the structure through which reality is constructed and organized. In the treatment dyad, it is not possible to be outside of the structuring of the transference/countertransference matrix.[2]

Likewise, it is not possible to view reality except through a subjective lens. It is the eye that sees, the apparatus that the psychoanalytic process aims to deconstruct. The question is whether or not this or that co-construction *makes sense* of the past and *works* in the present, not whether it is right or wrong. Because we spoke about her anxiety in these terms, my patient was not overly humiliated when Y2K dropped with a thud. She dreaded the date and I, though concerned about her, looked forward to it. Still, a week before New Year's, I bought an extra case of Pellegrino.

Notes

1 This essay was originally published in The Psychotherapy Forum, a publication sponsored by *The Boston Psychoanalytic Society and Institute*, Boston, MA, 1996.
2 See Essay 1, *Transference, real or unreal* (this volume).

Chapter 37

"Yes and ...." dreams [1]

My son is an improvisational actor. He has taught me the fundamental ethic of the improv world. It is called "*Yes, and* .... ." This is an attitude to which each actor commits, an affirmational stance that accepts anything that comes up. Sounds like our ethic – an affirmative receptivity to all that is in our patient's mind. But I want to call attention to one effect of this ethic, this "*Yes, and* ..." attitude that is conveyed when everyone adopts it. There proliferates an atmosphere of safety that allows for creativity and for taking risks. We tell our patients, "Say whatever comes to mind ...." and if we adopt an affirmative attitude, the atmosphere will be safe enough so that they might actually tell us something of what is on their mind. This safety is for us too, so that we may be receptive to *our own* minds, allow us to affirm an association, a reverie, a daydream that may have arisen *within us* because our patient unconsciously conveyed it *to* us. Do we dare risk affirming what comes from inside us on their behalf?

Stein, the wisened, alcoholic mentor to Conrad's *Lord Jim* (1924) tells Lord Jim, "We are born and we fall into a dream." Shakespeare observed that all the world's a stage. We tell our stories, narrate our lives and construct a universe in which we can live. These universes shift and sometimes radically change as we elaborate our perspectives. We evolve as we narrate our scripts. These universes have props, characters (not necessarily human) and exist in an enlargening field. We are creating a field now, between author and reader. Who is center stage, in a narrative with readers and where we regularly break the fourth wall?

To introduce Irene, I will tell you only briefly that she has been in analysis with a supervisee for several years for incapacitating depression and difficulty in interpersonal relationships (angry outbursts) which have stood in the way of her maintaining steady, satisfying love, life and work. She comes from a family where emotional resources were limited, her mother being preoccupied with (for her) too many children, depressed and unavailable. Irene has felt chronically unloved by her, making her father the primary, but sporadic love object. He is a commercial pilot and is often absent from the family. As a little girl, Irene would wait for him by the window when he left

DOI: 10.4324/9781003264095-41

for his trips and though she felt she was his favorite, there were traumas of separation and loss.

As one can imagine, the birth of Irene's third younger sister (four sisters in all) was a catastrophe as she had to compete for her father's limited attention and time. She retreated into books but was known to throw them against a wall in fits of temper. (I just had the image of the fourth wall; was she, then and now, trying to directly tell us something?).

Irene's parents divorced when she was a teenager, all the girls remaining with their mother. Her father, unfortunately for Irene, became more successful in his career, which included increasing travel, so he was unreliable and sometimes failed to visit her and her sisters for months. When Irene was older, she confronted him about this and he dismissed her, telling her she was always exaggerating and blaming. In later years, this pattern would play out in many of her romantic relationships, each blaming the other for a variety of failings. She had this same kind of trouble at various jobs, sometimes resulting in her being fired.

In taking up our story at this point, I would like to delineate a particular character that stands out to me. That is one of Irene's books – a *Nancy Drew* story involving the young detective searching under a stairwell for, ironically, a missing book. I consider books as prominent characters in the field because it is books that, to me, comprise Irene's universe, i.e., her way of narrating her story and delineating the idioms and meanings of her life. There are many books in Irene's universe. There is the book of her sisters' intrusions. There is the book that she and her analyst are writing together. There is her analyst's book – the collection of papers she has written about Irene to present at conferences and those she writes to present Irene to me. Many of these books have stories Irene cannot yet live with – she feels some stories have been stolen, some are stories by which she feels persecuted and some reflect dreams she is yet to realize.

There is a story in one book that speaks of Irene being dethroned. (I meant to write dethroned, d-e-t-h-r-o-n-e-d as in demoted from a throne, but misspelled the word as d-e-t-h-r-o-w-n-e-d, an unconscious slip with meaning we will weave into this fabric.) In this book, Irene is a Cinderella character, chosen by the prince [her father, as she sat on a bench close to him] until her [wicked step-]sister shoved her off [and the prince/father had no reaction]. Irene has this memory and has told it to her analyst. This is not a story she can as yet live with.

Another story from Irene's analysis is played out repeatedly. She wants to know personal details about her analyst's life. Perhaps she experiences her analyst's disciplined decentered focus (the asymmetry in the analytic set-up) as something like her father's absences, we don't know, but what we do know is that it is intolerable to her. She is hurt by the asymmetry in the analytic relationship and she often seems, to her analyst, to want an apology. She wants a new ending to the many losses, separations and absences – a new ending she can live with.

But Irene demands it, in a doer/done-to manner that constricts her analyst (my supervisee). This goes against my supervisee's usual warmth and receptivity toward her patients. Irene manages to constrict her, demands a response in a way that commands her analyst to submit to Irene. This scene reminds me of a scenario with one of my patients who wanted to know personal facts of my life and I found myself *less* revealing, *more constricted* with him than with any of my other patients. I felt guilty because he was so hurt by my refusals. How sadistic of me! I was responding, as my supervisee has for many years with Irene, with a *"No, but ....."* Similar to when Irene's father refused to apologize for disappearing from her life, he responded with a "No, *you!*" This is part of the story that repeats.

What of this repetition compulsion, the tendency to repeat patterns from the past in search of corrective, new outcomes? This is the underlying premise of my supervisee's understanding and formulation of therapeutic action. It is not wrong. It is an historical reconstructive model that underlies many theoretical orientations: Freudian, neo-Freudian, ego-psychological, self-psychology and relational to name a few. It requires a certain cognitive set, one that is rational, causal, somewhat linear and directed in the way it constructs links from the past to the present,[2] though these are not in one-to-one correspondence with actual events. The past is constructed in the present looking back, *après coup* and then transforms the present as well.

If we take the perspective that our unconscious is *potential*, that it is formed only in the moment that we access our experience in one of many multiple and diverse ways, another model comes to mind that fits this narrative as well. Irene has several dissociated self-states (herself as a little girl, her father's favorite – dethroned at her third sister's birth, another whose parents divorced when she was a teenager and her woman-self with too many romantic break-ups and job losses). These are all characters on the stage of her life and whom she cannot leave behind. She must pick them up, engage them where they are (herein lies the repetition) and write a script she can live with in a universe of benign, loving others who are transformed by her powers. The princes will find all the shoes that fit. An apology, a marriage of sorts, a story of love and acceptance, a *"Yes, and ... ."*

However, my supervisee (Irene's analyst) generally does not address Irene's anger, resentment and consequent dominant insistence. Instead, she attempts to provide Irene with a new interactive/relational experience in the dyadic interplay to counter the internalized self-other configurations she has constructed and that will be retranslated. This is evident in the ways my supervisee attends to historical repetitions. She tells me of the binds of doer/done and dominance/submission modes of interacting with Irene, how these are rooted in her past experiences, internalized and emergent in the here-and-now. She also describes how she tries to free herself and Irene by being the person Irene needs her to be. She apologizes and there, by her example, gives Irene the experience of the difference between surrender and submission. Irene is changed by this.

What would a more diffuse, receptive cognitive set add to this process? I was in Australia when I read my supervisee's most recent case write-up of Irene. The books, the dethroning (including my cognitive slip, spelling it as d-e-t-h-r-o-w-n-e-d), Irene's angry outbursts and all the losses. My being in Australia at the time enlarges the receptive field, the unconscious setting for my processing of Irene as I experience her. I associated to the children's book, *Alexander and the Terrible, Horrible, No Good, Very Bad Day* (Viorst, 2014) and the many times Alexander says that he'd rather be in Australia. My husband and I were out to dinner and struck up a conversation with a friendly waiter who told us he had just undergone a house fire in Perth – all his belongings lost. I thought of Irene's books up in flames – an image of all the losses she underwent. Then I thought about a part of the story that persistently vexes my supervisee and me about Irene. Why did she have so many losses in romance and all the difficulties at work? The idiom of *being thrown away* came to mind (as in my misspelling) and I also wondered about Irene's character, especially her ability to throw things away. Interpersonally, pushing away, throwing away, being thrown away came to my mind.

In our next supervisory meeting, I suggested that my supervisee use these musings and play with me, with the assumption of the supervisory field as an enlargement of the clinical field. In our discussion, we came to a potential intervention, such as, "It's better to be the thrower than the thrown." When my supervisee expressed this to Irene in the following session, Irene was able to hear something in this message, something about her tendency to push or throw others away. (I think she was able to hear my supervisee's benign intent because of the way it incorporated a "*Yes, and ...*" sentiment.) This also matched something of my supervisee's countertransference, immersed in the transference/countertransference dyadic doer/done-to interplay. We surmised that my supervisee's constriction probably had something to do with a fear that Irene might throw her away.

Embedded in my reveries is my imagining that I am Irene's analyst. What part would I play in Irene's drama, what part do I want or which part would be forced upon me? The [wicked step-]sister replacing her on the bench/throne would be one that she would need me to play out, no doubt. I would protest this one (as my supervisee did as well) and insist that gender does not define me any more than it does my supervisee. Why must I take *that* part? I want to be Stein, the wisened old man that has a meta-perspective, the one who knows we live in a dream – a waking dream of our own unconscious construction.

As I returned home, I began writing this essay and the images of a "diffuse cognitive set"[3] along with "unbidden affective states" kept reverberating in my mind. Did I have an example of that? Irene throwing people away is a relationally configured reverie ... but another one came to mind. I kept imagining Irene throwing her books. Throwing away the book, so to speak. Was this relevant? In the subsequent weeks, my supervisee and I played with that as well.

What parts would you take on, dear reader, as you question, reflect and let your mind wander through your own constructing paths? I hope the response you receive will be "*Yes, and ... .*"

Notes

1 A longer version of this paper was originally presented at *The Lawrence E. Lifson Psychotherapy Conference,* Boston, MA, March, 2018.
2 See Essay 14, *Stance and attentional set in analytic listening*, Essay 15, *Directed attentional set* and Essay 17, *Stance, set, transference* (all this volume).
3 See Essay 16, *Diffuse attentional set* (this volume).

References

Abram, D. (1996). *The Spell of the Sensuous*. New York: Vintage Books.

Akhtar, S. (2000). From schisms through synthesis to informed oscillation: An attempt at integrating some diverse aspects of psychoanalytic technique. *Psychoanalytic Quarterly* 69(2):265–288.

Akhtar, S. (2009). *Comprehensive Dictionary of Psychoanalysis*. London: Karnac.

Antonis, B. (2015). Controversial discussions: Independent women analysts and thoughts about listening to experience. *British Journal of Psychotherapy* 31(1):96–106.

Aragno, A. (2008). The language of empathy: An analysis of its constitution, development, and role in psychoanalytic listening. *Journal of the American Psychoanalytic Association* 56(3):713–740.

Arberry, A.J. (1947). *Discourses of Rumi*. London, England: RoutledgeCurzon. ISBN 0-7007-0274-1 (Print Edition).

Arlow, J.A. (1971). Character perversion. In I.M. Marcus (Ed.) *Currents in Psychoanalysis*. New York: International University Press.

Arlow, J.A. (1987). Trauma, play and perversion. *Psychoanalytic Study of the Child* 42:31–44.

Aron, L. (1991). The patient's experience of the analyst's subjectivity. *Psychoanalytic Dialogues* 1:29–51.

Aron, L. (1996). *Meeting of Minds: Mutuality in Psychoanalysis*. Hillsdale, NJ: Analytic Press.

Aron, L. (1998). The clinical body and the reflexive mind. In L. Aron and F.S. Anderson (Eds.) *Relational Perspectives on the Body*, pp. 3–38. Hillsdale, NJ: Analytic Press.

Aron, L. (2000). Self-reflexivity and the therapeutic action of psychoanalysis. *Psychoanalysis Psychology* 17:667–689.

Aron, L. (2012). The analyst's vulnerability: how "The Repudiation of Femininity" remains bedrock (Ghosts, monsters, mulattoes, queers, undecidables, and other thirds). Paper presented at the Lifson Conference, Boston, MA.

Aron, L. (2018). Beyond tolerance in psychoanalytic communities: Reflexive skepticism and critical pluralism. In L. Aron, S. Grand and J. Slochower (Eds.) *Decentering Relational Theory: A Comparative Critique*, pp. 200–215. London & NY: Routledge.

Aron, L. and Anderson, F.S. (Eds.) (1998). *Relational Perspectives on the Body.* Hillsdale, NJ: Analytic Press.

Ashby, H. dir. (1980). *Being There.* BSB, US.

Atlas, G. (2016). *The Enigma of Desire: Sex, Longing, and Belonging in Psychoanalysis.* New York: Routledge.

Bader, M.J. (1993). Adaptive sadomasochism and psychological growth. *Psychoanlaytic Dialogues* 2:279–300.

Bakewell, S. (2016). *At the Existentialist Café: Freedom, Being and Apricot Cocktails.* New York, NY: The Other Press.

Balchin, R., Barry, V., Bazan, A., Blechner, B.J., Clarici, A., Flores-Mosri, D., Fotopoulou, K., Sonia-Goergen, M., Kessler, R., Matthis, I., Munoz-Zuni, J.F., Northoff, G., Olds, D., Oppenheim, L., Reismann-Lagreze, D., Tsakiris, M., Watt, D.F., Yeates, G. and Zellner, M. (2019). Reflections on 20 years of neuropsychoanalysis. *Neuropsychoanalysis* 21(2):89–123.

Balsam, R. (2003). The vanished pregnant body in psychoanalytic developmental theory. *Journal American Psychoanalytic Association* 51(4):1153–1179.

Balsam, R.H. (2012). *Women's Bodies in Psychoanalysis.* New York, NY: Routledge.

Balsam, R.H. (2014). The embodied mother: Commentary on Kristeva. *Journal of the American Psychoanalytic Association* 62(1):87–100.

Balsam, R.H. (2019). On the natal body and its confusing place in mental life. *Journal of the American Psychoanalytic Association* 67(1):15–36.

Baranger, M. and Baranger, W. (2008). The analytic situation as a dynamic field. *International Journal of Psychoanalysis* 89:795–826 (original work published in 1961–1962).

Baranger, M., Baranger, W. and Mom, J. (1983). Process and non-process in analytic work. *International Journal of Psychoanalysis* 64:1–15.

Bassin, D. (1996). Beyond the he and the she: Toward the reconciliation of masculinity and femininity in the postoedipal female mind. *Journal American Psychoanalytic Association* 44 S:157–190.

Bataille, G. (1957/1986). *Erotism: Death and Sensuality.* New York, NY: City Lights.

Benjamin, J (1988). *The Bonds of Love: Psychoanalysis, Feminism, and the Problem of Domination.* New York, NY: Pantheon.

Benjamin, J. (1994). What angel would hear me? The erotics of transference. *Psychoanalytic Inquiry* 14:535–556.

Benjamin, J. (1995). *Like Subjects, Love Objects: Essays on Recognition and Sexual Difference.* New Haven, CN: Yale Univ. Press.

Benjamin, J. (1998). *The Shadow of the Other: Intersubjectivity and Gender in Psychoanalysis.* New York, NY: Routledge.

Benjamin, J. (2013). *Embodiment and Subjectivity, Discussion.* Paper presented at the American Psychoanalytic Association, Winter Meeting, New York, NY.

Benjamin, J. (2014). Beyond doer and done to: An intersubjective view of thirdness. In L. Aron and A. Harris (Eds.) *Relational Psychoanalysis Volume 4: The Expansion of Theory (Relational Perspectives Book Series)*, pp. 91–130. NY: Routledge.

Bernardi, R. (2017). A common ground in clinical discussion groups: Intersubjective resonance and implicit operational theories. *International Journal Psychoanalysis*, 98:1291–1309.

Bion, W.R. (1959). Attacks on linking. *International Journal Psychoanalysis*, 40:308–315.

Bion, W.R. (1965a). *Transformations*. London: Karnac.

Bion, W.R. (1965b). Memory and desire. In C. Mawson (Ed.) *The Complete Works of W.R. Bion: Vol. VI*, pp. 3–17, 2014. London, England: Routledge.

Bion, W.R. (1967). *Second Thoughts: Selected Papers on Psycho-Analysis*. London: Heinemann.

Bion, W.R. (1970). *Attention and Interpretation*. London: Tavistock.

Birksted-Breen, D. (1996). Unconscious representation of femininity. *Journal of the American Psychoanalytic Association* 44(s):119–132.

Blass, R. (2017). Committed to a single mode and open to reality. *Journal American Psychoanalytic Association* 65(5):845–858.

Bollas, C. (1982). On the relation to the self as an object. *International Journal of Psychoanalysis* 63:347–359.

Bollas, C. (1987). *The Shadow of the Object: Psychoanalysis of the Unthought Known*. New York, NY: Columbia Univ Press.

Bolognini, S. (1994). Transference: Erotised, erotic, loving, affectionate. *International Journal of Psychoanalysis* 75:73–86.

Bolognini, S. (2011a). The analyst's awkward gift: Balancing recognition of sexuality with parental protectiveness. *Psychoanalytic Quarterly* LXXX:33–54.

Bolognini, S. (2011b). *Secret Passages: The Theory and Technique of Interpsychic Relations*. [Gina Atkinson, trans.], NY: Routledge.

Bolognini, S. (2011c). The psychosexuality of mucous membranes. In *Secret Passages: The Theory and Technique of Interpsychic Relations*. [Gina Atkinson, trans.], pp. 107–117. NY: Routledge.

Bonaminio, V. (2017). Transference before transference. *Psychoanalytic Quarterly* 86(4):795–810.

Bressler, S.L. and Menon, V. (2010). Large scale brain networks in cognition: Emerging methods and principles. *Trends in Cognitive Sciences* 14(6):233–290. doi:10.1016/j.tics.2010.04.004

Britton, R. (2004). Subjectivity, objectivity and triangular space. *Psychoanalytic Quarterly* 73:47–61.

Bromberg, P. (1998). *Standing in the Spaces: Essays on Clinical Process, Trauma and Dissociation*. Hillsdale, NJ: The Analytic Press.

Butler, J. (1995). Melancholy gender-refused identification. *Psychoanalytic Dialogues* 5(2):165–180.

Carignan, L. (1999). The secret: Study of a perverse transference. *International Journal Psychoanalysis* 80(5):909–928.

Carnochan, P. (2013). Fields of thought and action in psychoanalysis: Commentary on paper by Donnel B. Stern. *Psychoanalytic Dialogues* 23:654–659.

Celenza, A. (2000a). Sadomasochistic relating: What's sex got to do with it? *Psychoanalytic Quarterly* 69(3):527–543.

Celenza, A. (2000b). Postmodern solutions and the limit-opportunity dialectic: The challenge of female penetration and male receptivity. *Gender and Psychoanalysis* 5:347–357.

Celenza, A. (2005). Vis à vis the couch: Where is psychoanalysis? *International Journal of Psychoanalysis* 86:1–14.

Celenza, A. (2006). The threat of male to female erotic transference. *Journal American Psychoanalytic Association* 54(4):1207–1232.

Celenza, A. (2007). *Sexual Boundary Violations: Therapeutic, Academic, and Supervisory Contexts.* New York: Jason Aronson.

Celenza, A. (2010a). The guilty pleasure of erotic countertransference: Searching for radial true. *Studies in Gender and Sexuality* 11(4):175–184.

Celenza, A. (2010b). The analyst's need and desire. *Psychoanalytic Dialogues* 20:60–69.

Celenza, A. (2014). *Erotic Revelations: Clinical Applications and Perverse Scenarios.* London: Routledge.

Celenza, A. (2017). *Book review, A teaching anthology: The Interpersonal Perspective in Psychoanalysis, 1960s–1990s: Rethinking Transference and Countertransference.* D.B. Stern and I. Hirsch (Eds.). New York: Routledge.

Celenza, A. (2019). From relation to the field: Modes of unconscious fantasy elaborations. *International Forum Psychoanalysis* 28(4):203–211.

Celenza, A. (2021). Shadows that corrupt: Present absences in psychoanalytic process. In C. Levin and M. Dimen (Eds.) *Boundary Trouble: Psychosexual Violations and Intimacy in Psychoanalysis.* New York: Routledge.

Celenza, A. (2022a). Maternal erotic transferences and the work of the abject. *Journal American Psychoanalytic Association* 70(1):9–38.

Celenza, A. (2022b). Necessary suffering, bravery of prey: Commentary on "Dominant perversions; perverse dominance: Eroticized schemata and dissociative phenomena in the case of Daniel." *Psychoanalytic Perspectives* 19:96–107.

Chase, D. dir. (1999). *The Sopranos.* US: HBO.

Chasseguet-Smirgel, J. (1970). *Female Sexuality: New Psychoanalytic Views.* London: Karnac.

Chasseguet-Smirgel, J. (1976). Freud and female sexuality: The consideration of some blind spots in the exploration of the 'dark continent.' *International Journal Psychoanalysis* 57:275–286.

Chasseguet-Smirgel, J. (1999). Oedipus and psyche. *British Journal Psychotherapy* 15:465–475.

Chica, A.B., Bartolomeo, P. and Lupiáñez, J. (2013). Two cognitive and neural systems for endogenous and exogenous spatial attention. *Behavior Brain Research* Jan 15, 237:107–123. doi: 10.1016/j.bbr.2012.09.027. Epub 2012 Sep 21.

Chodorow, N. (2011). *Individualizing Gender and Sexuality: Theory and Practice,* New York: Routledge.

Civitarese, G. (2008). *The Intimate Room: Theory and Technique of the Analytic Field.* D. Birksted-Breen (Ed.) The New Library of Psychoanalysis. London: Institute of Psychoanalysis. London: Routledge.

Coen, S. (2019). Creating meaning within the rules of the game: Psychoanalysis as playful rite to manage intimacy. Paper presented at *International Psychoanalytic Association,* London, England.

Coen, S. (2021). The hijacked infantile erotic and its management in adult analysis. Paper presented *at internationalPsychoanalytic Association,* Vancouver, BC.

Conrad, J. (1924). *Lord Jim: A Romance.* New York: Doubleday.

Cooper, S.H. (2013). Introduction to two-part panel on the concept of the "Analytic Field". *Psychoanalytic Dialogues* 23:485–486.

Cooper, S.H. (2015). Clinical theory at the border(s): Emerging and unintended crossings in the development of clinical theory. *International Journal Psychoanalysis* 96:273–292.

Cooper, S.H. (2016). Blurring boundaries or why do we refer to sexual misconduct with patients as "Boundary Violation". *Psychoanalytic Dialogues* 26:206–214.

Cooper, S.H. (2017). The analyst's "use" of theory or theories: The play of theory. *Journal American Psychoanalytic Association* 65(5):859–882.

Corbett, K. (2013). Shifting sexual cultures, the potential space of online relations and the promise of psychoanalytic listening. *Journal of the American Psychoanalytic Association* 61:25–44.

The Boston Change Process Study Group (CPSG), Bruschweiler-Stern, N., Harrison, A.M., Lyons-Ruth, K., Morgan, A.C., Nahum, J.P., Sander, L.W., Stern, D.N.N. and Tronick, E.Z. (2002). Explicating the implicit: The local level and the mircoprocess of change in the analytic situation. *International Journal of Psychoanalysis* 83(5):1051–1062.

D'Agostino, G. (2011). Analytic listening as a holding function of the dissociated parts of the patient. *International Forum of Psychoanalysis* 20(1):31–37.

Damasio, A. (1994). *Descartes' Error: Emotion, Reason and the Human Brain*. New York: Putnam.

Davies, J. (1996). Linking the 'pre-analytic' with the postclassical: Integration, dissociation, and the multiplicity of unconscious process. *Contemp. Psychoanalysis* 32:553–576.

Davies, J. (1998). Between disclosure and foreclosure of erotic transference-countertransference. *Psychoanalytic Dialogues* 8:747–766.

De Palma, B. dir. (1980). *Dressed to Kill*. US: Filmways

De Sade, M. (2013). *The 120 Days of Sodom*. New York, NY: Wilder.

Demme, J. dir. (1991). *Silence of the Lambs*. US: Orion.

Deutsch, H. (1942). Some forms of emotional disturbance and their relationship to schizophrenia. *Psychoanalytic Quarterly* 11:301–321.

Dimen, M. (1991). Deconstructing difference: Gender, splitting, and transitional space. *Psychoanalytic Dialogues* 1:335–352.

Dimen, M. (1999). Between lust and libido: Sex psychoanalysis and the moment before. *Psychoanalytic Dialogues* 9:415–440.

Dimen, M. (2003). *Sexuality, Intimacy, Power*. Hillsdale, NJ: The Analytic Press.

Dimen, M. (2008). Remarks on body-writing: Feminist, one-person, and two-person views. Paper presented at Division 39 Spring Meeting, New York, NY.

Dunn, P.B. (2015). The psychodynamics of voyeurism as portrayed in Hitchcock's *Rear Window*. Paper presented at the Massachusetts Institute of Psychoanalysis, Spring, Boston.

Eidelberg, L. (1948). *Studies in Psychoanalysis*. New York: International University Press.

Eiguer, A. (2007). The intersubjective links in perversion. *International Journal Psychoanalysis* 88:1135–1152.

Eissler, K.R. (1953). The effect of the structure of the ego on psychoanalytic technique. *Journal American Psychoanalytic Association* 1:104–143.

Eliot, T.S. (1943). *Four Quartets*. NY: Harcourt.

Elise, D. (2002). The primary maternal oedipal situation and female homoerotic desire. *Psychoanalytic Inquiry* 22:209–228.

Elise, D. (2015). Eroticism in the maternal matrix: Infusion through development and the clinical situation. *Fort Da* 21(2):17–32.

Elise, D. (2017). Moving from within the maternal: The choreography of analytic eroticism. *Journal of the American Psychoanalytic Association* 65(1): 33–60.

Elise, D. (2019). *Creativity and the Erotic Dimensions of the Analytic Field*. New York: Routledge.

Embry, E. (2016). The bull's eye is all around us: Do or do not. There is no try. Unpublished manuscript.

Erreich, A. (2003). A modest proposal: (Re)defining unconscious fantasy. *Psychoanalytic Quarterly* 72(3):541–574.

Etchegoyen, R.H. (1978). Some thoughts on transference perversion. *International Journal Psychoanalysis* 59:45–53.

Faimberg, H. (2019). Basic theoretical assumptions underpinning Faimberg's method: "Listening to listening". *International Journal of Psychoanalysis* 100(3):447–462.

Fairbairn (1952). *Psychoanalytic Studies of the Personality*. London: Tavistock. 312 p.

Faulkner, W. (1951). *Requiem for a Nun*. New York: Random House.

Federn, P. (1952). *Ego Psychology and the Psychoses*. London: Imago.

Fenichel, O. (1937). The scopophilic instinct and identification. *International Journal Psychoanalysis* 18:6–34.

Ferenczi, S. (1928). The elasticity of psycho-analytic technique. Lecture given to the Hungarian Psycho-analytic Society, 1927. In M. Balint (Ed.) *Final Contributions to the Problems and Methods of Psycho-Analysis*, pp. 87–101. London: Maresfield Reprints.

Ferenczi, S. (1932a). The language of the unconscious. In *Final Contributions*. London: Hogarth Press.

Ferenczi, S. (1932b). Suppression of the idea of the 'grotesque'. In *Final Contributions*. London: Hogarth Press.

Ferrari, A.B. (2004). *From the Eclipse of the Body to the Dawn of Thought*. London: Free Association Books.

Ferro, A. (2009). Transformations in dreaming and characters in the analytic field. *International Journal of Psychoanalysis* 90:209–230.

Ferro, A. and Civitarese, G. (2013). Analysts in search of an author: Voltaire or Artemisia Gentileschi? Commentary on "Field theory in psychoanalysis, Part 2: Bionian field theory and contemporary Interpersonal/Relational psychoanalysis" by Donnel Stern. *Psychoanalytic Dialogues* 23:646–653.

Foehl, J. (2009). Discussion of "Expression between self and other by Lisa Folkmarson Kall". Paper presented at *the Boston Psychoanalytic Society and Institute*, Boston, Massachusetts, February 25, 2009.

Foehl, J. (2013a). Introduction to the second panel on the concept of the "Analytic Field". *Psychoanalytic Dialogues* 23:627–629.

Foehl, J. (2013b). Field theory: Commentary on paper by Donnel B. Stern. *Psychoanalytic Dialogues* 23:502–513.

Folkmarson Kall, L. (2009). Expression between self and other: A phenomenological understanding of intersubjectivity. Paper presented at the *Boston Psychoanalytic Society and Institute*, Boston, Massachusetts, February 25, 2009.

Fonagy, P. (2008). A genuinely developmental theory of sexual enjoyment and its implications for psychoanalytic technique. *Journal American Psychoanalytic Association* 56:11–36.

Fonagy, P. and Target, M. (2007). The rooting of the mind in the body: New links between attachment theory and psychoanalytic thoughts. *Journal American Psychoanalytic Association* 55:411–456.

Foucault, M. (1978). *The History of Sexuality*. (Vol. I). New York, NY: Vintage.

Freud, S. (1895). Project for a scientific psychology. *Standard Edition* 1:281–387.

Freud, S. (1900). The interpretation of dreams. *Standard Edition*. 4 & 5.

Freud, S. (1905). Three essays on the theory of sexuality. *Standard Edition* VII (1901–1905):123–246.

Freud, S. (1907). Letter from Sigmund Freud to Karl Abraham, July 7, 1907. *The Complete Correspondence of Sigmund Freud and Karl Abraham, 1907–1925*, 1–4.

Freud, S. (1910). 'Wild' psycho-analysis. *Standard Edition, Volume XI (1910): Five Lectures on Psycho-Analysis, Leonardo da Vinci and Other Works*, 219–228.

Freud, S. (1912). Recommendations to physicians practicing psycho-analysis. *Standard Edition* XII:111–120.

Freud, S. (1914). On narcissism: An introduction. *Standard Edition* XIV:73–102. London: Hogarth Press, 1961.

Freud, S. (1915a). Observations on transference love. *Standard Edition* XII:157–171. London, Hogarth Press, 1961.

Freud, S. (1915b). Instincts and their vicissitudes. *Standard Edition* 14:109–140.

Freud, S. (1916–1917). Introductory lectures on psycho-analysis. *Standard Edition* 15 and 16.

Freud, S. (1917). Mourning and melancholia. *Standard Edition* XIV:237–258.

Freud, S. (1921). Group psychology and the analysis of the ego. *Standard Edition* XVIII(1920–1922).

Freud, S. (1927). Fetishism. *Standard Edition*. XXI:152–157.

Freud, S. (1931). Female sexuality. *Standard Edition* 21:223–246.

Freud, S. (1937). Analysis terminable and interminable. *Standard Edition* 23:209–254.

Gabbard, G.O. (1994). Psychotherapists who transgress sexual boundaries with patients. *Bulletin of Menninger Clinic* 58:124–135.

Gabbard, G.O. (2016). *Boundaries and Boundary Violations in Psychoanalysis*. Arlington, Virginia: American Psychiatric Association Publishing.

Gabbard, G.O. and Lester, E. (1995). *Boundaries and Boundary Violations in Psychoanalysis*. New York: Basic Books.

Gaddini, E. (1969). On imitation. *International Journal Psychoanalysis* 50:475–484.

Gallese, V. (2001). The "shared manifold" hypothesis: From mirror neurons to empathy. *Journal of Consciousness Studies* 8(5–7):33–50.

Gharaibeh, N.M. (2005), The psychiatrist's image in commercially available American movies. *Acta Psychiatrica Scandinavica* 111:316–319.

Gill, M. (1984). Psychoanalysis and psychotherapy: A revision. *International Review of Psycho-Analysis* 11:161–179.

Gillespie, C. dir. (2007). *Lars and the Real Girl*. US: Sidney Kimmel Entertainment.

Goldberger, M. (1995). The couch as defense and as potential for enactment. *Psychoanalytic Quarterly* 64:23–42.

Goldner, V. (1991). Toward a critical relational theory of gender. *Psychoanalytic Dialogues* 1:249–272.

Goodman, N., Beseeches, H., Ellman, P., Elmendorf, S., Fritsch, E., Helm, F.l. and Rockwell, S. (1993, July). In the mind of the psychoanalyst: Capturing the moment before speaking. Paper presented at the *38th International Psychoanalytical Congress*, Amsterdam.

Green, A. (1986). *On Private Madness*. London: Hogarth Press.

Green, A. (1995). Has sexuality anything to do with psychoanalysis? *International Journal of Psychoanalysis* 76:871–883.

Green, A. (1998). The primordial mind and the work of the negative. *International Journal of Psychoanalysis* 79:649–665.

Green, A. (2008). *The Chains of Eros*. London: Karnac.

Greenacre, P. (1958). Toward an understanding of the physical nucleus of some defence reactions. *International Journal Psychoanalysis* 39:69–76.

Greenberg, J. (1986). Theoretical models and the analyst's neutrality. *Contemporary Psychoanalysis* 22:87–106.

Greenson, R.R. (1966). A transvestite boy and a hypothesis. *International Journal Psychoanalysis* 47:396–403.

Greenson, R. (1967). *The Technique and Practice of Psychoanalysis*. New York, NY: International UP.

Griffin, F.L. (2016). *Creative Listening and the Psychoanalytic Process: Sensibility, Engagement, and Envisioning*. Abingdon, UK/New York: Routledge.

Grossman, L. (2015). The object-preserving function of sadomasochism. *Psychoanalytic Quarterly* 84(3):643–664.

Grotstein, J. (1994). Endopsychic structure and the cartography of the internal world: Six endopsychic characters in search of an author. In Grotstein J.S. and Rinsley D.B. (Eds.) *Fairbairn and the Origins of Object Relations*, pp. 174–194. New York, NY: Guilford.

Grotstein, J. (2000). *Who is the Dreamer Who Dreams the Dream?* Hillsdale, NJ: The Analytic Press.

Hamelmann-Fischer, D. (2016). Understanding and not-understanding: Oscillating between different forms of listening. *Romanian Journal of Psychoanalysis* 9(2):67–79.

Harlem, A. (2010). Exile as a dissociative state: When a self is "Lost in Transit". *Psychoanalytic Psychology* 27(4):460–474.

Harris, A. (1996). The conceptual power of multiplicity. *Contemporary Psychoanalysis* 32: 537–552.

Harris, A. (2005). *Gender as Soft Assembly*. Hillsdale, NJ: The Analytic Press.

Harris, A. (2009). You Must Remember This. *Psychoanalytic Dialogues* 19:2–21.

Harris, A. (2011). The relational tradition: Landscape and canon. *Journal American Psychoanalytic Association* 59(4):701–735.

Havens, L. (1997). A linguistic contribution to psychoanalysis: The concept of performative contradictions. *Psychoanalytic Dialogues* 7:523–534.

Heimann, P. (1950). On countertransference. *International Journal of Psychoanalysis* 31:81–84.

Helm, F.L. (2000). A continuum of listening and interventions. *Psychoanalytic Psychology* 17(4):730–749.

Hesiod (c. 730-700 BC/2018). *Theogony, Works and Days, and the Shield of Heracles.* H. G. Evelyn-White (trans.). Digireads.com Publishing.

Heusser, S. (2022). Dominant perversions; perverse dominance: Eroticized schemata and dissociative phenomena in the case of Daniel. *Psychoanalytic Perspectives* 19:76–95.

Hilferding, M. (1911/1974). Zur Grundlage der Mutterliebe. In *Protokolle der Wiener Psychoanalytischen Vereinigung III.* (On the basis of mother-love.) In (1974) Minutes of the Vienna Psychoanalytic Society III (pp. 112–125). New York: International Universities Press.

Hirsch, I. (1996). Observing participation, mutual enactment, and the new classical models. *Contemporary Psychoanalysis* 32:359–383.

Hirsch, I. (2015). *The Interpersonal Tradition: The Origins of Psychoanalytic Subjectivity.* New York: Routledge.

Hitchcock, A. (1954). *Rear Window.* Los Angeles, CA: Universal Studios.

Hoffer, A. (1996). Asymmetry and mutuality in the analytic relationship: Contemporary lessons from the Freud-Ferenczi dialogue. In P.L. Rudnytsky, A. Bokay and P. Giampieri-Deutsch (Eds.) *Ferenczi's Turn in Psychoanalysis,* pp. 107–119. NY: NYU Press.

Hoffman, I. (1998). *Ritual and Spontaneity.* Hillsdale, NJ: Analytic Press.

Horney, K. (1926). The flight from womanhood: The masculinity-complex in women as viewed by men and women. *International Journal of Psychoanalysis* 7:324–339.

Irigaray (1989). The gesture in psychoanalysis. In T. Brenman (Ed.) *Between Feminism and Psychoanalysis.* London: Routledge.

Jacobs, T.J. (1992). Contemporary reflections on the analyzing instrument: Isakower's ideas of the analytic instrument and contemporary views of analytic listening. *Journal of Clinical Psychoanalysis* 1(2):237–241.

Jewison, N. dir. (1985). *Agnes of God.* U.S.: Columbia Pictures.

Jiménez, J.P. (2004). A psychoanalytical phenomenology of perversion. *International Journal Psychoanalysis* 85:65–81.

Johnson, N. dir. (1957). *The Three Faces of Eve.* US: Twentieth Century-Fox.

Josephs, L. (2003). The observing ego as voyeur. *International Journal Psychoanalysis* 84:879–890.

Kaplan, L. (1991). *Female Perversions: The Temptations of Emma Bovary.* New York, NY: Doubleday.

Kaplan, L. (2006). *Cultures of Fetishism.* New York, NY: Macmillan.

Kasdan, L. dir. (1999). *Mumford.* U.S.: Touchstone Pictures.

Katz, H. (2004). Motor action, emotion, and motive. *Psychoanalytic Study of the Child* 59:124–142.

Katz, S.M. (2015). *Contemporary Psychoanalytic Field Theory: Stories, Dreams and Metaphor.* New York: Routledge.

Kernberg, O.F. (1994). Love in the analytic setting. *Journal American Psychoanalytic Association* 42:1137–1157.

Knafo, D. and LoBosco, R. (2016). *The Age of Perversion*. New York: Routledge.

Kohut, H. (1968). Evaluation of applicants for psychoanalytic training. *International Journal Psychoanalysis* 49:548–554.

Kohut, H. (1977). *The Restoration of the Self*. New York, NY: International UP. 345 p.

Kristeva, J. (2000). From symbols to flesh: The polymorphous destiny of narration. *International Journal Psychoanalysis* 81(4):771–787.

Kristeva, J. (2011). La reliance, ou de l'érotisme maternel. Available from http://www.kristeva.fr/reliance_film_galabov.html

Kristeva, J. (2014a). Reliance, or maternal eroticism. *Journal of the American Psychoanalytic Association* 62(1):69–86.

Kristeva, J. (2014b). Julia Kristeva comments on the "Maternal Reliance" section in JAPA. *Journal American Psychoanalytic Association* 62(3):NP60–NP64.

Kristeva, J. (2019). Prelude to an ethics of the feminine. Keynote address presented at the *International Psychoanalytic Association*, London, England.

Kulish, N. (1989). Gender and transference: Conversations with female analysts. *Psychoanalytic Psychology* 6:59–71.

Lable, I., Kelley, J.M., Ackerman, J., Levy, R. Jr. and Ablon, J.S. (2010). The role of the couch in psychoanalysis: Proposed research designs and some preliminary data. *Journal American Psychoanalysis Association* 58:861–887.

LaFarge, L. (2000). Interpretation and containment. *International Journal of Psychoanalysis* 81(1):67–84.

Lafarge, L. (2017). From "either/or" to "and": The analyst's use of multiple models in clinical work. *Journal American Psychoanalytic Association* 65(5):829–844.

Laplanche, J. (1989). *New Foundations for Psychoanalysis*, D. Macey, translator. Oxford: Blackwell.

Laplanche, J. (1989). *New Foundations for Psychoanalysis*. London: Blackwell.

Laplanche, J. (1994). Psychoanalysis as anti-hermeneutics. Paper presented at Cerisy colloquium. Also in Laplanche, J. (2015). *Between Seduction and Inspiration: Man*, J. House, (Ed.), 2015, pp. 203–218, New York: The Unconscious in Translation.

Laplanche, J. (1997). The theory of seduction and the problem of the other. *International Journal of Psychoanalysis* 78:653–666.

Laplanche, J. (1999a). The drive and its source-object: Its fate in the transference. In *Essays on Otherness*, pp. 117–132. London: Routledge.

Laplanche, J. (1999b). Transference: Its provocation by the analyst. In *Essays on Otherness*, pp. 214–233. London: Routledge.

Laplanche, J. (2017/2006). *Après Coup*. J. House and L. Thurston (trans.). New York: Unconscious in Translation.

Laplanche, J. and Pontalis, J.B. (1973). *The Language of Psychoanalysis*. D. Nicholson-Smith (trans.). New York: W.W. Norton.

Layton, L. (2004). *Who's That Girl? Who's That Boy? Clinical Practice Meets Postmodern Gender Theory*. New York: Routledge.

Lear, J. (1990). *Love and Its Place in Nature*. New Haven, CN: Yale University Press.

Lear, J. (1998). *Open Minded: Working Out the Logic of the Soul*. Cambridge, MA: Harvard University Press.

Lemma, A. (2015). *Minding the Body: The Body in Psychoanalysis and Beyond*. London: Routledge.

Lemma, A. and Caparrotta, L. (Eds.) (2014). *Psychoanalysis in the Technoculture Era*. London: Routledge.

Lester, E. (1985). The female analyst and the erotized transference. *International Journal of Psychoanalysis* 66:283–293.

Levenson, E.A. (2005). *The Fallacy of Understanding and the Ambiguity of Change*. New York: Analytic Press.

Levi, H. (2008). *B'tipul (In Treatment)*. U.S.: Leverage Management.

Levin, C. (Ed.) (2021). *Sexual Boundary Trouble in Psychoanlysis: clinical Perspectives on Muriel Dimen's Concept of the "Primal Crime."* London: Routledge.

Levine, H. (2013a). Comparing field theories. *Psychoanalytic Dialogues* 23:667–673.

Levine, H. (2013b). The colourless canvas: Representation, therapeutic action, and the creation of mind. In H.B. Levine, G.S. Reed and D. Scarfone (Eds.) *Unrepresented States and the Construction of Meaning: Clinical and Theoretical Contributions*, pp. 42–71, London: Karnac.

Levine, H. (2020). Reflections on therapeutic action and the origins of psychic life. *Journal American Psychoanalytic Association* 68(1):9–25.

Levenson, E.A. (2005). *The Fallacy of Understanding and the Ambiguity of Change*. New York: Analytic Press.

Lichtenberg, J. (2008). *Sensuality and Sexuality across the Divide of Shame*. New York, NY: The Analytic Press.

Lindbergh, A.M. (1955). *Gift from the Sea*. New York: Pantheon.

Lipton, S. (1977). The advantages of Freud's technique as shown in his analysis of the Rat Man. *International Journal Psycho-analysis* 58:255–273.

Litowitz, B.E. (2014). Introduction to Julia Kristeva. *Journal of the American Psychoanalytic Association* 62(1):57–60.

Loewald, H.W. (1960). On the therapeutic action of psycho-analysis. *International Journal Psychoanalysis* 41:16–33.

Loewald, H. (1970). Psychoanalytic theory and the psychoanalytic process. *Psychoanalytic Study of the Child* 25:45–68.

Lombardi, R. (2002). Primitive mental states and the body. A personal view of Armando B. Ferrari's concrete original object. *International Journal Psychoanalysis* 83:363–381.

Lombardi, R. (2008). The body in the analytic session: Focusing on the body-mind link. *International Journal Psychoanalysis* 89:89–110.

Lombardi, R. (2016). *Formless Infinity: Clinical Explorations of Matte Blanco and Bion*. London: Routledge.

Luborsky, L. (2001). The meaning of empirically supported treatment research for psychoanalytic and other long-term therapies. *Psychoanalytic Dialogues* 11(4):583–604.

Malcolm, J. (1980). *Psychoanalysis: The Impossible Profession*. NY: Knopf.

Mares, S. (2010). Home is where we start from: Early experience, play and creative living. *Attachment: New Directions in Psychotherapy and Relational Psychoanalysis* 4:216–231

McDougall, J. (1986). Identifications, neoneeds and neosexualities. *International Journal Psychoanalysis* 67:19–31.

McDougall, J. (1995). *The Many Faces of Eros: A Psychoanalytic Exploration of Human Sexuality*. London: Free Association Books.

McNamara, E. (1994). *Breakdown: Sex, Suicide, and the Harvard Psychiatrist*. New York: Pocket Books.

Meissner W.W. (1998). The self and the body: IV. The body on the couch. *Psychoanalysis and Contemporary Thought* 21:277–300.

Meissner, W.W. (2000). On analytic listening. *Psychoanalytic Quarterly* 69(2):317–367.

Meltzer, D. (1973). *Sexual States of Mind*. Perthshire, Scotland: Clunie Press.

Merleau-Ponty, M. (1961). Eye and mind. In G.A. Johnson (Ed.) *The Merleau-Ponty Aesthetics Reader*, 1993, pp. 121–164. Evanston: Northwestern University Press

Merleau-Ponty, M. (1962). *Phenomenology of Perception*. New York, NY: Routledge.

Merleau-Ponty, M. (1964/1945). *Signs*. R.C. McCleary (trans.). Evanston, IL: Northwestern University Press.

Merleau-Ponty, M. (2012/1945). *Phenomenology of Perception*. C. Smith, (trans.) New York: Routledge.

Miller, P. (2004). On analytic listening. *International Journal of Psychoanalysis* 85(6):1485–1488.

Mitchell S. (1991). Contemporary perspectives on self: Toward an integration. *Psychoanalytic Dialogues* 1:121–147.

Modell, A. (1990). Transference and levels of reality. In A. Modell, *Other Times, Other Realities*, pp. 44–59. Cambridge, MA: Harvard University Press.

Modell, A. (1993). *The Private Self*. Cambridge, MA: Harvard UP. 250p.

Moore, L. (1998). Which is more than I can say for some people. In *Birds of America*. New York: Vintage.

Moriatis, G. (1995). Prologue. *Psychoanalytic Inquiry* 15:275–279.

Morris, H. (2012). Constituting the ethics of psychoanalysis: Observations on "Observations on Transference Love," the story. Paper presented on Panel on Ethics, Boston Psychoanalytic Society and Institute, May, 2012.

Moya, P. and Larrain, M.E. (2016). Sexuality and meaning in Freud and Merleau-Ponty. *International Journal of Psychoanalysis* 97(3):737–757.

Ogden T. (1985). On potential space. *International Journal of Psychoanalysis* 66:129–141.

Ogden, T. (1986). *The Matrix of the Mind: Object Relations and the Psychoanalytic Dialogue*. Northvale, NJ: Aronson. 270 p.

Ogden, T. (1988). Misrecognitions and the fear of not knowing. *Psychoanalytic Quarterly* 57:643–666.

Ogden, T. (1994). *Subjects of Analysis*. Northvale, NJ: Aronson.

Ogden, T. (1996). Reconsidering three aspects of psychoanalytic technique. *International Journal Psycho-Analysis* 77:883–899.

Ogden, T.H. (1997). Reverie and interpretation. *Psychoanalytic Quarterly* 66:567–595.

Ogden, T.H. (1999). The analytic third: Working with intersubjective clinical facts. *IJP* 75:3–20.

Ogden, T.H. (2019). Ontological psychoanalysis or "What do you want to be when you grow up?". *Psychoanalytic Quarterly* 88(4):661–684.

Ogden, T.H. (2020). Toward a revised form of analytic thinking and practice: The evolution of analytic theory of mind. *Psychoanalytic Quarterly* 89:219–243.

Orgel, S. (1996). Freud and the repudiation of the feminine. *Journal American Psychoanalytic Association* 44(S):45–67.

Pajaczkowska, C. and Ward, I. (2008). *Shame and sexuality: Psychoanalysis and visual culture*. London, England: Routledge.

Pakula, A.J. dir. (1971). *Klute*. US: Warner Bros.

Parsons, M. (2000). Sexuality and perversion a hundred years on: Discovering what Freud discovered. *International Journal Psychoanalysis* 81:37–51.

Parsons, M. (2007). Raiding the inarticulate: The internal analytic setting and listening beyond countertransference. *International Journal of Psychoanalysis* 88(6):1441–1456.

Peltz, R. and Goldberg, P. (2013). Field conditions: Discussion of Donnel B. Stern's *Field Theory in Psychoanalysis. Psychoanalytic Dialogues* 23:660–666.

Perelberg, R.J. (2018a). Introduction: A psychoanalytic understanding of psychic bisexuality. In R.J. Perelberg (Ed.) *Psychic Bisexuality*, pp. 1–57. London: Routledge.

Perelberg, R.J. (2018b). Love and melancholia in the analysis of women by women. In R.J. Perelberg (Ed.) *Psychic Bisexuality*, pp. 103–121. London: Routledge.

Person, E.S. (1985). The erotic transference in women and men: Differences and consequences. *Journal of the American Psychoanalytic Association* 13:159–180.

Pirandello, L. (1921). *Six Characters in Search of an Author*. (1997), London: Dover Thrift.

Pizer, S. (1996). Negotiating potential space: Illusion, play, metaphor, and the subjunctive. *Psychoanalytic Dialogues* 6:689–712.

Pizer, S. (1998). *Building Bridges: The Negotiation of Paradox in Psychoanalysis*. Hillsdale, NJ: Analytic Press. 220 p.

Purcell, S.D. (2006). The analyst's excitement in the analysis of perversion. *International Journal Psychoanalysis* 87(1):105–123.

Racker, H. (1957). The meanings and uses of countertransference. *Psychoanalytic Quarterly* 26(3):303–357.

Redford, R. dir. (1980). *Ordinary People*. U.S.: Paramount Pictures.

Reis, B. (2020). *Creative Repetition and Intersubjectivity: Contemporary Freudian Explorations of Trauma, Memory, and Clinical Process*. New York: Routledge.

Renik O (1995). The ideal of the anonymous analyst and the problem of self-disclosure. *Psychoanalysis Quarterly* 64:466–495.

Renik, O. (1999). Playing one's cards face up in analysis: An approach to the problem of self-disclosure. *Psychoanalytic Quarterly* 68(4):521–539.

Resnick, S. (2006). *Biographies de l'Inconscient*. Preface par R. Kaes. Paris: Dunod.

Richards, A.K. (1993). Perverse transference and psychoanalytic technique: An introduction to the work of Horatio Etchegoyen. *Journal Clinical Psychoanalysis* 2(4):463–480.

Rilke, R.M. (1923). *Duineser Elegien*. Berlin, Germany: Insel-Verlag.

Ritvo, S. and Provence, S. (1953). Form perception and imitation in some autistic children: Diagnostic findings and their contextual interpretation. *Psychoanalytic Study of the Child* 8:155–161.

Roth, P. (2001). Mapping the landscape: Levels of transference interpretation. *International Journal Psychoanalysis* 82:533–543.

Saketopoulou, A. (2019). The draw to overwhelm: Consent, risk, and the re-translation of enigma. *Journal American Psychoanalytic Association* 67(1):133–167.

Saketopoulou, A. (2020). The infantile erotic countertransference: The analyst's infantile sexual, ethics and the role of the psychoanalytic collective. *Psychoanalytic Inquiry* 40(8):659–677.

Salomonsson, B. (2012). Has infantile sexuality anything to do with infants? *International Journal Psychoanalysis* 93(3):631–647.

Sanchez-Medina, A. (2002). Perverse thought. *International Journal Psychoanalysis* 83:1345–1359.

Scarfone, D. (2008). Transference and the reality of the message.

Scarfone, D. (2015). *The Unpast.* New York: The Unconscious in Translation.

Schafer, R. (1968). *Aspects of Internalization.* New York: International Universities Press.

Schafer, R. (1983). *The Analytic Attitude.* New York: Basic Books.

Schaverien, J. (1995). *Desire and the Female Therapist: Engendered Gazes in Psychotherapy and Art Therapy.* London and New York: Routledge.

Schmahmann, J.D. and Pandya, D.N. (1997). The cerebrocerebellar system [Review]. *International Review Neurobiology* 41:31–60.

Schoener, G.R., Milgrom, J.H., Gonsiorek, J., Luepker, E.T. and Conroe, R.M. (Eds.). (1989). *Psychotherapists' Sexual Involvement with Clients: Intervention and Prevention.* Minneapolis: Walk-In Counseling Center.

Schore, A.N. (2018). Moving forward: New findings on the right brain and their implications for psychoanalysis. Keynote Address, presented to the *American Psychological Association Division of Psychoanalysis at the 37th Annual Spring Meeting,* April 26–30, 2018, New York.

Schumacher, J. dir. (1999). *Flawless.* U.S.: Magnolia Pictures.

Searles, H. (1959). Oedipal love in the countertransference. *International Journal of Psychoanalysis* 40:180–190.

Shedler, J. (2004). *Clinical and Observational Psychoanalytic Research: Roots of a Controversy.* J. Sandler, A.-M. Sandler and R. Davies (Eds.) Madison, CN: International Universities Press.

Slochower, J. (1991). Variations in the analytic holding environment. *International Journal of Psychoanalysis* 72:709–717.

Slochower, J. (1996a). Holding and the fate of the analyst's subjectivity. *Psychoanalytic Dialogue* 6:323–354.

Slochower, J. (1996b). Holding and the evolving maternal metaphor. *Psychoanalytic Review* 83:195–218.

Smith, S. (1977). The Golden Fantasy: A regressive reaction to separation anxiety. *International Journal Psychoanalysis* 58:311–324.

Solms, M. (2000). Preliminaries for an integration of psychoanalysis and neuroscience. *Annals Psychoanalysis* 28:179–200.

Solms, M. (2010). Happy reading for a psychoanalyst. *Neuropsychoanalysis* 12(2):182–184.

Sperling, O.E. and Arlow, J.A. (1954). III. Perversion: Theoretical and therapeutic aspects. *Journal American Psychoanalytic Association* 2:336–345.

Stein, G. (1933). *The Autobiography of Alice B. Toklas*. New York, NY: Vintage Books.

Stein, R. (1998). The poignant, the excessive and the enigmatic in sexuality. *International Journal Psychoanalysis* 79:253–268.

Stein, R. (2005). Why perversion? 'False love' and the perverse pact. *International Journal Psychoanalysis* 86:775–799.

Stern, D. (1985). *The Interpersonal World of the Infant: A View from Psychoanalysis and Developmental Psychology*. NY: Basic Books.

Stern, D. B. (1990). Courting surprise: Unbidden perceptions in clinical practice. *Contemporary Psychoanalysis* 26:452–478.

Stern, D. B. (1997). *Unformulated Experience: From Dissociation to Imagination in Psychoanalysis*. Hillsdale, NJ: Analytic Press.

Stern, D. B. (2013a). Field theory in psychoanalysis, Part I: Harry Stack Sullivan and Madeleine and Willy Baranger. *Psychoanalytic Dialogues* 23:487–501.

Stern, D. B. (2013b). Field theory in psychoanalysis, Part 2: Bionian field theory and contemporary Interpersonal/Relational psychoanalysis. *Psychoanalytic Dialogues* 23:630–645.

Stern, D.B. (2015). *Relational Freedom: Emergent Properties of the Interpersonal Field*. New York: Routledge.

Stern, D.B. and Hirsch, I. (Eds.) (2017). *A Teaching Anthology: The Interpersonal Perspective in Psychoanalysis, 1960s–1990s: Rethinking Transference and Countertransference*. New York, NY: Routledge, 310 p.

Stoller, R. (1986). *Perversion: The Erotic Form of Hatred*. London: Karnac.

Stoller, R.J. (1966). The mother's contribution to infantile transvestic behavior. *International Journal Psychoanalysis* 47:384–395.

Troise, D. (2013). Field of vision: Radical uncertainty and the analyst's conduct: Commentary on paper by Donnel B. Stern. *Psychoanalytic Dialogues* 23:514–522.

Tuckett, D. (2008). Reflection and comparison: Some final remarks. In D. Tuckett, R. Basile, D. Birksted-Breen, T. Bohm, P. Denis, A. Ferro, H. Hinz, A. Jemstedt, P. Mariotti and J. Schubert (Eds.) *Psychoanalysis Comparable and Incomparable: The Evolution of a Method to Describe and Compare Psychoanalytic Approaches*, New York: Routledge, pp. 243–261.

Tutter, A. (2018). The erotics of knowing: A neglected contribution to analytic erotism. *Journal American Psychoanalytic Association* 66(3):407–441.

Viorst, J. (2014). *Alexander and the Terrible, Horrible, No Good, Very Bad Day*. New York: Little Simon.

Vossel, S., Geng, J.J. and Fink, G.R. (2014). Dorsal and ventral attention systems – Distinct neural circuits but collaborative roles *Neuroscientist* 20(2):150–159. doi: 10.1177/1073858413494269.

Watt, D.F. (1990). Higher cortical functions and the ego: explorations of the boundary between behavioral neurology, neuropsychology, and psychoanalysis. *Psychoanalytic Psychology* 7(4): 488–529.

Watt, D.F. (2017). Reflections on the neuroscientific legacy of Jaak Panksepp (1943–2017). *Neuropsychoanalysis* 19(2): 183–198

Watt, D.F. (2019). Reflections on neuropsychoanalysis at 20 years. *Neuropsychoanalysis*, 21(2):114–117.

Weissman, S. (1977). Face to face: The role of vision and the smiling response. *Psychoanalytic Study of the Child* 32: 421–450.

Widawsky, R. (2014). Julia Kristeva's psychoanalytic work. *Journal of the American Psychoanalytic Association* 62(1):61–68.

Wilson, M. (2014). Maternal reliance: Commentary on Kristeva. *Journal of the American Psychoanalytic Association* 62(1):101–111.

Wilson, M. (2018). The analyst as Listening-Accompanist: Desire in Bion and Lacan. *Psychoanalytic Quarterly* 87(2):237–264.

Winnicott, D.W. (1958). The theory of the parent-infant relationship. In *The Maturational Processes and the Facilitating Environment: Studies in the Theory of Emotional Development*, pp. 37–55. New York, NY: International Universities Press, 1965.

Winnicott, D.W. (1960). The theory of the parent-infant relationship. *International Journal Psychoanalysis* 41:585–595.

Winnicott, D.W. (1971). *Playing and Reality*. New York: Routledge.

Winnicott, D.W. (1986). *Home is Where We Start From*. New York: Norton.

Wittgenstein, L. (1953). *Philosophical Investigations*. G.E.M. Anscombe, translator. New York, NY: Macmillan.

Wrye, H.K. and Welles, J.K. (1994). *The Narration of Desire: Erotic Transferences and Countertransferences*. Hillsdale, NJ: Analytic Press.

Yamaguchi, S. (2012). Analytic listening and the five senses: Commentary. *Journal American Psychoanalytic Association* 60(4):813–815.

Yeats, W.B. (1928). Among school children. In R.J. Finneran (Ed.) *The Collected Poems of W.B. Yeats*, NY: Scribner. (1996).

Zeavin, L. (2019). The elusive good object. *Psychoanalytic Quarterly* 88(1):75–93.

Zimmer, R.B. (2010). A view from the field: Clinical process and the work of confluence. *Psychoanalytic Quarterly* 79:1151–1165.

Zimmer, R.B. (2017). The analyst's use of multiple models in clinical work: Introduction. *Journal American Psychoanalytic Association* 65:819–827.

Index

Page numbers followed by f indicate figure

Printed in Dunstable, United Kingdom